Seth Pancoast

The Kabbala

Or, The true Science of Light

Seth Pancoast

The Kabbala
Or, The true Science of Light

ISBN/EAN: 9783337172091

Printed in Europe, USA, Canada, Australia, Japan

Cover: Foto ©Lupo / pixelio.de

More available books at **www.hansebooks.com**

THE KABBALA:

OR,

THE TRUE SCIENCE OF LIGHT;

AN INTRODUCTION TO THE

PHILOSOPHY AND THEOSOPHY

OF THE

ANCIENT SAGES.

TOGETHER WITH A CHAPTER ON

LIGHT IN THE VEGETABLE KINGDOM.

By S. PANCOAST, M.D.

NEW YORK:
R. WORTHINGTON, 770 BROADWAY.

TO THE

TRUE SCIENTISTS,

NOT ONLY OF THE UNITED STATES, BUT OF THE ENTIRE WORLD—
THOSE WHO SINCERELY DESIRE TO DISCOVER THE TRUTHS OF
SCIENCE, WHOSE MINDS ARE NOT CLOUDED BY PRECON-
CEIVED NOTIONS AND THEORIES, BUT ARE OPEN TO
CONVICTION, READY AND ANXIOUS TO LEARN
ALL THAT MAY BE LEARNED FROM THE
ANCIENT PHILOSOPHERS AS WELL AS
FROM INVESTIGATION OF THE
PHENOMENA OF LIGHT;

ESPECIALLY TO THE

NOBLE ARMY OF TRUE PATHOLOGISTS, THOSE WHO FOLLOW THE
PHILANTHROPIC PROFESSION OF MEDICINE BECAUSE OF TRUE
HEARTFELT SYMPATHY WITH SUFFERING HUMANITY,

THIS LITTLE VOLUME, DEVOTED TO

THE TRUE SCIENCE OF LIGHT,

ESPECIALLY IN ITS

RELATIONS TO LIFE AND HEALTH, AND ITS APPLI-
CABILITY AS A REMEDY IN DISEASE, IS

Affectionately and Respectfully Dedicated

BY THE AUTHOR.

PREFACE.

THE Author does not deem an extended Preface requisite, in offering to the Public the result of Thirty Years' Patient Study of the Science of Light as taught not only by modern Scientists but by the Ancient Philosophers who, as the reader will discover, perhaps with astonishment, knew far more than readers of Popular Works on Scientific subjects would imagine, of the true facts of Science; in studying the Kabbala and Kabbalistic Literature, we have taken nothing for granted, but, by severe test-experiments and critical observation, have "tried all things and held fast that which was good"—that which stood the most exacting tests! We do not apologize to any one for our book—the only persons who can look for an apology are those *Scientists* whose pet-theories we controvert, but we decline to tender any apology to them because we have been influenced by no malice or prejudice, but have written purely in the interest of Truth; we believe what we have written is every word true, and only ask those who dissent from any of our views to apply the tests of careful experiments and investigation, and if these tests prove us in error we shall unhesitatingly, nay cheerfully, yield. Meanwhile we add but one word in the form of a familiar adage: "Truth is mighty and must prevail!" and we remain the Readers'

     Sincere Friend
        THE AUTHOR.

CONTENTS.

PAGE
INTRODUCTION... 9

CHAPTER I.
ANCIENT IDEAS OF LIGHT AND HEAT............................ 17

CHAPTER II.
THE TRUE SCIENCE OF LIGHT—TRUTHS AND THEORIES—
WHAT WE KNOW, AND WHAT WE BELIEVE..................... 54

CHAPTER III.
LIGHT MANIFESTED IN ATMOSPHERIC ELECTRICITY AND
IN TERRESTRIAL MAGNETISM....................................... 96

CHAPTER IV.
MATERIAL FORMS AND VITAL DYNAMICS......................... 127

CHAPTER V.
THE HUMAN ORGANISM AND ITS VITAL DYNAMICS............ 159

CHAPTER VI.
THE CENTRES AND ORIGINAL SOURCE OF VITAL DYNAMICS WITHIN THE HUMAN ORGANISM, AND THE GREAT
ACTUAL SOURCE... 185

CHAPTER VII.

How to Assist Nature in Banishing Disease from the Human Organism.................................. 225

CHAPTER VIII.

Light and its Rays Nature's Own and Only Remedies for Disease—How to Apply Light to the Human Organism.................................. 241

CHAPTER IX.

Light in the Vegetable Kingdom.................................. 283

CHAPTER X.

Light the Sole Source of Life—Light the Developer of Material Forms—Forms Developed Solely to Manifest Life—Light Nature's Means of Preserving Life—Hence, Light Nature's Means of Banishing Disease by Restoring the Equilibrium that constitutes Health.................................. 293

INTRODUCTION.

It is a trite saying that "There is Nothing New under the Sun!" Like many other familiar phrases, this is frequently uttered without any real perception of its scope—*nothing new*, indeed, and yet the world moves ever onward! then what is Progress, or is there any thing or any idea, to which the word Progress can be applied? Every now and then the world is electrified by some *new idea*, or some *new discovery!* then, lo! some delver in ancient lore, some seeker in forgotten mines, shows that the *new idea* is ages old, the *new discovery* nearly as old as the world itself. Facts are ascertained, demonstrated, taught, learned and ———forgotten; Theories, vague and uncertain even in the minds of their weavers, are accepted for Science! then, lo! the old-forgotten Facts spring again to view and the Theories flee to be forgotten in their turn, only with this difference that there is no resurrection for them!

It is not very many generations since, the world knew nothing of the Solar System and its marvelous revolutions and the laws that govern its Sun, Moon, Stars and Planets—Sir Isaac Newton made some astounding discoveries and there was doubt, astonishment, consternation; the world was not unwilling to believe, but unable. To-day, men look back and wonder how any one ever believed otherwise than in accord with the now accepted Science of Astronomy, which has made such acquisitions of facts since Newton assigned our Sun his rightful place and authority in the System that Astronomy is almost an Exact Science. Since Newton's day, it has been ascertained that many centuries before, even in the sixth century before the Era of "the Sun of Righteousness," the famous Ionian Philosopher, Anaximander, the first systematic writer on Philosophy, had an inkling of some of the marvelous facts of Astronomy; strangely mixed up with wild theories, were the ideas of the Solar centre with the earth and heavenly bodies revolving around it. Then we learn that the wonderful Pythagoras actually knew all the chief facts concerning the movements of the Sun, the Stars, the Planets—he even knew that the Stars were Suns of other Systems like ours, and that the Planets were worlds cheered and animated with life similar to, if not like, ours; he knew, too, the two Physical Forces, Attraction and Repulsion; nay, he knew, what modern Science has not yet fully rediscovered, that the visible Suns were emanations from and dependent upon an invisible original Central Sun, the Sun of the Universe, the Celestial Power whence the forces of Nature were derived. We learn that there were others, from time to time, who knew more or less of the truth, until Copernicus who knew nearly all, and Galileo who had to answer to the Roman hierarchy for knowing more than the Church. Indeed, so much of the Newtonian Philosophy do we find in the ancient, that we cannot doubt he had been exploring the old mines of Kabbalistic lore, and had arrived at his great discoveries by following up clews gained therefrom.

As we shall show, the old Kabbala, with its curious and comprehensive symbol language, is at once an elaborate System of Natural Philosophy and a profound system of Theology—an illuminated exposition of the mysterious truths of Nature and of that higher Science which the Book of Nature unfolds to the enlightened eye of the Soul, the Science of Religion. Our readers would be slow to realize, many of them even unwilling to recognize, the fact that the grand old Kabbalistic Theosophy was the native root, the central trunk, whence *all* the religions the world has ever known sprang, as shoots and branches from a parent-tree—yet this is absolutely true. The Holy Bible is a translation into words of the symbols of the Kabbala. The reader would be astonished if he could read the Sacred Book in the Light of the Kabbala; first, to discover their close accordance; second, to find internal evidences, so clear as to be irrefragable, that the Book of Nature (Science) and the Written Word are one in source and significance; and third, to learn that the Bible is not the book of enigmas, mysteries, concealments that ordinary commentaries would make us believe, with their forced, incongruous, mysterious definitions and *elucidations*, but that the *Bible is absolutely the written revelation of God's work, will, purposes and ultimate purpose in creation and redemption, and of His essential character and attributes as well.*

Our scope in this work, and its specific design, will

not permit us to set forth and make plain, in detail, the noble, incomparable Kabbala, but we have in contemplation the publication of a large, full, candid exhibit of what the Kabbala is, has done, is doing and shall do, for the world. We may, however, declare our honest conviction here, and show hereafter the grounds upon which that conviction is based, that a just appreciation and knowledge of the Kabbala would stop the terrible Infidelity that is defiantly stalking through the world, uprooting, tearing down, razing, actually burying, Faith in God and His salvation. Few intelligent men are inclined to adopt the absurdities of Infidelity, many yield a quasi acceptance, and consent not to believe the Bible, *because they do not understand its glorious truths and are not satisfied with the explanations and elucidations offered by unenlightened commentators*—THE KABBALA IS AN AUTHORIZED, DIVINELY ILLUMINATED COMMENTARY ON NATURE AND THE BIBLE, WHICH MAKES BOTH SO PLAIN AND INTELLIGIBLE THAT "THE WAYFARING MEN, THOUGH FOOLS, SHALL NOT ERR THEREIN." It is only "The fool that hath said *in his heart*, There is no God!" many others say so with their lips who would accept the truth if they could but understand it. It is an error, and the prolific source of Infidelity, to maintain that men endowed by God with reason must believe what is not revealed to their reason—the Bible is the Revelation, not the Concealment, of God, and all that is revealed therein may be comprehended by the illuminated reason! and we shall show that this illumination is not restricted to a few, but is within the reach of every man who will diligently and devoutly cultivate the Subjective, Godlike Faculties of his Soul; these Faculties, "Self-Consciousness, Conscience, Sanctified Intuition and Imagination, and Prescience," are implanted by God in every Human Soul, and only the Man who cultivates these can receive the high gift of inward illumination—only those who are "born again" from the death of sin can become "children of Light." But, of this we shall speak at some length and more than once, in the ensuing pages. It is very probable that, as before intimated, we shall publish a larger volume especially devoted to the discussion of the Kabbala and Kabbalistic Literature, in the course of a few months—a work that thirty years' patient, conscientious study has perhaps fitted us to undertake.

But, the special purpose of this volume is to promote the well-being of mankind in this probationary world, by advocating Light and its Rays as the best remedial means for the Human Organism, when from any cause, internal or external, the equilibrium of health is disturbed, and disease wastes the body and deranges the mind—nay, even when there is no clearly defined disease, but only the feebleness and indisposition for physical or mental effort. Of course, to apply any remedy successfully, it is essential to know the characteristics and qualities of the remedy itself and the features and functions of the Organism in the condition of health; there are idiosyncrasies or differences in individuals, but the Human Organism, in health, is much the same not only throughout each race but even throughout the family of Man, and, while some Medicines act promptly and effectively in some cases, refuse to act in others, and act injuriously in still others, where the symptoms are identical, yet Light and its Rays will be found exceptional in this: that they seldom fail to effect just what they are designed to effect, when rightly administered—we have, in fact, seldom found them to fail in our practice. We attribute this exceptional efficacy to the fact that Light is essentially and especially Nature's remedy, and, therefore, peculiarly adapted to assist Nature in banishing disease and restoring health.

In the ensuing chapters, we believe we shall follow the natural order in the discussion, first, of Light as known and taught in Ancient Philosophy; secondly, as we view it—our views being based upon study, experiments and observation; thirdly, as manifested in Electricity and Magnetism; and fourthly, as manifested in Vital Dynamics—in Life. Then, we shall define the true doctrine of Development, or Evolution, showing that Light is the Developer or Evolver of material forms, and that the purpose of Material Development or Evolution is simply to provide bodies for the Objective or *visible* manifestation of Light as Life. And then, we shall show that in Man's Organism the highest possible Material Development is attained, and that within that form are implanted certain Subjective Faculties that distinguish Man and place him on a plane higher than the highest Animal—far higher than the highest Animal as compared with the worm, is Man as compared with it, simply because in him the Life-principle that pervades all life is Individualized and Personified into a responsible, "Living Soul." We shall then proceed to show the characteristics and functional constitution of the Human body.

With the foundation thus laid, in the explanation of Light and its Rays in all their manifestations and operations, and of the Human Organism in its material composition and organic arrangement, we shall proceed to explain how the one can be best applied to the other, citing illustrative cases in which we have successfully applied the Red and Blue rays.

This will conclude our special subject, but, as considerable attention has lately been evoked to the applicability of Light-rays in the propagation of Fruits, Vegetables, etc., we shall add a chapter on "Light in the Vegetable Kingdom."

It will be observed, that we follow *no one individual* thinker or *class* of thinkers in our views—we accept the *established facts* of Science, but take issue with some of the *almost universally accepted theories*—for example, we cannot accept the "Undulatory" or "Wave Theory" of the transmission of Light, and we shall freely reject it. More important than this, however, is our dissent from all the "accepted" definitions of Light—we believe that Light is the Power or Force of Nature, whence are derived all forces, Physical and Vital, and, therefore, we believe that "The True Science of Light" comprehends all other Natural Sciences or Philosophies. But we ask no one to accept our views without investigation, and we shall state the grounds upon which we rest them frankly and in detail, so far as the design and scope of this work will permit.

The reader will observe, also, that we accord to

General Pleasonton the merit and honor of having made an exceedingly important discovery, but it must be borne in mind that others in this country and in Europe have long been experimenting with Light and Light-rays; some have failed, but others, especially in the direction of therapeutic application of the rays, have had most encouraging success. We have been studying, investigating and experimenting in this direction for more than thirty years, and we believe our successes have been such that we dare claim the merit and honor of determining the positive, absolute applicability of Light, and especially of the Red and Blue rays, in the treatment of Disease of almost every type, but notably in Diseases that have their rise, or localize themselves in their influences, in the Nervous System. We have studied, as we write, purely in the interest of Suffering Humanity to whose welfare we dedicated our time, talents and all that we have and are, when we adopted the profession of Medicine.

BLUE AND RED LIGHT.

CHAPTER I.
ANCIENT IDEAS OF LIGHT AND HEAT.

By many centuries antedating the Christian, and older than the Mosaic, Scriptures—earlier, indeed, in its origin than the Egyptian or any other system of religion or philosophy of which aught is now known, the Kabbala has all the claims to respectful consideration that antiquity can confer; and these claims are enhanced and intensified when we discover tokens, not merely of its earlier origin, but of its important influence, in their structure and teachings, upon the religions of all lands and ages. Yet but few, even of the thinkers and thought-producers of recent days, know enough of the wondrous Kabbala to have the faintest conception of the vast debt the world of all ages has owed to that grand system of religion and philosophy. Using the symbols, quoting the language, repeating the ideas,—nay, teaching and maintaining the very doctrines, of the Kabbala, writers of modern times are generally ignorant of the source of the symbols, language, ideas and doctrines, and hence, naturally, they fail to realize their beautiful significance, far-reaching scope, and more than marvelous harmony. Within the present century, the Germans have given the subject, or constellation of subjects, much thoughtful investigation, but as yet have not shown a clear perception of the magnitude and grandeur of the Kabbalistic Theosophy. The Rosicrucians are the last and most advanced of these investigators, and the present writer gratefully acknowledges his indebtedness to them, and to their careful and intelligent researches, for many of the Kabbalistic ideas of Light and Heat herein to be stated, as well as for a clearer insight into the religious and scientific system of the Kabbala.

The Kabbalists claim that the source from which their knowledge is derived is Divine; that God reveals it to the pure in heart alone, and that the fountain of the true Light of knowledge is itself known to those only who are illuminated by that Light within their souls. The philosophy of the Kabbala was expressed in symbols, some of which are in use among the Masonic and other secret fraternities of our day, though much of their olden force and beauty, which depended very largely, and in some cases entirely, upon their occult meanings, is lost by erroneous interpretations. The symbols of Masonry are Kabbalistic, and were known to Zoroaster, Pythagoras, Apollonius, Raymond Lulli, Solomon ibn Gabirol, Gaffaral, Cornelius Agrippa, Fludd, Behmen and others. Solomon's Temple, with its marvels of beauty and grandeur, its strikingly distinct and different parts, its still more striking diversities of material and style—all blending in one superb, gorgeous and absolutely harmonious whole—was the grand panoramic symbol, a complete epitome and miniature, of the universe as portrayed in the Kabbala. The history of its builder, Hiram, is a curious, strangely fascinating history, but it is foreign to our present subject, and we must pass it by with the single remark that he was a Kabbalist of the clearest type. He who exactly understands Solomon's Temple, in its details and in its entirety, is a true Mason and a true Kabbalist—therefore, an initiant of the highest order.

There is a key to Kabbalistic symbolism that will unlock the secrets of the Kabbala, open the sanctuaries of the East where the knowledge of its full significance is still hidden, and expose to the understanding eye the mysteries of occult philosophy. This key we shall use in giving the Kabbalistic ideas of Light and Heat, and the information we are enabled to impart will be found to differ materially from what has hitherto been published. We must here state that we belong to no modern secret order, and violate no obligation in speaking so freely upon the subject as we shall.

As we have intimated, the Kabbala treats of two distinct subjects: Religion and Philosophy. Though distinct, the two are in perfect accord as found in the Kabbala, and show the sublime harmony that must ever characterize the relations of true Religion and true Science—both from the one Divine source and having the one central theme, they cannot be antagonistic or even really diverge.

Light is the foundation upon which rests the superstructure of the Kabbalistic Theosophy—Light the source and centre of the entire harmonious system

Light was the first-born of God—His first manifestation of Himself in the universe. No man can know God except as He manifests Himself in Light—not visible or sensible light, seen by man's carnal eye, but intellectual and spiritual Light, apparent only to the inner vision of those illuminated by that Light. This is the Light of which John spake when he said: "The Light shineth in darkness, and the darkness comprehended it not," and elsewhere in the same chapter. Christ, too, spake of that Light, as distinguished from the visible, ordinary light, when He declared: "Light is come into the world, and men loved darkness rather than Light," etc.; "If a man walk in the night, he stumbleth because there is no Light in him;" "While ye have Light, believe in the Light, that ye may be the children of Light;" He calls it "the Light of Life;" "I am the Light of the world: he that followeth me shall not walk in darkness, but shall have the Light of Life." Indeed, the Bible, in both the Jewish and Christian parts, abounds in the Kabbalistic distinction between the outward or objective, and the inward or subjective, Light. The outward light is a manifestation of Himself by the same Supreme Being, but inferior in degree and in its influences, though glorious notwithstanding.

The "Wisdom of Solomon" has been said to have been written in Alexandria in the time of Jerome, and is attributed to Philo; but he could not have been its author, as his known views were clearly opposed to much that is found therein. The "wisdom" it enunciates is claimed to be that taught to Moses in Egypt. It describes God as *Illuminated Time;* no origin can be assigned Him; He is engulphed in his own glory, "dwelling in the Light which no man can approach unto." Creation is stated to have consisted in emanations from Him, which dispelled darkness, the antagonizing element to Light, as Evil is to Good—the one fleeing as the other makes its presence felt. The "Wisdom of Solomon" is of much value to those who would learn the marvels of Kabbalistic *Wisdom*, but the great Kabbalistic works are "The Sohar, or the Book of Light," and "The Sepher Jetzera, or the Book of the Creation." The former was first printed in 1558 at Mantua, and repeatedly reprinted; its writer was Simeon ben Jochai. "The Sepher Jetzera," according to Dr. Zurns, was written in the eighth century, or possibly at the beginning of the ninth; but this is a mistake, as though its origin is really unknown, yet internal evidence would justify the claim that it was written very much earlier, if not as early as a century before the commencement of the Christian era. In the Talmud, there is distinct mention of this remarkable work, and Shabthai ben Abraham, an eminent commentator of the tenth century, gives it as his carefully formed opinion that it is the oldest book of human literature; admitting this to be an exaggeration, we deem its language and style conclusive proof that it belongs to a period anterior to the first Mishnaists; it is not impossible that those writers are correct who regard it as a collection, made it may be in the eighth or ninth century, of fragments of very much earlier times. We have been so fortunate as to secure a good copy of each of the three editions of the Sepher Jetzera: 1. The Latin edition of Rittangel

(Amsterdam, 1600); 2. The Latin and German edition of John Friedrich von Meyer (Leipsic, 1830); and 3. An edition bearing neither name nor date. The opinion prevalent among Kabbalists is that the Sepher Jetzera is a monologue of the patriarch Abraham, and they believe that the contemplations recorded herein induced the patriarch of patriarchs to abandon the worship of the heavenly bodies and become the servant of the true God; the Rabbi Jahuda ha Levi, who flourished and wrote in the eleventh century, says: "The Book of the Creation, which belongs to our Father Abraham, demonstrates the existence of the Deity and the Divine Unity, by things that are, on the one hand, manifold and multifarious, whilst, on the other hand, they converge and harmonize; and this harmony can only proceed from One who originates it." The design of this work is to declare a system whereby the universe may be viewed in connection with the truths found in the Bible, in such a way as to show, by tracing the gradual and orderly process of creation and the harmony which characterizes its details and its perfection, that one God produces all and is over all. The order and harmony of creation is deduced from the analogy subsisting between the visible things and the signs of thought.

The Sepher Jetzera is regarded as the basis of, and key to, the teachings of the Sohar, though the arrangement and plan of the two works differ somewhat. In the Sohar, the *Sephiroth*, of which we shall speak fully directly, are unfolded with care and in detail. "The Sohar, or the Book of Light," dwells with great emphasis upon the Kabbalistic doctrinal teachings on

Light. The Kabbala declares that Light is the primordial essence of the Universe, and that all life and motion proceed from it—it is the vital dynamic force of Nature. It also declares that it is by the study of Light that we are enabled to acquire a knowledge of the unknowable or causal world. Light is Jacob's Ladder by which we ascend to Celestial knowledge, the upper rundle being in the fourth *Sephira*, represented by the Pentagram.

In considering the Kabbala and the Kabbalists, we must never lose sight of its intimate connection with the Bible; it is really an enlightened "Commentary" on the Sacred Scriptures—these have, running all through their inspired lines and words, a two-fold meaning: an outward meaning which may be perceived by any candid reader, and an inward or hidden meaning which "the carnal mind cannot receive, because it is foolishness to him;" being spiritual, it can only be "spiritually discerned"—it is the province of the Kabbala to shed the Light of Truth upon this second meaning.

Solomon ibn Gabirol, an Arabian philosopher, wrote, under the pseudonym of Avicebron, about the middle of the eleventh century, two works of value to those interested in occult philosophy; they were "Liber de Causis," or "The Book of Causes," and "Fons Vitæ," or "The Source of Life." He speaks of the unity of Light as it arises from the throne of the Most High, which subjectively becomes divided into nine categories. This united Light he calls "the substance of the intellect," on account of its having been the receptacle of the Divine Will when God said "Let there be Light." In his "Liber de Causis," in speaking of God, Gabirol states that He is wise, and from His Wisdom He has seen fit to make His Will manifest in Light, and all existences and substances in creation are created and sustained by God through Light. His Will, His Divinity, His Unity, His Eternity, and His very existence, are profound mysteries, and we can know Him only through His manifestations of Himself in Light. Gabirol speaks of the absurdity of a finite mind's attempting to define God—could it be done, it would make Him a finite being.

Plate I. shows the ten *Sephiroth* of the Kabbala, which illustrate in symbol the Kabbalistic conception of the universe as it came from the incomprehensible Supreme Will of the Most High. "The Crown" is called the *En Soph* ("the Endless, the Ineffable"), because, in it and by it God manifested the power of His Will in creation; as Light is His creative agent, so this *En Soph* is the source from which Light flows, the *Fons Lucis*. The *En Soph* was not created by God, but emanated from Him to manifest Him. In "the Crown," Light is pure white, utterly undiscernible by the physical eye, and in it reside the life and dynamic power of the universe. The ten *Sephiroth* comprise this *En Soph*, the Unity, and nine categories, or spheres, making ten in the complete figure, whence the number ten is called a "perfect number" and symbolized thus ⓪, representing the unity and synthesis of creation. Pythagoras in his "*Tetractys*" gives, besides the *Sephiroth*, a representation of the creation composed of the four letters of the Ineffable

Plate I.— THE SEPHIROTH.

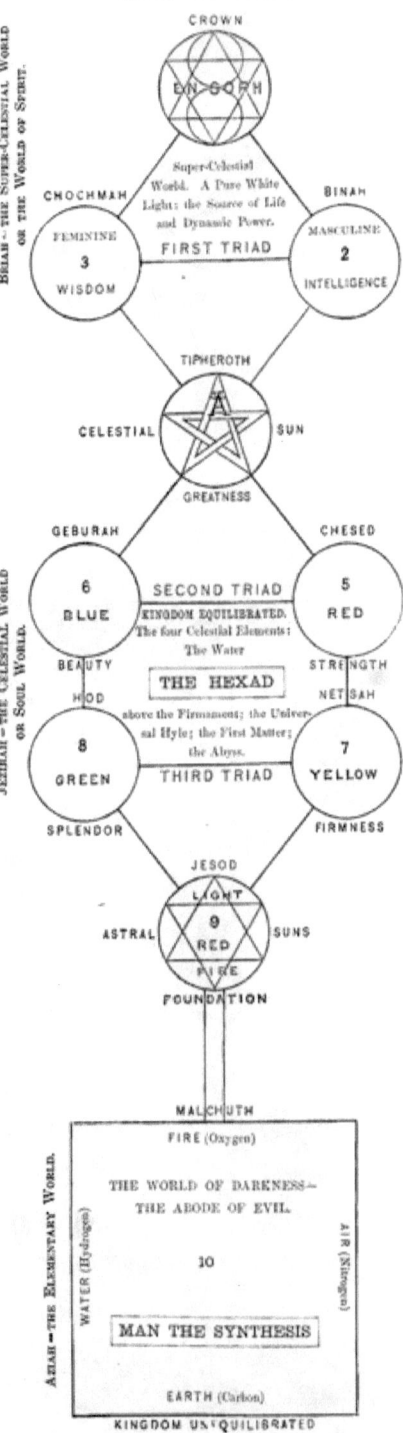

Name of God, the four-letter Name as it has been called, arranged and numbered as shown in Plate II., which we shall describe later in this chapter; this Name Pythagoras correctly pronounces the key to the mysteries of the Kabbalah. Pythagoras employed numbers in representing his ideas of creation, while the Egyptian Kabbalists used letters, words and numbers.

The Kabbalists represent the properties of Light as dual, calling the parts the two hands of Deity. Although it possesses duality, it maintains its unity and harmony until it becomes focalized in Astral Suns which we have illustrated by the sephirotic "Tree" in Plate I. We have said, the *En Soph*, or Crown, is the fountain or source of Light, which manifests itself in the two *Sephiroth*, *Binah* and *Chocmah*, "Intelligence" and "Wisdom," with masculine and feminine, or active and passive, functions—functions strikingly manifested in the light of our Sun, which must be understandingly distinguished before we can determine its various and diverse action and influence upon the human organism. *En Soph*, *Binah* and *Chocmah* form the first triad of the *Sephiroth*, and lines connecting them bound the World of *Briah*, the Super-Celestial World, or the World of Spirit.

Light is then focalized, forming the fourth *Sephira*, which is the Celestial Sun, called *Tiphereth*, "Resplendence," "Magnificence," because of the resplendent, magnificent whiteness of its Light, while its immensity is recognized in the farther designation "Greatness." This is the Central Sun of the entire universe, visible only to the spiritual or subjective sight, never to the natural or objective vision. It is to the Astral Suns precisely what they are to the respective planets which they control, illume and sustain, and which revolve around them; it controls, illumes and sustains the Astral Suns, and around it they revolve—without it they could no more maintain their equilibrium in space than could the planets hold their positions without their respective Suns.

This great Celestial Luminary possesses the dual properties of Light and Fire, but in absolute equilibration and perfect harmony. This perfect harmony embraces the rays of the Light, and chemics of the Fire; it is this harmony in the blending of the rays that produces the resplendent, magnificent white of which we have spoken as the characteristic of the Celestial Sun, and which justly gains it the appellation *Tiphereth*—the objective vision cannot conceive, as it could not endure, the white splendor of this glorious orb of orbs. When Moses desired to see the glory of God, this Celestial Light, God kindly replied: "I will make all my goodness pass before thee. . . . Thou canst not see my face; for there shall no man see me, and live." The near approach of the glory made the face of Moses so lustrous that, upon his return to the people, they could not endure the sight, and he was compelled to put a veil over his face while he talked with them. And when Saul and his companions were riding, upon their journey from Jerusalem to Damascus, suddenly there shone about them a beam from the Celestial Sun; so intense was its Light that they all fell to the ground, and Saul's eyes were temporarily blinded and permanently affected by the

Light, which he describes as: "a Light from heaven, above the brightness of the Sun."

We have already alluded to the fact that the one attribute which pre-eminently distinguishes the Kabbalistic system is its complete and absolute harmony: But more may be claimed: This harmony is not only the strongest evidence, but it is an all-sufficient and conclusive proof of the Divine origin of the Kabbala; for in God's universe, in its every department, separately and collectively, harmony is the one positive law which is never disobeyed without immediate and inevitable evil consequences exactly proportioned to the extent and nature of that disobedience. No merely human system of action or ethics, of living or believing, has ever been or can ever be devised wherein this Divine harmony is not evidently wanting; the most skilfully and cunningly planned and practised counterfeit bears this evidence upon its face of the absence of the Divine hand in its construction. It has been well said: "Harmony is God's unique law." So, when we find in the *Sephiroth* a positive unity, in their relation to each other and to the universe a positive accord, and in the system throughout, of which these are the symbolic declaration, a like oneness arising from marvelous harmony and sublime concord, we can believe that God, the God of harmony and concord, has inspired the Kabbala, and can believe no less and naught else until we discover some known-to-be-human system equally perfect in this particular.

But let us pause very briefly to note the operations of God's law of harmony around us: In the movements of the heavenly bodies, as we are wont to call the planets and their suns and moons and satellites, none question or can question the importance of this law. With the slightest defect in this respect, not only would their respective order and movements be disarranged and confusion ensue, but the very existence of some of the weaker ones would be destroyed by contact with their stronger neighbors, while the stronger ones would necessarily suffer immeasurably. In fact, set aside the law of harmony in the planetary system, and chaos would soon prevail. The same law is vital, too, in each individual member of the universe; take our Sun for an illustration; place discord instead of harmony in its structure, and beauty would give place to distressing ugliness, utility to horrible destructiveness; its orderly movements would become wanderings through space to the peril of our earth itself. And so with any one of the Suns or their planets, the loss of harmony would inevitably destroy its beauty and usefulness in the universe.

As God is one, so is this law uniform in all His works—in what we are wont to call the laws of Nature, His Will is seen in the presence and influence of this same law of harmony; every positive has a negative, every active a passive; every destroying element is opposed or corrected by a restoring principle —just in proportion as the opposing principles or forces are in exact equipoise do we see Nature move in beauteous and regular order; for example, let the forces of attraction become weak or impaired, will not the repellent forces work destruction? and the converse is no less sure; let the centrifugal force in any instance fall below the centripetal, or the latter yield to the former, and the consequence will soon be apparent; let the polarizing ray in light lose its influence, and decay and death come speedily to tell the story of the absence of harmony to the most ignorant and the most unobservant. It is this harmony that gives us all of beauty and beneficence we see in Nature; harmony amidst its constituents gives us beauty in Light, sweetness in sound, and all else that we enjoy in life is equally dependent on this law of God.

In the Moral World, the same God exacts obedience to the same law of harmony as the price of order and propriety, and disregard of its stringent requirements, even in what we are prone to call "trivial matters," is as surely and as swiftly followed by a proportionate penalty as in the Planetary and Natural Worlds. Even in the matter of Divinely-ordered penalties, do we not see this law ever exemplified?

And of the World of Eternal Peace and Blessedness, we cannot doubt the assurance that "order is Heaven's first law." The law of harmony finds there its most complete fruition, because there it is never disregarded, and that fruition is joy and happiness unspeakable, glory ineffable, and perfect life forever and forever—well may we believe that there is no sorrow or sighing, no pain or sickness, no decay or death, in that happy land where God's unique law of harmony is perfectly and absolutely and always obeyed.

The *Rouach Elohim* which brooded over or "moved upon the face of the waters" was held by the Alchemists to have been Light from the Celestial Sun shiting thereon. John, in his narrative of the life and ministry of Christ, tells us: "There is at Jerusalem by the sheep-market, a pool which is called in the Hebrew tongue Bethesda, having five porches. In these lay a great multitude of impotent folk, of blind, halt, withered, waiting for the moving of the water. For an angel went down at a certain season into the pool, and troubled the water: whosoever then first after the troubling of the water stepped in was made whole of whatsoever disease he had." Now, as Christ did not deny or question the popular notion as to the curative property imparted to the water of this pool, but tacitly acknowledged its correctness, and as the word rendered "angel" signifies literally "messenger," and the "messenger" was certainly invisible to the objective sight of those visiting the pool, may we not believe that this "messenger" was a healing ray from *Tiphereth* of the Kabbala? Commentators have offered various explanations of this "miracle" of Bethesda, but they speak with a degree of uncertainty which indicates that they are not quite satisfied with their own explanations; many of them are disposed to get rid of the difficulty by rejecting the story as "an interpolation;" we see no necessity for rejecting the passage, and cannot see that to believe that the curative principle was imparted by a ray "sent" from the Celestial Sun of the universe, does any violence to the most orthodox faith, as God's benevolent and omnipotent Will is as truly recognized in such a belief as in any "miraculous" theory we have ever seen or heard advanced. The same John, in his book of Revelations, states that there were seven angels to whom were given seven trumpets, the sounding of each of which brought a dire calamity upon the earth; "And the third angel sounded, and there fell a great star from heaven, burning as it were a lamp, and it fell upon the third part of the rivers, and upon the fountains of waters; and the name of the star is called Wormwood; and the third part of the waters became wormwood; and many men died of the waters, because they were made bitter." Was this "star" a destructive ray from the mighty *Tiphereth*? the supposition is certainly as reasonable as the suppositions of some of the popular commentators; and our suggestion is made still more probable by the fact that, according to the Kabbalists, the star symbol within the *Sephira Tiphereth*, in its upright, proper position representing the principle of good, when inverted represents the evil principle; our readers will find it interesting to note carefully the star, then invert the plate and observe how different and how much less pleasing the star appears.

The five-pointed "Star" seen on the disk of *Tiphereth* is the "flaming Pentagram" of the Kabbalists and of the Magi of the Orient; it was the glorious "Star of Bethlehem" that, as the Celestial forerunner of the "Light of the World," the "Light of Life," made known to the Wise Men the birth of Jesus. Miniatures of the Pentagram constitute favorite talismans, but to be effective they must be most accurately made and carefully placed; it was to a picture of this star, placed as a talisman, Goethe referred in the famous interview between Faust and Mephistopheles in the former's study; the latter had entered unbidden and unannounced, but when he wished to retire found an obstacle:

Meph.—...... Might I be permitted this time to depart?
Faust.—I see not why you ask ...... Here is the window, here the door; there is also a chimney for you.
Meph.—To confess the truth, a small obstacle prevents me from walking out—the wizard-foot upon your threshold.
Faust.—The Pentagram embarrasses you? Tell me then, thou child of hell, if that repels thee, how camest thou in? How was such a spirit entrapped?
Meph.—Mark it well; it is not well drawn; one angle, the outward one, is, as thou seest, a little open.

The Apocalypse is full of passages which can be read with ease by the help of the Kabbala; indeed there are passages which indicate that John was a Kabbalist of a high order. Among these we must cite one; he tells us of a most remarkable vision: "And there appeared a great wonder in heaven, a woman clothed with the sun, and the moon under her feet, and upon her head a crown of twelve stars," etc. The Rosicrucians call the Light of the Celestial Sun the Divine *Sophia*, "Wisdom," because of its purity and its passivity in matter. The Egyptian Kabbalists called this light *Isis*, and represented *Isis* as a pure woman; as the Light of the Celestial Sun is invisible to mere mortals, seen only by the subjective sight of the illuminated, they clothed *Isis* with an objective Sun; as the Celestial Sun is "greatness" and majesty, they placed under the feet of *Isis* the Crescent, beneath which, but outside the sacred circle, was a vanquished Fiery Serpent; then, as a token of the supremacy of *Tiphereth* in the universe, they surrounded the head of *Isis* with a halo of twelve Stars. (See the Frontis-

piece.] Doubtless, our reader readily sees *Sophia* of the Rosicrucians and *Isis* of the Egyptian Kabbalists in John's vision of the wondrous woman, and if he read John's narrative of that vision a little farther he will find the vanquished Serpent beneath *Isis's* feet in the Apocalyptic "great red dragon." The figure of *Isis* clothed with the Sun is one of the most interesting of the symbolic pictures of the Kabbala; when a person by self-denial, meditation and devotion has attained to the high privilege of subjective vision, he sees *Isis* or the Light of the subjective Sun—this is "lifting the Veil of Isis."

The Celestial Sun, we have seen, is the fourth *Sephira*; the fifth, sixth, seventh and eighth, called respectively *Chesed*, "Strength," *Gebureah*, "Beauty," *Netsah*, "Firmness," and *Hod*, "Splendor," represent four of the component colors of Light: Red, Yellow, Green and Blue; the Kabbalists fully understood the colors, their influence in Light and in Nature, their distinctive properties and their action together and separately; this is indicated in a singularly forcible manner in placing the Red and Yellow in the masculine or active column and the Green and Blue in the feminine or passive column—recognizing the active, polarizing quality of the heat colors and the passive, decomposing quality of the chemical colors. The non-recognition of the Orange, Indigo and Violet does not indicate that the Kabbalists knew not of them, for we know from other sources that they were thoroughly aware of the seven colors of the chromatic scale, and of the proportion, position and character of each color; but Orange is only a combination of the Red and

Yellow, and Indigo and Violet are close akin to Blue. The Celestial Sun having thus given forth the colors, they come together again, or are focalized, in Astral Suns, which appear as the ninth *Sephira*, designated *Jesod*, "Foundation," because they are the centres of their systems, the life-producers, -propagators and -sustainers for the worlds that depend upon them. *Tiphereth*, *Chesed* and *Geburah* form the second Triad, and *Jesod*, *Netzah* and *Hod* the third; these two Triads combined constitute the Hexad, which is the Soul of the world, and of it are derived the souls of all individualized existences. The second Triad depending upon the Celestial Sun is subjective, the third sustained by the Astral Suns is objective; the Hexad composed of the two contains both the subjective and objective principles, and souls consequently are likewise dual in their character, properties and impulses— the objective part receives material impressions, and through it we obtain our knowledge of the material universe, the world of effects not causes, while the subjective part receives spiritual impressions, called intuitive perceptions, and it urges us to earnest seeking after illumination and Divine Wisdom. Our reader will recollect that the Rosicrucians call the Light of the Celestial Sun *Sophia*, "the Wisdom of God," and the subjective part of man's soul partakes of this essence of Deity, while the objective part partakes in like manner of the antagonistic evil principle, and this evil part is in the ordinary man most active. Each part of the soul has its own faculties to be cultivated and nourished, or neglected. The unfolding of the objective faculties makes a man "carnal-minded," sensual, and he comes to be satisfied with the follies and views of this world, oblivious to the true interests of his soul; in proportion as these faculties develope and strengthen, man becomes blind and dead, spiritually, and when once under the domination of the objective part of his soul he is in such a state of spiritual death that he must be "born again" and become a "new creature," ere he can even "see the kingdom of God." Could a man cultivate and develope both his subjective and objective faculties equally he would be an inhabitant of both worlds at one time; but this is scarcely possible, for the unfolding of the subjective faculties opens to the soul visions of such glory and bliss in the Celestial World that the Terrestrial World ceases to interest him.

We have within a few months witnessed a most noteworthy case of this triumph of the subjective over the objective faculties within the soul: A lady of superior intellect and culture, of exceptionally kind and affectionate disposition, genial and ever cordial in her bearing to all, dearly loving and devotedly beloved by her husband and children, esteemed by all who came within the influence of her goodness—all her associations were such as to strengthen earthly ties, yet fully two weeks before her death these ties were completely sundered and all interest in this world evidently ceased, except only that her love for her faithful husband was undimmed—she was permitted subjectively to behold her Celestial Home and to realize the happiness and glory there laid up for her, and immediately her earthly home, with all its happy and enticing associations, lost its hold upon her—the side remaining tie was not sufficiently strong to lessen her intense longing for her Home in Heaven; with the view of that Home, she was enlightened as to the time of her departure, and she foretold the exact hour. She was a Kabbalist, with her subjective faculties in healthful exercise for years before her sickness, and her experience was what is called *illumination*. So in every case, if the subjective faculties of our soul be unfolded, we shall have our "conversation in Heaven," "lay up our treasures" there, and while still "in the world," we shall not be "of it." With our prize ever in view, we shall never "weary in well-doing," but "press on," calmly and uncomplainingly "bearing the cross," assured that we shall "wear the crown"—"the sufferings of this present time are not worthy to be compared with the glory which shall be revealed in us." The "children of Light" are not exempt from the trials and sufferings of the earthly pilgrimage, but they do not "walk in the darkness" of despair or uncertainty. May the "God of Light" illumine our dark minds with beams from His Celestial Glory, and fit us to enjoy a foretaste of Heavenly blessedness even in this world of darkness, and thus the more truly to enjoy the ineffable perfections of our Eternal Home.

The Kabbalists maintain that the want of harmony within the soul, caused by the activity of the evil faculties and the passivity of the good faculties, is sin or its direct cause, and results in placing him in bondage in darkness and error. The mission of Christ, they claim, was to deliver man from this bondage and make him "free indeed," by restoring the equilibrium or harmony within his soul. Those who achieve this deliverance and become obedient to the subjective or Divine principle, are called by the Kabbalists *Illuminati*, because their souls are illuminated by the Light of the Celestial Sun, the Divine *Sophia*, and by Christ they are designated "children of Light." Man himself can materially promote this deliverance "by self-denial, meditation and religious exercises," or, as Christ expressed it, by "taking up his cross and following Him."

The duality of the soul is one of the most beautiful and impressive doctrines of the Kabbala, and it is a Scriptural doctrine. James, in his Epistle, emphatically affirms the presence of the evil principle, when he declares: "The spirit that dwelleth in us lusteth to envy," and he recognizes that this evil part of the soul is of the devil, the evil principle in the world, when he admonishes us, in the same connection: "Resist the devil and he will flee from you." He clearly, too, teaches the dual principle in the soul: "Purify your hearts, ye double-minded." Paul's epistles abound in recognitions of the two antagonistic principles in the soul: "I delight in the law of God after the inward man; but I see another law in my members, warring against the law of my mind, bringing me into captivity to the law of sin which is in my members." There is a constant warfare between these two principles within us, until the good or the evil finally triumphs; the good must overcome the evil if we would attain to life in the Celestial World, and Paul urges Timothy "Fight the good fight of faith, lay hold on eternal life," and for his encouragement he declares: "For I am now ready to be offered, and the time of my departure is at hand; I have fought a good fight, I have finished my course, I have kept the faith." But a greater than Paul or James, their Master and ours, even Christ, counsels us: "Watch and pray, that ye enter not into temptation; the spirit indeed is willing, but the flesh is weak." The *flesh* cannot signify the body, because that cannot take part in leading us into, or keeping us out of temptation; the objective part of the soul, "the carnal mind," which is "enmity against God," and "whose God is the belly," is appropriately denominated "the flesh"—"the flesh lusteth against the spirit, and the spirit against the flesh, and these are contrary the one to the other." We need not Peter's testimony to the fact that "fleshly lusts war against the soul." The story of the "war in heaven," when "Michael and his angels fought against the dragon, and the dragon fought and his angels," is a beautiful allegorical picture of the unceasing warfare in the world, and in each soul of man, between Light and darkness, Truth and error.

As we have learned, pure white Light is the characteristic of *En Soph* and its Triad, of the Super-Celestial World, and of *Tiphereth* and its portion of the Hexad—this Light, too pure and dazzling for mortal vision, we know is seen alone by the subjective vision. Coming down to the objective portion of the Hexad, we find that Light loses its pure intense lustre and becomes visible to the human organ of sight and this is because the Fire principle becomes ascendent. Thus in the subjective portion of the soul Light rules, and in the objective portion Fire is dominant—of the one prevails, "the fruits of the Spirit" testify to its benign influence, but if the other prevails, "the works of the flesh" bear witness to its evil power. The Kabbalists aptly call the soul wherein the Celestial *Sophia* reigns, a Light Soul, while they as aptly style the soul wherein the subjective is subdued by the objective a dark Soul. The former, the "Child of Light," the Illuminatus, cannot "hide his Light under a bushel," it will shine forth in his works and make him a "Light of the World." So long as the Fire principle predominates, the Kabbalists tell us, the soul cannot soar above the earth's atmosphere, in which the Divine Light is never manifested, but it remains in bondage in darkness hovering around this world of darkness—but of this we shall speak hereafter. Meanwhile, we note that Fire appears as an evil principle, according to the Kabbala, but the reader must not imagine that it is necessarily, in itself, evil—it becomes an evil when the law of harmony no longer restrains its power, when it becomes master instead of servant. In *Tiphereth* and in the Celestial World, there is Fire as well as Light, but perfect harmony keeps it in its place, so to speak, and it performs its assigned work in obedience to the law of harmony.

What we have said of the duality of the soul, suggests a few words concerning the Kabbalistic doctrine of probation: the Kabbala teaches that the mundane life is one of probation for the development of the spirit and purification of the Soul, as the fœtal and embryotic life is a probation for the development of the physical form. Just as during the embryotic life, the development of the body may be retarded or stopped by an evil influence or power, so in the mundane life, evil within or without often hinders or stops the development of body, soul or spirit,—there is this important difference in the two probations to be kept in mind: the foetus can do nothing towards promoting or checking the development of its parts, but this must be subject entirely to good or evil influences outside of itself and beyond its control; the being, once born into the mundane existence, on the other hand, has it in his power materially to promote, or fatally to prevent, his progress towards the higher life; man is endowed with a will, and contains within his soul the germs of good and evil, the principles of Light and Fire, of good and evil, and it rests with him, in no small degree, to determine whether the good or the evil shall unfold and fill him with Light or darkness, with Life or death. Christ, "the Sun of Righteousness, with healing in His wings" [beams], has come to "bring Life and Immortality to light," and if man will but let His beams shine in his soul, the germs of good will unfold, the principle of good will be victorious, and he will be filled with "the Light of Life."

Lines connecting the fourth, fifth, sixth, seventh, eighth and ninth *Sephiroth*, the Hexad, bound *Jezirah*, the Celestial or Soul World. It is composed of the four Celestial elements, the universal Hyle (the Ether of modern science), the first Matter, the Abyss and the "Water above the Firmament" (the "fiery water" of the Alchemists); these elements are represented by the fifth, sixth, seventh and eighth *Sephiroth*, and correspond to the four elements of the material world, air, earth, fire and water. The *Rouach Elohim* broods over "the waters above the firmament," and the angels, laving themselves in their pure depths and quaffing Celestial nectar from their sweet fountains, preserve their perfect health and ever refresh and renew their strength, vigor and vitality.

The ninth *Sephira*, *Jesod*, "Foundation," so named because it is the life-source and sustainer of the life of and upon the Terrestrial Worlds, represent the Astral Suns, or the Suns of the material worlds. These are emanations from the Celestial Sun, and receive their Light and all their powers from that Central Orb; the Light of the Central Sun being too pure for mortal eyes, it is modified in the Astral Suns by permitting the Fire principle to prevail sufficiently to adapt it to human sight—the law of harmony is thus made less stringent in the Astral Suns not only to make them objectively visible, but to render their elements capable of separation and decomposition, and thus suit them, as we shall see, to the necessities of the material worlds. This relaxing of the law of harmony enables us to use the two elements, Light and Fire, in a measure separately, and farther enables us to analyze or separate the constituents of Light and Fire and apply them to multifarious and important uses; later we shall notice some of the immense advantages that the world derives and may derive from the relaxing of the law of harmony and the consequent privilege we enjoy of utilizing the constituent elementary powers of Light and Heat. Meanwhile, it is for us to notice that, though God thus relaxes His law of harmony, it is only for the good of His

creatures He does so, and He wisely maintains the
law sufficiently in force to hold the Sons in their
places and keep them to the work He requires of
them in His universal economy; though He permits
them to send forth destructive elements, He compels
them to send likewise elements which, intelligently
applied, counterbalance and antidote their power
for evil, or compensate and remedy evil wrought.
Such is the teaching of the Kabbala, and that it is
borne out by scientific tests and practical experience
will be shown later in this work.

The Astral Suns are truly, though in less or inferior
degree, manifestations of the Divine Will, and
we should not overlook the evidence of His Goodness
in that God adapts His manifestations of Himself to
the necessities and capacities of those to whom they
are vouchsafed. As "no man can see Him and live,"
He will not show even Moses all His glory, though
He manifests himself in a special manner to him, and
in an entirely different and less glorious manner to
the Israelites as a people. So now to those who can
behold it and live He manifests himself in the Celestial
Sun, and to those spiritually blind and incapable
of receiving or enjoying so glorious a manifestation,
He appears in the less glorious Astral Suns. He has
often chosen the element of Fire as His medium, for
example, at His first appearing to Moses in the Burning
Bush, and upon Mount Sinai to the children of
Israel, when " the sight of the glory of Jehovah was
like devouring fire on the top of the mount in the
eyes of the children of Israel;" in numberless instances,
when His presence was specially required, He

come in fire to consume sacrifices upon altars, as when the prophet wished to attest His true majesty and prove the Baal counterfeit. It was, no doubt, in consequence of God's frequent manifestation of Himself in and by Fire that the Persians and other people learned to regard Fire as the special symbol of God's presence, and worshipped Fire, or, as some affirm, worshipped God in Fire.

Zoroaster regarded the astral Suns as emblems of the Sun of Truth, or the True Sun, the great Central Orb of the universe—a shadow of the first source of all Splendor. For this reason, the "Wise Men" of the olden time saluted the rising of the Sun in the East and the dawning in the West, and for doing this "they have been accused by barbarians as Sun-worshippers."

The tenth *Sephira* is *Azirah*, the material world, the world of darkness, because the Divine or Celestial Light is not visible therein. Science teaches us that White is the harmonious blending of all the colors of Light, and that Black is the absence of all the colors, and where all the colors are absent, Light is certainly absent. Utter darkness is positive Blackness; hence, darkness is the absence of Light. The Kabbala tells us that when man disobeyed His Creator in attempting to steal forbidden knowledge, God punished him justly by withdrawing from him the Celestial Light in which he had hitherto basked, and enforced the promised penalty of disobedience by depriving him of the Light of Life, and thus of *real* Life itself—for spiritual Life is the *real* Life and it is dependent absolutely upon Celestial Light. Man, having now fallen from the condition of harmony with God, and thus lost the capacity to enjoy close communion with Him, he was "cast out of the garden" of Divine association and fellowship; the "flaming sword" which inhibited his approach to the "Tree of Life" was the prevalence in and about him of the Fire principle, which excluded him from farther partaking of the Divine *Sophia*, that teaches the law of harmony and thus imparts the ability to "live forever." Man, having lost spiritual sight and life, could not bequeath these to his posterity, and all his race are consequently "born blind." But the All-Wise did not will that man should be perpetually blind and dead spiritually, and while His Justice was punishing, His Mercy announced a plan of again bringing "Life and Immortality to light" by a new manifestation of Himself. He declared that though Satan, the evil principle, should still have the power to bruise the woman's seed as to the heel (checking his aspirations after a better life), the woman's seed should have the greater power of bruising him (Satan) as to the head (fatally in destroying his will-power or the power of freely exercising his will). This announcement has generally been understood to refer to the coming of Christ, "the Word made flesh," who was to be put to death physically, by the influence of Satan, but was to inflict far greater injury upon Satan by restoring the Celestial Light to the world of darkness; but while Christ was pre-eminently the promised Seed, the promise of God has had innumerable lesser fulfilments; in all ages there have been striking exceptions to the general rule of darkness; there have been individuals, and indeed communities, illuminated by that Light that bruises the head of the Prince of Darkness—there have been Goshens in the dark Egypts, wherein the "children of Light" have "not stumbled" though all around was dark with a darkness that was felt. Since the coming of Christ, the number of "children of Light" has been much increased by reason of His "preaching to the spirits in prison," His triumphs over demons, His imparting the "Light of Life," His work of Redemption, His final triumph over the Prince of Darkness, and His glorious outpouring of the Holy Spirit. But even yet darkness reigns over the earth, and "men love darkness rather than light."

Our world is also called the Synthetic World because man, its inhabitant, is a Synthesis in that he contains within him the properties of the kingdoms above, Soul and Spirit. Moreover it is called the Kingdom Unequilibrated, because it is purely objective, being the objective manifestation of the objective portion of the Hexad, just as the Soul World is called the Kingdom Equilibrated on account of its being subjective and therefore under the strict law of compensation or harmony.

Kabbalists maintained that water contains earthy matter, and that the inorganic matter of the planets was precipitated from water. This has been positively contradicted by modern Science. We can confidently affirm that the Kabbalists were absolutely correct in claiming that water contains earth, and it is at least possible that the inorganic matter of the planets was obtained from that source: we have produced a copious earth precipitate from pure oxygen and hydrogen in hermetically-sealed glass, and it is simply adamic earth. We have successfully continued the experiment by repetition.

We must now fulfil our promise to describe the "Tetractys" of Pythagoras.

Pythagoras correctly regarded the Ineffable Name of God, the Tetragrammaton, or Four-letter Name, as it has been called, as the key to the mysteries of the universe and of its creation and preservation, the mysteries of God whose Name it is. This is "the word" which so many have sought, that they might unlock the mystic secrets of Magianism, discover the treasures of Symbolism, and fathom the depths of Oriental Learning and Wisdom; Swedenborg declared "the word" to have been lost, but he erred—it was only its pronunciation, and unfortunately its import, that were lost or had become obscured. "And God spake unto Moses, and said unto him, I am the LORD: and I appeared unto Abraham, unto Isaac, and unto Jacob, by the name of God Almighty, but by my Name JEHOVAH was I not known to them." This Name in the Hebrew has but four letters only, the consonants alone being letters in the Hebrew tongue, the four letters are rendered in English by J (or more correctly Y), H, V, and H; the vowels did not appear in the earlier written language, and in this Name the loss of the pronunciation was due to the superstitious reverence the Hebrews entertained towards the word itself, which induced them whenever it occurred to substitute an entirely different word, ADONAI, for it in the reading; and from this dread of the word, and avoidance of it, in

ANCIENT IDEAS OF LIGHT AND HEAT. 47

time its awe-inspiring signification was lost; unenlightened commentators have made repeated attempts to discover this lost meaning, but until they show that *they believe* they have succeeded we need not give the definitions they have offered. The Kabbala has symbolized this awful Name of the Almighty, Incomprehensible One. We are by no means satisfied that the Tetragrammaton has been correctly vocalized JEHOVAH; the Name occurs in one of David's grand Psalms in the abbreviated form יה, vocalized יָהּ, in English JAH or more exactly YAH, and we suspect that the full name should be vocalized יהוה, English YAHVEH, rather than יהוה English JEHOVAH, as we have it. The English translators appear to have had the old Jewish superstitious dread of the word, for they almost always translate it into "The LORD," the only exceptions being in Exodus 6:3, Psalm 83:18, Isaiah 12:2, and Isaiah 26:4.

Fig. II.—Tetractys of Pythagoras.

But, to turn to the Diagram of Pythagoras: this great and singularly learned man took the four letters of the name יהוה and, arranging them as a pyramid or cone within a double circle, derived the ten numbers of creation from them. These ten numbers represent the *sitros* or principles of all things; these principles are unequal and equal, active and passive, masculine and feminine, expressed by the terms Unity and Duality; numbers 1, 3, 5, 7 and 9 express Unity, 2, 4, 6, 8 and 10 (separately considered), express Duality; the unequal numbers are limited and complete, equal numbers unlimited and incomplete; the absolute principle of all perfection is Unity, while Duality is imperfection; it is by the latter that forces are produced by which differentiation is perfected in the number 10, which, as the sequel or sequence of the entire system, is regarded as a perfect number and represents man, the synthesis of all created energy. The letter Jod (י) represents the *Monad* or Unity, the fountain of all things—the *En Soph* of the *Sephiroth*; the two letters (ה and ו) form the *Dyad*, the cause of increase and division, the two properties of Light, active and passive, the *Binah*, "Intelligence," and *Chocmah*, "Wisdom," of the *Sephiroth*; the three letters (י, ה and ו), containing the *Monad* and *Dyad*, form the *Triad*, and being thus a manifestation of *En Soph*, constitute the *Tiphereth* of the *Sephiroth*, the Central Sun of the Universe; the four letters (י,ה,ו and ה) separately represent the *Chesed*, *Geburah*, *Netsah* and *Hod*, which are polarized into *Jesod*, the Astral Suns; the product of the *Monad, Dyad, Triad* and *Tetrad*, is the *Decad*; as the sum of the four primary numbers it takes the name *Tetractys*, and as the complement of creation becomes the perfect number 10, which, as we have seen, represents man as the Synthesis; it comprehends, too, all musical and arithmetical proportions, and illustrates or denotes the system of the world. Pythagoras defines God to be *absolute Verity*, or *Truth* clothed with Light, and THE WORD embodied in the Light is the power that manifests forms; or to state it differently: THE WORD is the Divine Executive, and at the same time the Revealer of the mysteries of the Divine Will, the "hidden things of God." "No man hath seen God at any time; the only begotten Son, which is in the bosom of the Father, he hath declared [ἐξηγήσατο = "shown out" or "manifested"] him."

Pythagoras was one of the most remarkable men of his day; not only was he learned in the ordinary sense beyond his time, but he was a Kabbalist of the highest order. He is said to have been initiated into the Divine secrets of Nature by Daniel and Ezekiel; he was subsequently, after much opposition, admitted to the Egyptian mysteries upon the personal recommendation of King Amosis. His "Tetractys" is a fair illustration of his thorough acquaintance with Theosophic Science, as well as of his independence of thought. But the most notable fact we know of him was his knowledge of the truth in relation to the movements of the heavenly bodies which science did not make known for centuries after his death, and, if he was mistaken in reference to some of the details, his substantial correctness was none the less wonderful. He was the founder of the renowned School of Crotona, upon the south-eastern coast of Italy, about 500 B. C. He held that the Sun is the centre of the system around which all the planets revolve; that the stars are Suns like ours, each the centre of a system; that the earth revolves yearly around the Sun and daily on its axis; that the planets are inhabited, and that they and the earth are ever revolving in regular order, "keeping up a loud and grand celestial concert, inaudible to man, but, as the music of the spheres, audible to God." He was not permitted to declare publicly what he knew and believed, but taught his immediate pupils all the wonders of his philosophy, under the most binding obligation of secrecy. Pythagoras was especially forbidden to divulge this knowledge because it would reveal the law of attraction and repulsion, which constituted one of the great secrets of the sanctuary; Newton was led to the discovery of these forces by his studies of the Kabbala.

Speaking of Pythagoras calls to our mind the following singular Kabbalistic enigma written by Plato and sent to Dionysius: "All things surround our King [God]. He is the cause of all good things: Seconds for seconds and thirds for thirds." This expresses the complete philosophy of the *Sephiroth*. Plato was an earnest and most intelligent Kabbalist.

In concluding upon this portion of our subject, we cannot forbear offering a few thoughts upon the ten *Sephiroth* as a single entity. The group of categories or spheres, as seen in Plate I., has been styled the "Tree of Life," because it exhibits the true source of life and the means for the preservation and prolongation of life indefinitely into immortality: the Source is the Almighty Will of God as manifested in Light, and the means for the preservation and

prolongation of life is the Divine *Sophia* declaring
itself in the beautiful law of harmony as applied to the
creation and sustaining of the universe. The *Sephiroth*,
though ten in appearance are but one in fact—a manifestation of the Omnipotent Will in ten aspects; just
as the flame and sparks of a fire appear as several
objects to the eye and yet manifest but one fire, so the
ten *Sephiroth* are apparently plural and are actually
one with the *En Soph*, the Endless, Ineffable, Incomprehensible emanation from the God of Light and
Life.

Turning again to the plate, we observe that the
spheres range in three columns or pillars: the central
one, comprising the "Crown," and the Celestial and
Astral Suns, has been called the Pillar of Hercules,
and more aptly the Life Pillar. At the right of this
central one, is the Active Pillar, consisting of *Binah*,
Chesed and *Netzach*, "Intelligence," "Strength" and
"Firmness," representing the Fire principle, the masculine or active forces in creation and providence.
At the left is the Passive Pillar, representing the
Light principle, the feminine or passive properties in
creation and providence, as expressed in *Chocmah*,
Geburah and *Hod*, "Wisdom," "Beauty," and "Splendor." The two side pillars being in exact equilibration, the active and passive qualities equally performing their functions, the universe came perfect from the
Creator and moves in sublime beauty and complete
utility, in undeviating accord with the Will that called
it into being by the Word, and just as long and as far
as the two principles are in absolute equipoise everything must continue "very good" in God's sight.

This equilibrium is exactly maintained until we reach the Astral Suns, when we find it disturbed, but it still is upheld and respected in part—when, however, we pass to the material world we find the blackness of darkness, because God's law of harmony has been broken by man, and inharmony has brought disease, decay and death upon every species of life—nay, even upon the earth the seal of doom is set, change, dissolution are seen on all hands, and ultimately it shall pass away.

We have seen that, though God's Justice must be visited upon the world, and sickness and suffering, disease, decay, and death must follow the breach of the law of harmony, yet His Mercy and Goodness came to the rescue of the offender and his race by providing a remedy for spiritual blindness and death; nor did His Infinite Kindness stop here: He has also furnished suitable remedies for the physical ills resulting from man's fall; some of these remedial agents were long since discovered and have been successfully applied for many years, some even for many centuries, others have but recently been found out by science, and doubtless there are many the health-giving properties of which man has never yet discovered. Among those natural remedies which are only now in course of discovery are the color-rays of the objective light of our world, which we believe are destined, at no very distant day, to work a sensible change in the therapeutic practice not only of our country but of the world; so-called scientists may oppose their use in this important field, and may scoff at the startling facts that experience is reporting of their virtues, as their peers, in all ages of the world, have mocked at new discoveries not set down in their philosophy; but despite all opposition whatsoever they are to meet, the colors of the light will force and win their way into the effecting of a great, beneficent work among the sick and suffering. And there seems to us a peculiar fitness in this appropriation of the Sun's bright beams: the withdrawal of the Light of the Sun of Suns entailed sickness, pain and death upon man, and now shall not the beams from that Sun's offspring, the Sun of our system, be placed under tribute for relief? It is the purpose of this book not only to prove that the mild, gentle Blue ray has curative properties for some disorders, and the strong, warm Red ray for others, but to demonstrate just why they, and not the Green or Yellow, must be employed, and how they act, and then to explain the best methods for applying them.

CHAPTER II.

THE TRUE SCIENCE OF LIGHT — TRUTHS AND THEORIES—WHAT WE KNOW, AND WHAT WE BELIEVE.

THERE are those who question the Divine Source and Authority of the Bible, because they find within its pages statements that appear to be contradicted by known facts of Science. The cavillers, when sincere, lose sight of the real design and purpose of the Scriptures; and so those who dispute or deny the Divine origin of the Kabbala, fail to appreciate its true purpose and scope. The Kabbala was not designed to teach Natural Philosophy; Physical Science is only recognized therein in so far as it is directly related to or bears directly upon the higher Philosophy of Spirit and Soul Life. It is worthy of remark and of thoughtful consideration, that, while scientific research has, in a sense, added to what may be learned from the Kabbala, it has, in no one instance, established a fact antagonistic to a single tenet of that grand old system.

There is but one God, revealed in Nature and in the Holy Bible, and it is human blindness that fails to realize that oneness—the Kabbala is no more than an authorized interpreter, an expounder of the two harmonious Revelations, and the most enthusiastic Kabbalist claims no more for it. God manifested Himself in Light, and it became His direct Agent in creation and providence; He shed beams of that sublime Light into "holy men of old," illuminating them to see and know the mysteries of Creation, Providence and Redemption, and thus *inspired* them to pen the Sacred Scriptures; but the "natural man" could not receive "the things of the Spirit of God" "because they are spiritually discerned," and men were disposed to "wrest the Scriptures to their own destruction." And now God further testified the infinitude of His love, in that He illuminated men with the same Celestial Light to see and know and interpret the mysteries of the two Revelations.

It is also worthy of note that no inconsiderable number of the "discoveries" of Scientific seekers within modern times are but recoverings of old truths that were once known and forgotten; Pythagoras, as we have stated in the preceding chapter, knew the facts concerning our solar system, and that the stars were suns with systems similar to ours; that the planets were worlds peopled and probably much like the one we inhabit. Anaximander, too, of the School of Miletus, earlier than Pythagoras, taught much the same. Numa Pompilius knew of Electricity and the laws governing it; Pliny tells an ancient tradition of Pompilius: that he used an electric battery with success against a monster named *Vofta* who had desolated the countries belonging to Rome. [*Query*—Can this Phœnician Volta be a myth, or a reality? can the name of the Voltaic Pile date back to the time of Numa Pompilius, the sixth century before Christ, or can the Italian physicist have had any association with the "monster" of Pliny?]

During his study of Occultism, extending over a period of thirty years, the present writer has learned that the ancient philosophers knew much more of the universal cosmogony than modern scholars are usually disposed to admit. Indeed the ancients (I refer to those of the Mystic School) knew more of light, heat, electricity, magnetism and kindred topics, and of the original of matter and of its unfoldment into material forms, than Scientists of modern times have ever dreamed of. Little as Scientific men of our day know or are inclined to believe it, the greatest discoveries of the last century and a half can be traced directly to the ancient system of Occultism; few indeed know how very much modern science owes to the old Mystics. There is much more yet not learned by modern Scientists, that will in time be brought from the same source and set down as "discoveries." In our studies in this most interesting field, we have received aid from a source we do not desire at present to divulge, but to this source we are under obligations which forbid our telling some things we should otherwise much like to tell.

We have one important caution to urge upon the consideration of our reader: Always notice critically the distinction between the indisputable, immutable *facts* of Science, and the *theories* of Scientists—the former change not and constitute *absolute knowledge*, while the latter change often and may almost be styled *guesses*. From time to time a theory is advanced that is not swept away, but grows into or is proved to be a fact, but a vast majority of theories, after an uncertain life, fade away or are pushed aside by new theories, until ultimately the Truth is discovered. One fact established is worth more than hundreds of theories; it is the act of a fool to dispute a fact, and it is little less foolish to be excessively tenacious of a theory—not even a Newton's theory is too sacred to be disputed by the merest tyro in Science, for Newton has been found to have been mistaken in some of his theories. In Science, as in Religion, it is wise to "Prove all things; hold fast that which is good."

God is "the same yesterday, and to-day, and forever;" all Nature is controlled by fixed laws, called the laws of Nature, and these are laws of God; as God is one and unchangeable, so His laws are uniform and unalterable; the laws which God enacted when He said "Let there be Light," when He made "the greater Luminary to rule the day, and the lesser Luminary to rule the night," and when he called vegetable and animal life into action, are still in force and shall continue in force until He wills that natural life shall cease; Nature in its every phase, in life and in death, obeys the laws of the Supreme. While the laws of Nature, or, to be more specific, the laws of Light, for these comprehend all, have not changed, human understanding of these laws has undergone repeated and marvelous changes. The present scientific comprehension and definition of the laws of Light are comparatively of very recent origin; many of the views entertained and advanced, concerning Light and its functions, by Scientists, and supposed to have been proved by them, within but a few years, have been discovered to have been erroneous, and we have no doubt whatever that some of the to-day accepted teachings of Science will prove to-morrow equally untenable. Continued seeking will discover now hidden truths, and new floods of light will be shed upon the grand mysteries of Light, until the day of perfect and complete knowledge shall come and all the glories of glorious Light shall be seen and known, to the joy of the whole earth.

A few lines above, we have said that the laws of Nature are all comprehended in the laws of Light, and this is true. Light is the source, the sustainer, the renewer, of the universe and of all life therein—Light is the universal motor, the one prime source and cause of every motion and operation in and of the universe—motion and operation are life, and, hence, Light is the fountain of Life. But this universal motor is the Celestial Light of the infinite Central Sun of the universe—upon that glorious orb depends directly all spiritual life, and indirectly all natural life upon the earth and upon the planets—it is the source of the Astral Suns which control and sustain their worlds. Light is not Spirit, as the Indian Hierophants believed, but it is called the "substance of the intellect," because it is the instrument of Spirit—the substance through which the Divine Intellect and the Word operate. It was the first manifestation of the Divine Afflatus by which God eternally creates with His Will. The Light of the Celestial Sun is invisible to mortal eye, except in and through the Light of the Astral Suns; the Sun of our world is one of those Astral Suns, and it, in common with them, receives its Light and derives its power from that unseen chief Sun. The Celestial Light is pure and perfect in the harmony of its principles, and is incapable of being divided or separated into distinct rays, and to meet the requirements, the absolute necessities, of the objective worlds, it was necessary that it should manifest itself in the Astral Suns, wherein the relaxing of the law of harmony should make it possible to separate their light, into rays of various colors and various qualities—but for this adaptation of light to the exigencies of our degenerate world, we should not be able to apply the actinic rays to certain uses and the calorific to others. The fact that God has thus permitted the relaxation of His essential law of harmony, in order to place the special virtues of each ray of our Sun at our disposal for beneficent purposes, is sufficient reason why we should strive to learn how we may best avail ourselves of His gracious kindness. We shall more particularly discuss the several colors and the uses to which we may and should apply them later; before passing to the consideration of the facts demonstrated in modern Science and the theories of modern Scientists, we cannot but remark that light was the secret and universal medicine of the Ancients; they knew all its properties far better than modern Science is yet capable of teaching them; with it they were enabled to cure the most inveterate diseases; they knew how to condense, or *fix*, light so as to administer it in wine and oil. The medicinal qualities of light and modes of applying it, were among the great secrets of the Kabbala and of the Eastern Wise Men.

But, if Light be the great power of Nature, what is the nature of this light, and how does it act—how does it impart and sustain life? These are proper questions, and we propose to answer them, not precisely as the Scientists of our day answer them, and yet in a Scientific manner. Accepting the facts of Science, and judging critically the theories of Scientists, we shall submit some ideas that are not theirs; we shall reject some of their theories the more fearlessly, because it is certain that they have not attained that degree of complete knowledge which shall in due time forbid differences and dissent. The patent fact that such Scientists as Newton, Malus, Laplace, Biot and Brewster have been found to have been mistaken in some of their theories, supposed to have been discoveries and deductions, justifies us in believing that Huyghens, Thomas Young, Fresnel, Bunsen, Kirchhoff, Huggins, Janssen, Tyndall, Schellen and the others now accepted as authorities, may prove fallible —indeed, upon some points these eminent discoverers and teachers are themselves not in positive accord, while on others they evince that caution which must indicate lack of confidence in their own conclusions.

Tyndall tells us: "*Luminous* bodies are independent sources of light. They generate it and emit it and do not receive their light from other bodies. The sun, a star, a candle-flame are examples." Farther on, under the caption "Nature of Light," he does not really attempt to tell what its nature is, but he speaks of it as "the sensation of light," which it certainly is not, though it excites "the sensation of sight." Schellen, in his admirable work on "Spectrum Analysis," says: "Although the theory of light is now so completely understood that we are able to explain the most complicated optical phenomena, yet an elementary reply to the question, What is the nature of light? still presents some difficulty." Perhaps this difficulty has been felt by the several writers who have attempted to tell us precisely what light is, for they all content themselves with telling what it is not, adding sometimes "the theories generally received" upon the subject. The nearest approach to a direct statement we find is by Dr. Charles L. Hogeboom in Appletons' Cyclopedia; he says, it is "that force in nature which, acting on the retina, produces the sensation of vision." How very weak is this definition! But let us try Schellen again: "Every substance which sets the ether in powerful vibration is luminous; strong vibrations are perceived as intense light, and weak vibrations as faint light, but both of them proceed from the luminous object at the extraordinary speed of 186,000 miles in a second, and they necessarily diminish in strength as they spread themselves over a greater space. Light is not therefore a separate substance, but only the vibration of a substance, which, according to its various forms of motion, generates light, heat or electricity." This is about the weakest paragraph we have met with in Schellen's truly excellent work, and yet this is the nearest approach to the truth we have been able to find; "Light is not a separate substance"—true! neither is it "only the vibration of a substance"—the vibration (if there be a vibration, which we do not believe for reasons we shall give) is simply the means assisting the ether in carrying and disseminating light. Behind the vibration and superior to the luminous body which sets the ether in motion is *Light, the positive power or force in Nature*, which, emanating from the Almighty Creator, has a grand, mighty mission—no less than the originating, controlling, directing and perfecting of all the movements, operations and processes of Nature. Light is the mysterious power which, setting aflame the Sun, imparts to it its special characteristic—the Sun is it visible representative, its agent, and the other its messenger to carry it to its destination. Light itself is, like the ether, invisible, and it makes itself seen, manifests itself, in everything we see; everything in Nature is a manifestation of this all-pervading, all-producing, all-controlling, all-invigorating power, just as it is the manifestation of God Himself. Luminous bodies, therefore, are not "independent sources of light;" they do not "generate it," though, as the agents of Light, they do " emit it." They are reservoirs to receive and distribute the luminous essence— of the Astral Suns this is most strikingly true, as they are the vast reservoirs of light for their worlds. None of the "accepted" theories, we venture to affirm, can be made to account for the vast influence of Light in any one department of Nature, to say nothing of its stupendous work in the worlds of the universe: a "Sensation" could not give to the blade of grass its delicate tint, much less could it cause its germ to develope into a thing of beauty and utility—a "vibration" could not paint the rose or shape and adjust its petals, much less could it carry it forward from its embryotic to its perfect state, and what proportion of all the varied and wonderful processes of Nature's vast laboratory could be ascribed to "that force in nature which, acting on the retina, produces the sensation of vision"? But, recognize Light as "a positive power or force in Nature," an actual and active manifestation of the Omnipotent Will of "the Creator and Preserver of all things," His agent and instrument in creation and providence, and we have an ample, all-sufficient *causal power or force* for all the wonders of Nature. Nor will this definition of Light antagonize any of the known facts of Science, or, in itself, necessarily militate against "accepted theories" as to the methods of the dissemination and action of light. It is but necessary to keep in mind the distinction between Light, *the power or force*, and its apparition or visible representative, the light we see. The former is what the Kabbalists call CELESTIAL LIGHT, or SUBJECTIVE LIGHT, and the latter they style OBJECTIVE LIGHT—we know of no better way to keep the important distinction in view than by adopting the name CELESTIAL LIGHT for that mighty, invisible something that we have defined as "the power or force," and "its apparition or visible representative" we shall speak of by its common designation, light.

There is in nature no vacuum—none is possible; as a learned writer has expressed it "Nature abhors a vacuum." The spaces throughout the universe wherein there is no other matter are occupied by an impalpable, invisible substance called Æther, or Ether. Schellen says: "The whole universe is an immeasurable sea of highly attenuated matter, imperceptible to the senses, in which the heavenly bodies move with scarcely any impediment. This fluid, which is called ether, fills the whole of space—fills the intervals between the heavenly bodies as well as the pores or interstices between the atoms of a substance." Tyndall calls this something "luminiferous ether," and declares that "it extends, without solution of continuity, through the humors of the eye." This ether is the *hyle* of the ancient philosophy. We do not know why Schellen calls ether a "fluid," or why Tyndall says "its mechanical properties are rather those of a solid than those of an air;" the most that can be known of it is that it is luminiferous when in requisition as the light-bearer, absolutely invisible except when polarized, and impalpable at all times—whether it be solid, fluid or gas, we opine, depends upon the substance with which it is associated. However, we have here to notice it in its employment as light-bearer, and to state how it performs the duty assigned it.

Newton supposed that light consisted of minute particles shot out by luminous bodies, fine enough to pass through the pores of transparent bodies—this is the famous "Emission Theory" which was accepted and maintained by Laplace and other Scientists of deservedly high repute. But Huyghens, and after him others of equal eminence, notably Thomas Young and Augustin Fresnel, successfully opposed the "Emission Theory," advocating what is known as the "Wave Theory" or the "Undulatory Theory." The former is now entirely discarded, and the latter almost universally adopted by Scientific authorities. According to this theory, a luminous body being in a state of incandescence, its molecules become agitated, the ether between them partakes of this agitation and passes it to the ether without the body, and it is then borne in every direction by the ether, moving in waves; as the ether fills space, occupies all the intervals between bodies of matter, and actually fills the pores between the atoms of all matter, of course the waves roll on and bear their glorious burden not only through space and to the surfaces of bodies but actually into their pores; as the ether "extends, without solution of continuity, through the humors of the eye," the light is borne to the retina and the sensation of sight is produced.

We confess to no little diffidence in calling in question a theory which is received and maintained by all the distinguished Scientists of the present day, and is sustained by a very strong array of arguments. One of its most eminent champions, Professor Tyndall, however, appears not to feel over-confident that it will permanently establish itself as a fact of Science. He says: "The justification of a theory consists in its exclusive competence to account for phenomena." We think the word "exclusive" could well be omitted, and the word "general" might be substituted, in this "justification." We believe that we shall show that there is a "theory" that, though not hitherto advanced, so far as we know, by any recognized Scientific authority, stands on quite as strong a foundation of fact and reason as the "wave theory," and is more justifiable even than that "now universally accepted theory," because it more exactly and more completely "accounts for phenomena." We have long studied Light in all its workings and in its every phase, and long since found an insurmountable objection to the "wave theory" in the well-known fact that two or more sets of waves, in any element or produced by any influence, coming together at any point must weaken, and are apt to destroy each other. In the transmission of light, ether-waves must constantly meet this sort of opposition not only from other light-waves, but from sound-waves as well, for if an ether-wave bearing light meet an air-wave bearing sound, unless their undulations happen, as is scarcely possible, to be in perfect harmony, the stronger air-wave must suppress the ether-wave; in this connection it is well to bear in mind that, according to Scientific opinion, the air in carrying sound moves in *longitudinal* waves, while the ether in carrying light moves in *transverse* waves—hence, harmony between a set of air-waves and a set of ether waves is really out of the question; it is well also to bear in mind that the destroying influence of collision or attempted commingling would be the more inevitable on account of the unquestioned fact of Scientific knowledge that the ether-atoms in the atmosphere are actually within the spaces between the air-atoms—this would render independence of wave-motion impossible, and the ether would necessarily lose its own waves in accommodating itself to the stronger air-waves. Again, it is a well-known fact that wind interferes with sound-waves, and as ether is incalculably lighter than air, we shall have to look to the wave-theorists to explain why light is not checked or driven out of its course by even a hurricane.

Besides, we have never been able to understand how ether in the pores of a solid could vibrate or undulate at all, much less at the rate of from 39,000 to 57,500 waves to the inch (the wave-theorists tell us the ether bearing the Red ray makes 39,000 waves to the inch, and that bearing the Violet makes 57,500 waves to the inch, the other colors having numbers between these extremes), especially when the necessary lack of strength that must characterize *waves of impalpable ether* is taken into account; then can any one not an enthusiastic wave-theorist conceive of such a tremendous agitation in that delicate piece of mechanism called the eye when seven rays, each with a distinct wave-motion of its own, attempt to pass through to the retina at the rate of 37,000 to 57,500 waves per inch, and at a uniform speed of 186,000 miles a second? What eye could survive such a commotion amid its *humors* and such an onslaught upon its retina? Could we believe the "wave theory" we should desire for our own eyes, and should advise others to wear, the deepest blue spectacles and thus exclude six of the waving rays with their quarter of a million waves.

These two objections are, in our estimate, fatal to the "wave theory," and yet there is another more weighty than the two: light, as it comes from the great Solar reservoir, is a unit—not seven rays, but one Sunbeam; though it contains the dual attributes, the active and passive, the positive and negative, the polar force and the chemical function, they are so exactly equilibrated, so perfectly in harmony, that they form absolutely a unit; this unity is slightly affected by contact with our terrestrial atmosphere, which extracts from it *in transitu* a small amount of its chemical Blue, and a portion of its calorific ray as

well, still the unity is substantially maintained until
actual contact with the earth and earthly objects, when
it is interrupted, and the beam distributed, in order to
permit each virtuous principle to perform its part in
Nature's vast laboratory; before the prism was devised
to analyze the Sunbeam, and Science learned to test
and judge of the special qualities and virtues and
functions of each ray, before the God-given penetration of man enabled him to ascertain what were the
several principles and what was the mighty Agent,
the seven faithful workers and the potent Light-unit
were busy throughout the world accomplishing the
grand, beneficent work required of them; the prism
has not changed the light or its united and separate
nature and attributes—it has only shown us that the
great unit has seven members, so to speak, working in
perfect harmony, obediently to the laws of the Supreme.
The smallest blade of grass and the mightiest oak, the
tiniest mite and the huge elephant, the scarce-formed
fœtus and the intellectual giant—all Nature owes its
every form and feature of physical life to Light, the
mighty Unit, not to seven rays. The ancients fully
understood this, and they never thought of light as
seven rays riding through space on seven broomsticks
or waving on seven distinct sets of waves; they knew
accurately and perfectly all that man can know of the
secrets and mysteries of Nature—of the essence and
nature of Light as well as of its great work in creation
and providence; as we have said earlier in this chapter,
the ancients knew vastly more of the causal world
than all the Scientists from Galileo or Newton to the
present day have ever learned—incalculably more

than the Tyndalls, Schellens and other wave-philosophers will learn for centuries to come unless they go to those old sages and learn of them, verifying what those old marvels of knowledge teach by all the means that Scientific research and study and inventive genius have placed at the command of students in this *enlightened* century.

Theories are well enough when certain knowledge is out of reach, but theories are at best most unsatisfactory, while knowledge satisfies the longings of our best intellectual and spiritual parts; knowledge is attainable by all who seek it aright at the right sources. There are a few points wherein theories are permissible because the knowledge we may attain to is, in a measure, incomprehensible by our limited perceptions, but steady seeking will discover the truth that shall establish or dissipate our theories in due time, even in the most incomprehensible mysteries of Nature and of Nature's grandest power, Light. We conceive that the one fact of the unity of Light utterly suppresses the waves or undulations of modern Scientists—a Sunbeam cannot come in seven parts upon seven sets of waves.

But, we do not reject the "wave theory" and its several subordinate theories, without having ready to offer a better; a "theory" doubtless some may deem it, but it is really more—it is, we firmly believe, a Scientific fact; we claim no credit for originality or authorship—all we claim is such credit as may be due to patient study of the old Philosophy, out of which study it has grown (just as Newton's "discovery" grew out of his studies in the same old mines of knowledge), and to careful application thereto of Tyndall's "justifying" test as cited above; we believe that " the justification of a theory consists in its competency to account for actual phenomena," and we only ask for this "theory" that it be submitted to that test. For the sake of greater ease in reference to, and criticism of, this "theory" we will call it "*the impulse and tension theory ;*" but, as we consider it a fact or truth, rather than a theory, we shall state it accordingly:

When a luminary sends forth a beam of light, it imparts to that beam an impulse, in exact proportion to its own power, sufficient to send it to the limit of the periphery of the space illuminated by the luminary, subject to opposing and interposing influences— *e.g.*, the Sun imparts to every Sunbeam an impulse sufficient to propel it to any and every point within the vast circle comprised in the solar system, and every beam, obedient to its impulse, travels to the outermost verge of that circle in a direct line unless turned aside by a denser medium intercepting its course or stopped by a body that will not afford it passage through its pores ; so a taper gives to its tiny light-ray an impulse proportionate to its own brilliance, which is the measure of its power. But a beam of light must have a conductor as well as an impulse, and this conductor it provides for itself, calling in requisition the all-pervading ether ; upon contact with ether, the first resistant substance it meets, light excites tension with it, temporarily polarizing it into an infinite network of ether-wires in all directions, along which, as a system of perfect conductors, it travels, at the rate of 186,000 miles per second, whithersoever its Divinely-appointed mission calls it, if but a Sunbeam to bless the worlds of the solar system, if but a taper-ray to bless the individuals within its reach. The ether-wires, like the ether at rest, are impalpable and invisible, until, upon contact with opposing influences, their polarity is in different degrees modified and new poles are established, when the ether may be polarized in color, as we shall see, or incorporated with soil or other substances into the pores of which it has borne the light. As ether fills space and occupies every spot not occupied by any other substance, actually filling the interstices between the atoms of every substance, and these light-conductors lead wherever ether is found or can enter, so wherever they lead, light goes quietly, peaceably, without being agitated or producing agitation. The Sun is the mighty battery, the ether-wires the conductors to bear its light with its countless and incalculably precious blessings to all parts of the solar system; or, to employ an illustration all may understand, the Sun is to the solar system what the heart is to our physical organism, and the ethereal conductors serve as the arteries—this difference must be noted: *each bearer of light creates its own conductors out of the Divinely-provided ether, and the ether-wires are but temporary, decomposing into their ether-atoms as soon as their work is done or changing their polarity to color objects or to mix with the earth or some of its products.*

The thoughtful reader will see that the impalpable ether-wire in passing through the air may readily adapt itself to such motion as it may meet without impeding or impairing the light in transit; that it may pass into or through the pores of any solid, fluid or gas, with much greater ease than could seven sets of waves with independent and different motions; that it can pass through the humors of the eye "without solution of continuity," to the retina, and not agitate or disturb that most sensitive organism; and that it conducts the beam of light undivided at a uniform speed through a homogeneous medium until contact with a denser body, medium or otherwise, modifies its polarity. And the candid Scientist who will carefully investigate the matter will find that "the impulse and tension theory," so far from antagonizing any known fact of Science, actually simplifies and makes easy of comprehension many phenomena and operations of light that have hitherto taxed the ingenuity of skilful Scientists to explain or reconcile with their pet theories. There is one argument in support of "the impulse and tension theory" that alone entitles it to thoughtful consideration: the ablest Scientists now recognize electricity as a product of light or a form of light—now, no wave can be conceived of capable of carrying an electric flash, while tension of ether provides a suitable conductor.

As we have said everything is made visible by light; without light there could be no sense of sight. The Sunlight, as it shines around and about and upon us, shows but one brilliant color, while it is really seven colors in one, nay, an innumerable variety of colors, tints and shades beautifully blended in the one we see. Objects around us appear red, blue, white, black, green, gray and of every conceivable hue, but in reality color belongs exclusively to light, and light is the incomparable artist that, with matchless skill, imparts, of and from its own glorious self, to each object the hue or tint or positive color best suited to it. The apple-tree, with its dark brown trunk and lighter brown branches, its green foliage, its pale blossoms, its fruit changing from green to brilliant crimson or delicate blush; the rose, with its brown stalk, green dress and red, pink or white flower; the modest violet, tiny-blossomed alyssum, the gaudy rhododendron and the simple grass; the marble, the granite, each precious gem; the beasts, the birds, the fishes, the reptiles, and the smallest mite; even man of every race and clime—all Nature, of every known species, owes to Light its endless variety of color and tint and hue and shade. *Color is simply light polarizing the ether in the bodies it enters*, and converting darkness into light. Not only Nature, but man's vaunted Art owes all of its claims to admiration to the glorious and glory-creating beams of Sunlight; the genius of a Raphael, a Rubens, a Bierstadt, a West, a Hamilton, or a Rothermel, or the combined genius of all the world-renowned artists of all ages and climes, could not produce a single "gem of art" if denied the boon of obtaining colors from Sunlight.

The popular teachers of Science unite in telling us that every body possesses, in a greater or less degree, a certain quality they call *selective absorption*, which, they tell us, enables each body to *select* certain rays of the light that enters its pores, which it absorbs, while the other rays it casts out and reflects from its surface; they tell us that these ejected rays give or lend to the body its color—that is, when the seven colors have entered its pores, the body absorbs one or more, and casts out the rest, the latter pass out and are reflected, and as a reward for this rejection the discarded ray or rays impart to the body the beauty of their own color: if the Green alone be reflected, the body appears Green, and if two colors be reflected, the body appears of the shade produced by combining those two, and so on; the colors absorbed have no influence upon the color of the body. Moreover, those teachers tell us that light only *lends* its colors to objects while it shines upon them.

Now the facts are, in our opinion, diametrically opposed to all these *selective absorption*, *reflection* and *lending* theories: The several bodies have no voice or choice in determining what colors or shades of color they shall assume—Light is independent in the exercise of its art, recognizing no authority but that of the laws of Nature; in deference to that code, it paints the mineral, the vegetable, the animal. Borne by its ether-conductor, light reaches a body; the polarity of the ether is broken, and the Sunbeam is divided at the surface, certain colors enter and polarize the ether in the pores, imparting to it their own colors, or the shade produced by their combined colors; the colors that do not enter shed their smiles upon the surface, increasing its lustre, and then pass on to other objects which they in turn enter and paint. When a single color enters an object it imparts to it its own color; hence, objects become Red, Yellow, Green, Blue, etc. The infinite variety of tints and shades of color are produced by the harmonious combining of two or more colors within an object. When all the colors enter and are harmoniously fixed in an object, in the proportions of the *Spectrum*, the object becomes White; when all refuse to enter a body, it remains Black, as in darkness, except that the light on its surface makes the Black visible; the many shades of Gray are caused by the colors entering and being fixed harmoniously but not in the proportions of the *Spectrum*; White is often produced by the mixture of but two colors (*e. g.* Indigo and Yellow, Orange and Blue), or of more than two though less than all (*e. g.* Red and Greenish Blue, Greenish Yellow and Violet, Green and Purple), and so, too, a body may appear Black though all the colors do not refuse to enter its pores and abide therein—if two or more inharmonious colors, or colors that will not combine harmoniously, thus enter a body, they destroy each other's influence, and the body remains Black. As the color of a body or a substance is the polarization of ether in its pores by light, so the color may be changed by decomposing the ether in a body or substance, and removing the color, or part of it, or adding a color, and then repolarizing the ether: the bleaching of a piece of linen or muslin is an interesting illustration of the action of Sunlight in thus changing an object from a Yellowish or Brownish shade to a pure White. Two or more colors that produce White are called complementary colors, a recognition of White as the *complement* of colors.

In the case of a transparent body or substance, the light-bearing ether passes through its pores and, none being posited in its passage, it remains absolutely colorless and invisible; pure unpolarized ether is the only substance that is colorless and invisible in the presence of light, and it is therefore the only truly transparent substance known. But, as ether is impalpable as well as invisible, we must take a substance that, though not truly transparent, is sufficiently so to serve as an illustration of what we desire to explain.

Glass must serve us: prepared with care, it is sufficiently transparent to permit the luminiferous ether to pass through with scarcely perceptible effect upon either; it is on account of this quality, that glass is made into panes for our windows. Now, when we wish to impart a color to glass we introduce matter of the desired color among the materials in process of manufacture, or we apply a pigment to the surface of the manufactured glass. In either case, especially in the former, we find that the glass has assumed the color of the pigment, and that the glass is transparent now only to its own color, except that it permits very small quantities of the colors next above and below it in the scale to pass through—the other colors of the light are arrested at the surface and are said to be "thrown down." Thus, a pane of glass colored Blue is fully transparent to the Blue light-ray, to a very small extent to its congenial neighbors, the Indigo and the Violet, and to a still less extent to the Green; all the other rays are "thrown down." But of this and its advantages, we shall speak when we come to tell how light-rays must be utilized in the treatment of disease; we must now explain how the glass becomes Blue, and why it is now transparent only to the Blue ray and its immediate neighbors: The pigment introduced or applied, has already incorporated with it Blue-ray-bearing ether before it is combined with the glass, the combination does not disturb the polarity of the ether, and thus the Blue becomes a constituent part of the glass; the ether now in the pores of the glass, being especially devoted to the transmission of the Blue-ray, it only can pass through—the passage of the Green, Indigo and Violet can readily be understood by any one who examines the color-scale shown by a prism, as described below; it will be seen that the color-bands are not separated by sharp lines, but shade off into one another.

The atmospheric envelope of the earth is transparent, but not perfectly so; it is warmed by the calorific and very slightly tinted by the Blue ray in the passage of light through its pores; but this Blue can only be perceived by the eye when the air is seen in mass; hence the color of the sky which is simply the limit of our vision, in looking towards which we look through the mass of atmosphere. The beauteous luminous appearance that surrounds us during the interval between dark and Sunrise, and between Sunset and dark, is not in any sense or degree independent of the Sun, as some suppose and as a writer has recently suggested; the vapors ever in the air form a perfect reflector and refractor, and they borrow from the Sun, before it is itself visible and after it has passed from view, the delightfully subdued light that makes the dawn and the twilight. The more or less obscure or dim light that is apparent when clouds hide the Sun is due to the partiality of Sun-rays for vapors and the responsive disposition of the vapors to quench or retain light; more or less of the Sunlight forces itself through even the densest clouds, the amount being of course in proportion to the density; the occasional Reddish appearance of thick clouds is owing to the tension of the Red-ray ether; the superior luminosity of the Yellow ray often gives dense clouds a Yellowish cast. The Red appearance borne by late evening and early morning clouds is due to the tension of the Red-ray ether and its consequent less refrangibility, which makes the Red disappear, last and appear first upon the vapory reflector as the Sun retires or approaches. So, too, the Red aspect of the Sun seen through a fog is occasioned by the greater tension of the ether bearing the Red rays, the other rays having a disposition more or less pronounced, in proportion to their tension, to stop with the vapor. One of the most pleasing effects produced by the disposition of some of the rays to cling to clouds is the bluish silvery appearance light, floating clouds often present.

The writer referred to above cites the account of the Creation in Genesis, to show that there was light before there was a Sun, and argues from that fact that there is light now independent of the Sun.—Yes! there was Light before our Sun was created, just as there was water before the oceans, seas and lakes were formed; and there is a grander more glorious Light than our Sun can produce or show forth. But that Light was and is the Celestial Light which no mortal eye may behold—which only the "children of Light" may see and they only with the subjective eye of the Soul. There is not, and there never was, objective light independent of the Sun, except that of his co-suns, which we call stars.

Before passing to the consideration of the *modus operandi* of analyzing Sunlight and ascertaining the colors and properties of the separate rays, we wish to allude briefly to the remarkable analogy between light and sound as seen in their respective scales of seven—seven tones in music, the harmony of sound, and seven colors in beauty, the harmony of light. Hargrave Jennings says: "There is a singular and mysterious alliance between color and sound." Substituting the word light for color, this is a happy way to allude to one of the most striking illustrations of the harmony that is the characteristic of all that is produced by the Supreme Will of God—of course, the light we allude to is the visible light, for the Celestial Light, as we have shown, is the universal motor, and, therefore, the author of sound as well as of light. As we shall see presently, light, when divided, shows seven colors, ranging from Red to Violet, and invariably occupying the same relative position in the scale, and so sound, when analyzed, shows seven tones, ranging from the deep bass to the alto, and always occupying the same relative position in the sound scale. The seven colors harmoniously and naturally blended represent beauty to the eye, and so the seven tones harmoniously and naturally produced represent music to the ear.

All visible light may be analyzed or separated into rays, but we have here to consider only Sunlight and its rays:

The Sunbeam is a unit comprising nine rays in perfect harmony, and travels in a direct line upon etherwires formed by its own polar principle exciting tension of ether, sustaining its unity while traversing the homogeneous ether; but, upon passing into the atmospheric envelope of the earth, the increased density of the air modifies the polarity of the conductor, and the beam begins to divide; it leaves in passing a portion of its calorific ray to warm the air, a small portion of its Blue ray to tinge the sky, such light, floccy clouds as it passes through it paints in fading tints of Red, or Yellow, of a rich golden or a mild silver hue, and the vapors that pervade the atmosphere borrow and reflect portions of the entire beam, the reflection producing the beauteous, delightful sheen of dawn and twilight. The Sunbeam, upon reaching us, however, betrays no lack of beauty in consequence of its generous bounty by the way; but upon contact with the earth or earthly objects, the beam entirely throws aside its unity and distributes its rays with their several colors and virtues wheresoever they can do the most good in beautifying the world and its objects and in making the earth happy in the fruitfulness of its fields and the prosperity of its cities.

Sunlight has seven clearly defined colors, and two colorless rays of most pronounced qualities; the colors are seen in the Rainbow which is the reflection, upon a cloud-screen, of Sunlight that has been divided into its colors by a natural prism consisting of raindrops falling between the Sun and the cloud-screen; but, as the moisture-prism or the screen vary in density, the colors are not always defined with equal clearness, though they invariably appear in the order of the spectrum (except that sometimes a second Rainbow shows the spectrum inverted). For the purpose of exactly analyzing a Sunbeam and measuring its rays, an artificial prism is employed, consisting of a wedge-shaped piece of glass or other transparent substance, and the separated rays are thrown upon a suitable white screen, where they appear in seven color-bands—these seven bands form the *Solar Spectrum*. The spectrum always shows the seven colors, not in sharply drawn lines of equal width, but the colors shade off into each other, while, as we shall note, the widths of the bands are very different. The colors are: 1. Red, 2. Orange, 3. Yellow, 4. Green, 5. Blue, 6. Indigo, 7. Violet, and the colorless rays are: a *calorific*, which is found below the Red, and an *actinic*, above the Violet; those below the Green are the positive rays and the others are the negative rays—heat is the most noticeable quality of the former and actinism, or chemical action, of the latter. The colorless rays are the extremes of the positive and negative portions of the spectrum. The Red is the positive polar ray, and the three Blue rays are the negative; the Yellow is the most luminous, and the Orange combines the Red and Yellow in character as well as color; the Green is negative, but is influenced by the Yellow. We shall have occasion in later chapters to speak at some length of the specific properties of the several rays, of their functions in Nature, and of their respective values in the treatment of disease, and therefore will not dwell longer now upon this part of the subject.

The tension of the luminiferous ether excited by the lightbeam upon first contact is not entirely relaxed until the beam has reached its ultimate destination; when light is reflected or refracted, the ether-wire being elastic is bent not sundered, and when the light is distributed, portions becoming fixed in color, while other portions assume their duties in carrying forward the operations and processes of Nature, there is simply a suitable change of polarity. We have seen that, upon passing from the ether-mediums into the air, the increase of density affects the polarity of the ether-wire sufficiently to enable the beam to posit portions of its rays in the air and clouds; so, upon passing from the air into glass, a still denser medium than the air, we see that, though the polarity of the conductor is maintained, the increased density evidently affects it, variously according to the form of the glass and its position in relation to the beam—if the glass be in the form of a square block or flat sheet, with parallel sides, and the beam enter at right angles, it is merely retarded and, upon its escape into the air, goes on its way just as if it had met no obstruction; if the sides are parallel and the beam strikes obliquely, the conductor is bent according to the angle of incidence, the beam passing directly not obliquely through the glass—the rays resist this bending in exact proportion to their tensive power, the Red ray being the most positive is therefore the least bent and the Violet being the most negative is the most bent; upon escaping into the air, the Red straightens its wire and, its influence assisting the tendency of the elastic ether-wires to recover their course, brings the other rays to itself, the unity of the beam is restored and it proceeds towards its destination; but when the sides of the glass are oblique, the rays are so much refracted and their conductors so bent that the Red has lost its power to draw the others to itself, and the wires unaided, though they show their former tendency by a partial straightening, cannot recover their original line; hence, the beam is divided, so that, unless a lens of suitable focus is made to lend its aid, the division is permanent, and the separate rays go forwards on constantly diverging lines; by placing a white screen at a proper distance from the prism, the spectrum of seven colorbands is reflected upon it. Now, as we have seen, the Red ray has the greatest power of resisting the refracting power of the glass, because it is the active, positive ray, while the Violet being its extreme opposite, the most negative ray, its conductor is consequently least tense and offers the least resistance to the bending; hence, the Red is invariably seen at the foot of the spectrum and the Violet at the top, the other rays coming in between according to the tension of their conductors. Thus, we see at a glance just why the order of the chromatic scale is invariable. We may see in the foregoing explanation, also, why the Red is the most heating and the Violet, the most cooling of the color-rays in their influence: resistance developes heat and the former offers the most resistance, and the latter the least, to antagonistic influences. By means of a lens of suitable focus placed at the right point, the unity of the beam may be restored—this proves what we have said above as to the continuance of the tension of the ether conductor; the tension is only controlled by a superior force during the separation, and as soon as the assistance of the lens enables it to overcome that force it reunites the beam.

It is interesting to note here an illustration of the

law of harmony suggested by the spectrum: the Red ray being the most potent is proportionately smaller in bulk, so to speak, than its chief opponent, the Blue, and much smaller than the Violet. Dividing the spectrum into 170 parts, we find the rays occupy the following portions: Red, 20; Orange, 20; Yellow, 30; Green, 20; Blue, 25; Indigo, 20; Violet, 35. The difference appears the more marked when we consider that the Blue, Indigo and Violet are all decidedly, and the Green essentially, chemical in their character, while the Red is but slightly sustained by the Orange and very slightly by the Yellow; this would show that the chemical rays, not including the Green, are as 80 to 20, or if we include the Green with the chemical and the Orange and Yellow with the calorific Red, we find the proportion 100 negative to 70 positive.

We have defined, with sufficient clearness and emphasis our views, or we may say our knowledge, of the mighty power in Nature, the universal motor, the life-producer, life-preserver, life-promoter, life-restorer, Light—we have also noticed briefly the light we see, the apparition or visible representative of that Celestial Power. We must be distinctly understood in this: When we speak, in the ordinary way, of what light does, or what this or that color does or is capable of doing, we recognize always that it is Light, the power or force, that is the active, though unseen, principle, operating through and by the visible light and its several colors.

We have spoken of Light as the Power or Agent wherein God manifested Himself in Creation, and the propriety of this will be seen in a later chapter where we treat of Universal Dynamics, as we therein show that water is generated by the combustion of Hydrogen with Oxygen (such as no doubt is constantly in progress in the Sun's photosphere), and that earth is a precipitate of water; thus by the Word of His Will God called into existence Light, and endowed it with the power, operating through the Astral Suns, to produce Water, and from that Water to precipitate Earth, causing "dry land to appear." The thoughtful Bible student will readily see that this tracing of the process of Creation does not derogate from the Supreme Power and Will of the God of Light, as it does not ascribe to Light any power independent of God—it is Light manifesting the Power and Will of the Almighty and the Divine One working in and by Light.

He sees fit ever to work in and by instrumentalities. But we are not now discussing Universal Dynamics; our present theme is rather the visible light, the manifester of the Celestial Light. We have shown what this visible light is, what are its component rays as discovered and measured by the prism, how it is sent from the great Light reservoir, the Sun of our Solar System, and how it makes for itself a suitable conductor to carry it throughout the space belonging to our Sun.

We may form a partial estimate of the power of the Sun by endeavoring to comprehend the extent of space under his influence and control and the number and size of the worlds that owe their existence, their preservation, their places in space, and every form and sort of physical life upon them to the light and heat he sends forth. The span of the space over which the Sun is lord, has been computed at six thousand millions (6,000,000,000) of miles. Now, taking Dr. Child, a very able English astronomical mathematician, as our pilot, let us make a rapid tour of this space, and take a flying peep at the worlds that revolve within:

We take the Sun for our starting-point, and, for the sake of comparison, estimate his size as that of a *globe two feet in diameter*. At the *short* distance of thirty-seven millions (37,000,000) of miles, we find the little world which is called *Mercury* on account of the tremendous swiftness (100,000 miles an hour) of its motion around the Sun; compared with the two-foot globe, Mercury is but a *grain of mustard-seed*. The next world we behold is the beautiful *Venus*, the most dazzling of the Sun's train; this world is as a *pea* in size and is the nearest neighbor of our Earth. About ninety-two millions (92,000,000) of miles from the Sun, we find another *pea* a little larger than neighbor Venus, and we readily identify it as our own little world, the Earth. We travel now to a distance of about fifty millions (50,000,000) of miles, when we discover the ruddy little *pin's-head* called *Mars;* Venus and the Earth consume about the same time in moving around the Sun, and hence their years are almost of an equal length, but Mars, though his mean orbital speed is 54,000 miles an hour, nearly that of the Earth, takes nearly two of our years to get around the Sun. We have now travelled so far from the Sun that his light is very perceptibly less than we are used to. But we have yet to go to an immensely greater distance from the grand centre; on our way through the "asteroid" zone, we pass by smaller planets at the distance of two hundred and sixty millions (260,000,000) of miles, because we as yet know but little about them, and hasten on to the giant *Jupiter*, whose size is that of a *small orange* as compared with our pea and with the two-foot globe; he is nearly five hundred millions (500,000,000) of miles from the Sun, and the light from the great central reservoir has grown so faint that four brilliant reflectors (moons or satellites, one of which is always *full*) have to contribute to his necessities; his orbital path is three thousand millions (3,000,000,0000) of miles long, and his year is equal to about twelve of ours. Travelling now nearly as far as Jupiter is from the Sun, we find a *smaller orange* more than nine hundred millions (900,000,000) of miles from the Sun; the name of this world is *Saturn*; his share of Sunlight is but one-ninetieth of what we enjoy, and no less than eight satellites and a vast mysterious luminous "ring" surrounding him come to his relief; his year is nearly thirty times as long as ours. But far as Saturn is from the Sun, *Uranus* is twice as far, and so far is he from the Earth that though he is nearly four times as large as our world, we can seldom see him with the naked eye, while, looking from him, the Earth cannot be found; he has to traverse ten thousand millions (10,000,000,000) of miles to get around the Sun, and it requires *eighty-four* of our years to make the journey—hence, his year is eighty-four times as long as ours; it is not uninteresting to estimate the possible tenure of life of the inhabitants of Uranus—the three-score-and-ten limit assigned by David to life in our world would give nearly six thousand years as the possible limit in that far-away world. Until a little more than thirty years ago, Uranus was reasonably thought to be the farthest planet from the Sun, but in 1846 *Neptune* was discovered, three times as far as Saturn and one-half farther than Uranus, or nearly *three thousand millions* (3,000,000,000) *of miles* from the centre of light, heat, and motion. As time rolls on, possibly other worlds may show themselves, but we have permitted Dr. Child to pilot us far enough, and we return to our starting-point, the Sun, where we may well pause awhile and ponder upon the wonderful source and centre of this wonderful system of worlds.

If we are lost in wonder and admiration when we thoughtfully contemplate the Sun's marvelous and beneficent influence and operations in our little world alone, what must be our feelings, and what words can we employ in giving adequate expression to our sensations, when we recollect that this world of ours is but an insignificant portion of the vast, magnificent system of worlds, to all and each of which that Sun is light, heat and life! Truly, "God moves in a mysterious way His wonders to perform," and not the least mysterious are the constantly recurring mysteries of His ways in the heavens and upon the earth. Then, when we recollect, too, that our Sun is but one of many, perhaps millions, and that each has its system, aggregating perhaps billions of worlds, each world as full of wonders as ours! well may we laud and magnify Jehovah's Name! for He manifested Himself in Light, and through it and by it He hath created the Universe; nay, far more! that Light still, in His Power and Might, sustains the innumerable Astral Suns and they sustain the countless thousands of millions of worlds that move in, though they do not fill, space. And just here we cannot but realize with renewed force the inestimable importance of the law of harmony in the Universal System, and in the Solar Systems that make the Universe: with millions of Suns and billions of worlds moving in space, how small a violation of that law might entail universal disaster and ruin!

Among the undetermined questions in Astronomy, not the least important is the number of Suns that, like ours, derive light and life-power from the Central Sun and dispense them to the worlds dependent upon and controlled by them; and, while Science has discovered many valuable facts as to these Suns and their Systems, it has failed to ascertain with any approximation to certainty, just what these Suns are, of what they are made, what is the nature of their luminosity, whence they derive their light and how they disseminate it. The ancients instruct us upon some of these points and afford us clews to the determining of others; but modern Scientists, instead of learning of them and testing the lessons learned by their improved apparatus, prefer to grope in the dark for "discoveries," and of the "discoveries" they herald a large percentage prove to be but theories, and the few that stand as facts, if not actually discovered by the aid of the Kabbala and Kabbalistic teachings, could have been found with their assistance with much less labor than has been expended in seeking without it.

Of the lessons yet unlearned by the Science of our day, by study of the old fathers of philosophy and exploration of the mines they have opened for those who will seek therein, we have learned whence the Astral Suns derive their light and how they disseminate it; these lessons we have conveyed to our readers in the earlier portions of this chapter. We believe, too, that, by following clews supplied by the old Philosophers, with the assistance of more recent Scientists, we can learn just what these Suns are, of what they are made, and what is the nature of their luminosity. Of course, what is true of one is equally true of the other Astral Suns, for they are all undoubtedly alike in every particular, and, for the sake of convenience we shall speak specially of our Sun.

As to the size of the Sun it is sufficient to say: it has been variously calculated that it is from 600 to 750 times as large as the sum of all the worlds under its control; as compared with the earth, its volume is 1,253,000 as great, while its mass is 316,000 times that of the earth. Gravity at the visible boundary of the Sun exceeds that at the earth's surface 27 times; a body dropped within the influence of the Sun's gravity would fall through 436 feet the first second and acquire a velocity of 872 feet the next second, or about ten miles a minute.

Sir John Herschel tells us that the Sun appears to consist of an immense globe surrounded by two atmospheres, the inner non-luminous and the outer one a vast photosphere, or atmosphere of perpetual flame; he deems it probable that the inner atmosphere is a sort of screen to shield the globe from the glare and heat of the outer, and thinks it not impossible that animated life may exist upon the globe in some form. Other eminent astronomers corroborate his theory as to the sphere and two atmospheres, though we do not recall one who believes that animated life exists in any form upon the globe; a medical gentleman of New York, we believe, who writes well in support of the absurd notion, attempted some years since to prove that the globe of the Sun is heaven and its photosphere hell. Careful observations have shown that the Sun is a globe with two atmospheres, but nothing beyond this has been demonstrated. Accepting what has thus been proved, we cannot fully accept any one of the popular theories as to the material of which the globe is composed or the character of the incandescence of the photosphere. We feel confident that the Sun was created for specific purposes: to make of itself the source and centre of a grand system of worlds, and to produce and sustain physical life in all its forms upon each by shedding light and heat and through these pouring blessings innumerable upon all its worlds; and feeling thus, we are no less confident that every portion of it contributes to those specific purposes. The photosphere is unquestionably a vast flame of intense fire—a living and perpetual incandescence, the fuel Hydrogen and Oxygen; Hydrogen is the negative, and Oxygen the positive, polarization of ether— the all-pervading ether of the universe thus furnishes an inexhaustible supply of fuel. Chemistry teaches us that the burning of Hydrogen in Oxygen, in the proportions of two volumes of the first to one of the second, produces steam which is readily condensed into pure water—every school-boy who has acquired only the rudiments of chemistry knows that water is composed of Hydrogen and Oxygen. Thus, we have the photosphere of flame, and the product, steam, for the inner atmosphere, and the steam condensed, water, for the globe; this water is in turn is decomposed, and, escaping, replenishes the universal ether. (It takes 1200 quarts of pure Hydrogen and 600 quarts of pure Oxygen to produce 1 quart of pure water.) But the flame of Hydrogen in Oxygen is very faint, though very hot, and it is possible other substances enter into the flame of the Sun's photosphere to increase its luminosity. The experiments of Spectrum Analysis have been thought to indicate the presence of Lithium to produce the Red; Sodium to produce the Yellow and, with the Lithium, the Orange; Thallium to produce the Green, and Indium to produce the Blue, Indigo and Violet, because those minerals in a colorless electric flame produce the respective colors—we do not consider the experiments conclusive, nor do we realize the necessity for believing that any substances except the gases, Hydrogen and Oxygen, enter into the photospheric flame; still we shall not here call in question the Scientific theory upon this point, beyond the mention of our doubt, and adding that it is only a theory with little chance of ever attaining the rank and authority of a fact. In this connection it may not be amiss to note what none will deny, though many have doubtless never thought of it: Red and Blue are the only absolutely independent colors.

Before dismissing this part of our subject, we have a few words to say in reply to the notion that the globe within the Sun is Heaven. The strongest argument adduced by the writer we have referred to as advancing this absurd theory is that astronomers have never discovered a planet or other object they could denominate "Heaven." He says: "Considering that it would require three hundred thousand years, travelling with the rapidity of three hundred thousand miles a second, to reach the extent of space surveyed by the eye through the telescope," it would be impossible to entertain "the supposition that Heaven was still far out beyond." Neither the writer quoted nor the astronomers who have been searching for "Heaven" will ever discover it with the carnal, objective eye; like God Himself, like the Celestial Sun and its Light, like all things "belonging to the Spirit," Heaven is only "spiritually discerned;" while the astronomer may use his telescope in vain, the humblest, when "born again," shall "see the kingdom of God;" "children of Light" alone can see the "realms of Light." We venture to affirm that none who are fitted for Heaven will experience any difficulty in finding or reaching that Celestial Home.

The prism enables us to analyze the Sunlight, to ascertain the colors of a Sunbeam, and their respective proportions and refractive positions in the Scale; but it does not teach us how to apply or assist us in applying Sunlight or its separate rays in therapeutics or agriculture. Careful, conscientious study and practical experience, during a long term of years, have convinced the author that as curative agents Sunlight and its component rays have no rivals in Materia Medica, but that, like the simples and compounds of the pharmacopœia, to apply them successfully the physician must apply them wisely, and to do this he must know the character and properties of each ray, exactly and thoroughly, as well as have a complete general knowledge of the nature and functions of Sunlight as a sublime aggregation of marvelous virtues. We have found that the application of Sunrays does not do away with the necessity for the use of mineral and vegetable medicines, but that the judicious harmonious use of both Sunrays and medicines will generally effect the desired cure most surely and effectually. We believe, indeed, that the most effective medicines, especially those from vegetable substances, owe their qualities to virtues imparted to them by the rays of the Sun. We have learned that even the clothing upon a patient may contribute to or hinder the effect of a Sunray. The most convenient medium for the application of specific rays in the treatment of disease is colored glass. We have already spoken of the modes of preparing glass so that it shall permit only the Blue, or the Red, or any desired color-ray to pass through, and we shall describe in a later chapter (Chapter VI.) when and how the Red or the Blue or other color must be employed. Here we propose merely to offer a few general remarks:

The Red ray is specially demanded in cases where it is desired to induce excitation of the nervous system, the Blue where it is desired to produce an opposite effect. We have employed the Red ray as often and with as decidedly beneficial results as the Blue ray. The precise effect of the use of colored glass may be stated in few words thus: Sunlight possesses cer-

tain positive qualities which, in certain conditions and
under favorable circumstances, produce certain known
effects upon objects in Nature, upon the human organism as certainly as upon objects in the vegetable kingdom; the qualities of Light are in perfect harmony
and, when an object is in a responsively harmonious
state, to state it more explicitly, when, in the case of
a human being, the body is in perfect health, the combined qualities of Light promote that health. But,
let that harmony in the object be suspended or deranged, let the body become diseased, and the case
assumes at once a different phase; some of the properties of Light now favor, while others are prejudicial to,
the restoration of the equilibrium, and with it a return
to health. A ready illustration of this suggests itself:
a patient has the Small Pox, and the calorific and luminous rays are known to be pernicious in their effect;
it has been customary to darken the room and to deprive
the patient almost entirely of light—but the chemical rays would unquestionably be beneficial; shall we
not admit these and exclude the others? But our
reader is familiar with a recognition of this principle
of accepting one ray and rejecting the rest: a man's eyes
have become diseased, so that the brilliant and heat
rays of the Sun not only cause him pain but aggra-
vate the disorder; he does not shut himself up in a
dark room, but he procures a pair of Blue, or still
better Violet, spectacles, which exclude the injurious
rays and admit the beneficial ray. The use of colored
glass, then enables us to assist Nature in reinstating
the Divine law of harmony in the human system, and
with it duly enforced disease is impossible.

CHAPTER III.

LIGHT MANIFESTED IN ATMOSPHERIC ELECTRICITY AND IN TERRESTRIAL MAGNETISM.

IN the preceding chapter we have discussed Light as manifested in the light we see and in the Sun, the great reservoir of light for, and dispenser of light to, the system of worlds of which the earth is one. In this discussion we have accepted the facts of modern Science, and some of the theories of Scientists, but we have not hesitated frankly to dissent from, and to advance views in conflict with, some "generally received theories"—views, too, which have never, so far as we know, been advanced by recognized Scientific authorities. And, in this chapter, we shall accept only those of the teachings of modern Science that are certainly facts and such theories as, in our judgment, "account for the phenomena" of Electricity, and shall no doubt advance some ideas that are new to the Scientists of the present time, ideas that we believe will stand the strictest tests fairly applied, though there may be those who, considering themselves Scientists or being close sticklers for *authority*, will reject them without investigation, if they do not actually deride them, simply because they do not coincide with their own preconceived notions or with the theories of those whom they esteem as apostles of Science.

Electricity, in all its forms and phases, is a manifestation of Light. The writer on "Lightning" in Appletons' Cyclopædia tells us: "Of the nature of lightning the ancients knew nothing; its disastrous effects were associated rather with the terrific sound of the thunder than with the flash." This would be an unpardonable blunder, but for the addition of the words "and the Greeks and Romans attributed them to the thunderbolt hurled by Jupiter to the earth." This shows the said writer's mistake to be the common one of regarding the Greeks and Romans as "the ancients." "Of the nature of lightning," as of all the operations, processes and phenomena of Nature, "the ancients," properly so called, knew far more than modern investigators have yet discovered, and, as we have before said, the old Philosophy comprehends vast stores of knowledge not yet embraced in our Science. The ancients knew not only that Electricity was a manifestation of Light, and that the phenomena of Lightning were phenomena of Electricity, but a passage found among the fragments of Ctesias shows that the utility of lightning-rods was understood four centuries before the Christian era; this passage tells of a fountain in India from the bottom of which was obtained a sort of iron, made into rods and "set up in the ground, averted clouds, hail and lightning." But it is true that not only the Greeks and Romans, but the learned of much more recent times, knew nothing "of the nature of lightning," or of its cause, Electricity. The knowledge was lost until the Abbé Nollet in 1746 began to notice the identity of effects produced by thunder-clouds and the prime conductor of an electrical machine; then Winckler noticed that the principle of the powers of Electricity and Lightning was the same. Our own Dr. Franklin, in 1749-50, satisfactorily demonstrated the similarity of the two, and three years later he made his famous kite experiment. But, before he had experimentally tested them, others proved the correctness of his theories: Dalibard, May 10th, 1752, obtained sparks by means of an iron rod forty feet high in the garden at Marly, and by the same means charged Leyden jars; as early as 1751, M. Romas is said to have constructed a kite seven feet five inches high and three feet, at its widest part, in width, with a surface of eighteen square feet —this kite was raised, on the approach of a storm, to a height of 550 feet, and sparks were obtained accompanied by violent shocks, and, as the storm increased, flashes of fire, with explosions, darted to the ground (the French Academy of Sciences awarded to M. Romas the credit of the invention of the electric kite, though subsequently the French medal awarded to Franklin said "*Eripuit cœlo Fulmen*"). Franklin made his kite experiment June the 15th, 1752. He had before suggested the feasibility of employing lightning-rods, and afterwards demonstrated it most satisfactorily. Thus, after a lapse of more than two thousand years, Lightning was rediscovered to be Electricity, and lightning-rods were reinvented.

Careful investigations have shown a close relationship subsisting between Atmospheric Electricity and Terrestrial Magnetism, and they can be most satisfactorily traced to a common source, which we shall see is the great source of objective light, the Sun, and the Stars. It is interesting to note, without going into tedious details, the various contradictory theories of Scientists as to the nature and sources of Electricity, and no less interesting is it to ascertain wherein the various popular theories are alike wrong:

First, as to the nature of Electricity—what Electricity *is*, there have been two popular theories: The one now most generally received is that it consists of two imponderable fluids which mutually attract each other; they never penetrate bodies, but locate themselves upon the surfaces; bodies of similar electricity repel each other, and bodies to approach each other must be charged with opposite fluids. The other theory, of which Dr. Franklin was the eminent exponent, is that Electricity consists of but one fluid; each body contains a certain quantity,—when in excess it is plus, or positive, and when a deficiency exists it is minus, or negative; that the tendency is always to equilibration.

In giving our views of Electricity, we must recognize the relationship between Electricity and Magnetism, noticed above: We believe that ELECTRICITY IS A PERIPHERAL POLAR FORCE MOVING OUT OF EQUILIBRIUM, AND MAGNETISM IS A POLAR FORCE MOVING IN EQUILIBRIUM. The attraction of bodies charged with the opposite electricities for each other, and the repulsion of those charged with either electricity, are *facts* with which all observers must be familiar; and that the positive electricity is strictly excluded from entering, and is confined to the surfaces of, bodies is true, and affords a strong illustration of the Wisdom and Beneficence of the Author of the laws of Nature: were the positive force permitted to penetrate bodies, it would annihilate the negative, and the universe of matter would soon pass back into chaos. When the positive and negative forces of Electricity harmonize, they move in equilibrium, as in Terrestrial Magnetism; when they are separated, they become antagonistic, and positive Electricity becomes a "blind force," as the ancients termed it—they symbolized Electricity in equilibrium by a Serpent swallowing its tail. Positive Electricity is the active, polar force, and the Negative is the passive, depolarizing force. Positive Electricity is ether tensely polarized, and when pushed to its utmost tension Fire is produced.

Now, as to the source or origin of Electricity: No question in nature has evoked such earnest antagonism among modern Physicists, and not one has so utterly failed to receive a satisfactory solution, as this. The ancients knew all about it, and, if our modern investigators could be induced to study the old Philosophy more and theoriæ less, this question, like many others, would soon be settled. Lavoisier, Laplace, Volta, De Saussure and others have endeavored to show that Electricity is derived from the earth by evaporation, which appears really absurd in the light of the fact that the Electricity at the earth's surface is purely negative. Pouillet advanced a modified version of this theory; he held that "evaporation to produce electricity must be accompanied by chemical decomposition, as when it occurs from saline mixtures, from the surface of heated iron, which becomes oxidized, and more especially when the vapor proceeds from the leaves of growing plants." We copy this statement of Pouillet's views from Appletons' Cyclopædia; the writer of the article in which it occurs adds: "Combustion also is a source of atmospheric electricity, as is seen upon a large scale in the constant flashes of lightning that sometimes play around the summits of volcanoes during their eruptions. The rushing of currents of wind past each other, or against opposing objects, also generates electricity by the friction it occasions." In reply to Pouillet, we need but to say that the action of Light in decomposing matter does generate electricity in small quantities, but not, in the smallest degree, in proportion to the vast quantities that fill the air, to say nothing of space beyond. "Combustion also," we admit, "is a source," but, as the writer alludes only to combustion in this little world of ours, we must add: while combustion does develope Electricity it is only as the candle-flame produces light and heat—all that is developed by the trifling combustions in our world, with all added that can be derived from the "rushing of currents of wind" and the decomposition of matter, would not in a hundred years be sufficient to meet Nature's requisitions in a single month. Yes! Combustion does produce the vast stores of Electricity that fill space and provide Nature with one of her most important means of working—but it is a combustion beyond the ken of "accepted" Scientists!

De la Rive believes that the Sun is the source of Electricity, but he admits that he can give no reason for his belief. Schönbein attributes its origin to the chemical rays of the Sun, because Oxygen under the influence of light is capable of producing Ozone. De la Rive nearly approximates the truth and Schönbein needs but to omit the word "chemical" to be correct as nearly as his conception of the Sun will permit.

LIGHT IS THE SOURCE OF ELECTRICITY! The original source is the great invisible Celestial Sun, but as the Astral Suns are the visible manifestations of that original Luminary, we may say, without violence to the truth, the Sun and Stars are the source of Electricity! The positive rays of Light produce positive, and the negative rays produce negative, Electricity; the former is absorbed by the aqueous vapor of the atmosphere, water having a strong affinity for it, while the latter is absorbed by the earth which has an equal affinity for it.

We repeat: Electricity is a manifestation of Light! We cannot conceive how many of the known phenomena of Electricity can be accounted for upon any other hypothesis. The single fact that Electricity is found to be more and more positive as we get further from the earth can be explained only when we realize that it is most tense near its source and loses in tension as it spreads over space; the theory that evaporation has anything to do with originating positive Electricity is sufficiently refuted by the fact that when the rain conveys to the earth the positive, the earth brings it into harmony with its own negative, Electricity. It is worthy of remark that the modern Scientific authorities are coming to recognize the true source of Electricity: Schellen, one of the most learned and deservedly popular writers on Light, in his work on "Spectrum Analysis," says "the vibrations of a substance [ether] which according to its various forms of motion, generates light, heat or electricity." We have declined to receive the "vibration" or "wave theory," and only accept the statement that ether "generates light, heat or [and] electricity," with the explanation that as ether, in its forms of Oxygen and Hydrogen, is the fuel of the Sun's flame, it may be said to "generate" light, heat and electricity. But our purpose in here citing Schellen is simply to show that he, one of the most distinguished Scientists of modern times, assigns *one origin* to light, heat and electricity; and others are more or less disposed to learn the great lesson that Electricity is a manifestation of Light!

Notwithstanding their mistaken theories as to the nature and source of Electricity, however, we must acknowledge our obligation to many modern Scientists for a vast amount of most valuable information they have obtained by patient painstaking investigation and given liberally to the world. In noticing some of the phenomena of Electricity and Magnetism, we shall have occasion specially to mention some of those to whose indefatigable researches the Scientific world is indebted for the progress made in this important department of learning, and we shall mention them with the single regret, mingled with our esteem and admiration, that they did not simplify their labors and no doubt amplify the extent of their knowledge by availing themselves of the teachings of the Wise Men of ancient times.

There are, as we have already learned, throughout Nature two distinct forces or principles: the positive, or active, and the negative, or passive, the masculine and the feminine—and we find these two in Electricity. We have seen, too, that the atmospheric envelope of the earth is charged with positive Electricity, the higher the stratum the more positive the Electricity, and we have seen why it is so; the tension of this positive force varies, however, and at times it is intense near, or intense currents move towards, the earth. The earth is full of electricity; at the surface it is *null* or negative. In the open country, where foreign influences are least felt, the equilibrium is found about three feet from the ground; trees, houses, etc., carry the negative upwards, and place the equilibrium at a higher point. Thus we see that the earth and the air are oppositely charged; so long as the positive and the negative hold their places, and the equilibrium is maintained, all is serene, but let this equilibrium be disturbed, by heat or other influence, and immediately the electric flash visibly notifies us that Nature is enforcing her law of harmony by the restoration of the equilibrium.

De Saussure was the first to study systematically variations in the electric tension; Ronalds at Kew, Clark in Ireland, Romershausen and Dillmann in Germany, and Palmieri in Naples, have followed up the study most satisfactorily; from them we learn that the diurnal variations in atmospheric electricity under a serene sky in the several countries, differ very slightly as to the hours of maxima and minima. The observations of Ronalds are critically exact; he employed the ordinary electroscope in communication with an insulated conductor elevated above ground, by means of which he collected electricity from the surrounding air; his observations covered a period of five years and included 15,170 quantities; of these,

14,515 are of positive and 655 of negative electricity. He took his observations at the even hours, Greenwich mean time, throughout the day of twenty-four hours, and the result is given thus: The tension of Atmospheric Electricity [see Plate III.] is at its minimum at 2 A. M., and there is a gradual increase until 6 A. M.,

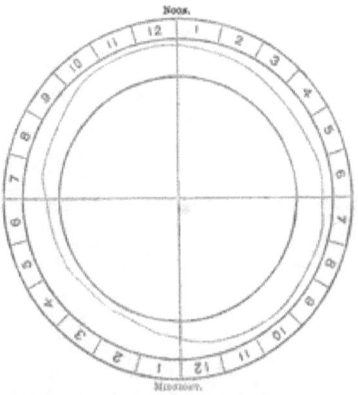

Plate III.—VARIATIONS IN ELECTRICITY OF THE ATMOSPHERE.

from which hour the increase is more rapid, so that at 8 it is more than double what it is at 6; it then increases more slowly until 10, when it has attained its first or morning maximum; it then diminishes gradually until 4 P. M., when it has reached its afternoon minimum, which is not nearly so low as at 2 A. M., and indeed scarcely below the degree at 8 A. M.; it then rises until 6, and from that hour until 10, which is called its evening maximum, it varies imperceptibly; then it falls until at 2 A. M. it has returned to its starting-point, its lowest tension. The diurnal variations in the magnetism of the earth are equally marked; Graham, in 1722, was the first to note them, and M. Arago has since added important observations, by which we learn that herein, too, there are two maxima and two minima in the variations: starting from 11 P. M., the north pole of the needle travels towards the east until at 8.15 A. M. it reaches its minimum declination; it then returns and travelling westward to its maximum at 11.15 P. M.; going again to the east it reaches its second minimum between 8 and 9 P. M., and thence westward it attains its second maximum at 11 P. M.

Besides the diurnal variation in tension, there is also a monthly variation in the quantity of electricity in the air; the difference is shown by M. Quetelet, of Brussels, in the table on the following page, the observations being made each day at about noon:

We have shown that positive Electricity proceeding from the luminous heavenly bodies charges the atmosphere to about three feet from the ground where it meets the surface Electricity which, proceeding from the earth, is negative; that, under a serene sky, the tension of the positive current varies diurnally and the quantity increases and diminishes month by

Months.	1844.	1845.	1846.	1847.	1848.	Mean.
January	"	471°	562°	957°	437°	605°
February	"	548	256	413	295	378
March	"	361	96	282	164	206
April	"	93	94	221	155	141
May	"	163	49	67	59	84
June	"	51	39	47	48	47
July	"	58	33	43	61	49
August	90°	99	57	11	64	62
September	91°	95	62	39	63	70
October	110	299	98	107	120	131
November	127	334	274	160	152	209
December	340	742	799	356	281	507
Annual Mean	"	267	202	225	162	204

month; that the negative keeps pace with it in its fluctuations; that so long as these two forces are held in equilibrium, each performs its allotted task quietly, and that so soon as the equilibrium is disturbed, lightning is produced in the effort of Nature to restore the equilibrium. We presume every reader realizes that Lightning, so destructive to property and life at times, is nevertheless one of God's best and wisest provisions for the welfare of His creatures, in that it is an invaluable means of purifying the atmosphere and thus promoting health and life on the earth. We shall see other tokens of the value of Electricity later in this chapter.

Moisture, in the form of fog, mist or rain, has a direct influence upon the electric condition of the atmosphere. Vapor consists of small globules or small spherical balloons filled with air; these unite to form fog or mist. The outer surface of each of these globules is charged with electricity, and they form, as it were, myriads of Leyden jars charged; a cloud is an aggregation of these cells. In a storm, the electricity upon the cloud surface is discharged and the inner globules send out a fresh supply with more than military promptness and precision; thus the surface is again and again recharged by its globular battery. Then each drop of rain, hailstone or snowflake bears with it to the earth positive electricity which assists in neutralizing the negative condition of the earth's surface.

There are three variations in the electrical state of the atmosphere before, during and after a thunderstorm: before the air about us is negative, during the storm, it is positive, and immediately after the cessation of the rain, it is again negative. As the electricity is drawn from the atmosphere directly surrounding the cloud, sometimes when the cloud is of extended magnitude the air becomes negative for twenty or thirty miles around. Negative zones always exist when rain-clouds are floating in space; hence, moisture always modifies the electricity of the atmosphere. The condition of the air under a clouded and a serene sky, as indicated by an electrometer, is shown in the following table:

	January	February	March	April	May	June	July	August	September	October	November	December
Clouded sky	20°	22°	125°	17°	8°	9°	15°	50°	45°	12°	99°	111°
Serene sky	143	216	364	129	65	22	25	61	74	148	226	373

Water, a powerful absorber of positive electricity, collecting in vapor from the surface of the earth and the sea and inland streams and lakes, ascends into the colder regions, and absorbs positive electricity—then it falls in rain, hail or snow, and its discharge of positive, neutralizes the earth's negative, electricity; thus an excessively negative condition is prevented, a condition that is prone to court epidemics of the cholera and gastro-enteric type. And in this, we see one way in which Light fulfils its beneficent work.

M. Quetelet has observed strong responsive relations between the barometrical and electrical conditions of the atmosphere; although temperature and wind influence the barometer as much as moisture, he has ascertained that, as the barometer rises so does the positive condition of the air increase. Peltew, for this reason, attributes barometric changes to the electric changes produced by moisture and not to moisture itself.

That a strong reciprocal relation exists between Atmospheric Electricity and Terrestrial Magnetism is readily demonstrated—indeed they are one manifestation of Light in two aspects; as we have said, the one is a polar force moving out of equilibrium, the other a polar force whose dual principles are in a perfect state of equilibration. There are several instructive natural demonstrations of the reciprocal relation we refer to: M. Arago states that in the Vicentin Hills there is a fountain which at times, especially after a long drought, is quite dry, and then, on the approach of an electric storm, it suddenly overflows, the overflow filling a canal with a turbulent stream. At a short distance from Perpignan there is an artesian well, which was furnishing a large amount of water, when the supply suddenly diminished, and it was feared that some obstruction had gotten into the lower part of the hole; but, as suddenly as it had diminished, it returned to its former yield: one day, on the approach of a storm, a rumbling noise was heard underground about the well, then an explosion, and a plentiful flow of water came. Thermal springs often announce the approach of a storm by becoming strongly agitated, and the agitation subsides immediately after the storm. The vapor which issues from the crater of Vesuvius is strongly positive and frequently vivid lightning belches forth, with terrific thunder at times. The great fog of 1763, which covered the greater part of Europe, was strongly positive; a volcanic origin was suspected.

It is well known that Lightning is the flash, or series of flashes, that is evoked by the discharge of Electricity from a positive into a negative cloud or into the negative surface-vapors of the earth; that the air being a non-conductor, the discharge creates a vacuum, and, as "Nature abhors a vacuum," the chasm is immediately closed with a report more or less loud in proportion to the volume of the discharge and the consequent extent of the chasm, and this report is what we call thunder; that between the opposite Electricities there is always a mutual attraction, and between two volumes of the same Electricity there is a mutual repulsion. We have said that Lightning is the immediate consequence of a want of equilibrium between opposing currents of Electricity, and is caused by Nature's act of producing equilibrium—the ordinary Scientific statement that between the two "fluids" "the tendency is to equilibrium" is true, and is a recognition simply of the fact that the law of harmony obtains here as throughout Nature's domain. Between two opposing currents there is always a space of neutral quality, of which the positive ingredient repels the positive current, and the negative ingredient repels the negative current—thus the neutral forms a resistance to the coming together of the opposite currents; this resistance successfully opposes the attraction, until it becomes weakened or the attraction intensified. Whatever the condition of the Electrical charge of the atmosphere, the surface negative corresponds in condition; when a positive current of great tension descends towards the earth, the earth responds, the attraction overcomes the resistance, the forces meet, and the flash and report attest the violence of the concussion; or, intense heat rarefies the air, the resistant neutral becomes attenuated and weak, whereupon heat-lightning follows, gratefully cooling the atmosphere and neutralizing the excess of negative electricity in the air we breathe.

The importance, and value to us, of the law of harmony is in no one respect more evident than in the maintaining or restoring of the equilibrium between positive and negative Electricity; an excess of the former in the air we breathe brings into our midst epidemics and diseases of the inflammatory type, such as Scarlet Fever, Diphtheria, Small Pox, etc., while an excess of the latter as surely brings epidemics and diseases of the gastro-enteric order and excessively debilitating and wasting type, such as Cholera, Dysentery, Typhus and Typhoid Fevers, etc. A healthful season, one in which we escape epidemics and in some measure diseases not of the epidemic types, is one wherein the two electric forces maintain their equilibrium or Nature promptly enforces her law of harmony when either exceeds its just proportions.

In the preceding chapter, we closed our arguments against "the wave theory" and in support of "the impulse and tension theory," with the remark : " No wave can be conceived of capable of carrying an electric flash, while tension of ether provides a suitable conductor." Just as the Sunbeam receives an impulse from the Sun and upon contact with ether excites tension with it, creating conductors upon which to travel upon its errand of blessing, so when the electric contest gives forth its flash, in precisely the same way and of precisely the same material the flash of light provides for itself conductors upon which it travels, whether to destroy property and life or to scatter benefits in its path. The zigzag course it often takes does not militate against our view, because the elasticity of the ether conductors allows it liberty to select its course, selecting as it does the congenial vapors that are not themselves already charged, and shunning alike the clouds whose positivity repels it and the obstructions that would hinder its swift flight.

There are not several kinds of Lightning, as popular text-books seem to teach—there is but one kind, assuming different aspects, according to the distance at which the discharge occurs, and the density or rarity of the medium or media through which it has to travel. It is well known that rarefied air is peculiarly favorable to the movements of electric flashes, and when the atmosphere is subtile the discharge of a large, tensely charged cloud is prone to move in mass, and the flash to assume the appearance of a ball of fire—this is called "ball-lightning," and is naturally the most destructive form of Lightning; when the discharge occurs at a considerable distance from us, and the atmosphere intervening is dense or loaded with positive Electricity, the flash chooses a zigzag course, and is called "zigzag-lightning;" it takes the name of "forked-lightning" when the flash divides to avoid an obstruction near its source; when the discharge is at a great distance and vivid flashes occur in rapid succession, they seem to be blended, appearing as one vast sheet, and this is appropriately called "sheet-lightning," so, also, the reflection of flashes below the horizon presents the same appearance, though less vivid, and bears the same name; when the discharge is near us, the flash often moves in a direct line and is designated "straight-lightning;" the flashes of "heat-lightning" may be like those of the zigzag, straight, or sheet, though they are comparatively faint, and often are so faint that they constitute what is known as "glow-lightning," because the clouds are smaller

and not heavily charged; "glow-lightning" is usually
unattended by thunder and is not followed by rain.
Lightning changes the surrounding clouds, lessening
their capacity to hold water, and the excess falls in
rain, and it disturbs the air which in recovering its
balance creates a more or less violent wind.

We have spoken of the affinity of the vapors that
pervade the atmosphere for positive Electricity: water
in every form is an excellent conductor of positive
Electricity, but especially so when tepid or warm;
substances that, when dry, repel it, when moist or wet,
attract it—it is for this reason that Dr. Franklin declared: "It is safer to be in an open field [during a
thunder-storm, than sheltered from the rain by a tree
or wall, because] when the clothes are wet, if a flash
in its way to the ground should strike your head, it
may run in the water over the surface of your clothes,
whereas, if your clothes were dry it would go through
the body."

We have, in the preceding chapter, stated that a
Sunbeam, on its way to the earth, gives some of its
Blue ray to color the atmosphere and some of its calorific ray to the vapors that pervade it—but we did
not state that the vapors actually absorb about two-
thirds of the calorific ray. In consequence of this
heavy draft upon the heat ray, the vapors become
warm and attract positive Electricity, which is de-
posited upon the surfaces of each globule, and, when
thus charged, the vapors cease to act as a conductor. We have explained, earlier in this chapter,
how the vapors ascend into the regions of the heavenly
bodies, absorb Electricity, and, coming down to the

earth again, bear their load with them; we have stated, too, that each drop of rain, hail-stone and snowflake brings down fresh supplies of positive to harmonize with the earth's negative and produce Magnetism.

The earth itself and all solids and liquids upon it and gases about it are negative, with a few exceptions, among which are dry air and dry earth, and this is the reason why the earth and its contents and inhabitants attract the positive and are good conductors; the ground where a lightning-rod is intended to discharge must be moist or it will not receive the positive, because dry earth is positive, like dry air, and is therefore a non-conductor. The metals are all good conductors, but pure platinum and copper are the best. So remarkable is this characteristic of copper that it has been observed that men working in copper-mines or factories never have an attack of Cholera or similar diseases: the copper attracts to itself the positive and imparts it to man, the fluids in whose body are among the best of conductors, and the positive, harmonizing with the negative always present in man, tends to equilibrate the physical forces and principles within him, and thus to render him less liable to disease; but if he receives an excess of the positive he becomes liable to inflammatory disorders. Notwithstanding the fact that the fluids in man's body are perfect conductors, when a flash of lightning strikes him it seldom spares his life—the reason is that in passing through him, its action upon his nervous system is so violent that it succumbs, and he dies. It is worthy of remark that, while a living man or beast is one of the best conductors of positive Electricity, the corpse of either absolutely rejects it—the reason is: the moisture in the one case makes the body strongly negative, and therefore it attracts the positive, while at death, decay having commenced, the body becomes more or less positive and rejects its kind.

That water itself is strongly negative, its great affinity for the positive amply shows, and doubtless in the large proportion of water that everything in Nature contains we may see one reason why the earth and almost everything in or upon or about it is negative: In the Vegetable Kingdom we find the proportion of water is from 20 to 99 per centum; and animals consist largely of water—e. g. a man weighing 150 pounds contains 116 pounds of water. The water of the sea and of large lakes and streams is positive at and a little below the surface and negative from that point to the bottom; the Sunbeam that strikes the surface of water has but about one-third of its calorific ray with it and the water quickly absorbs that—hence the water just as far as the heat ray has penetrated is warmed, and attracts positive Electricity from the air, but below that it is cool and negative. It is well for us that the vapors of our atmosphere are so partial to the calorific ray, for were it not for the moisture in our air, our delightful earth would be completely ice-bound and become a frozen, lifeless waste.

Among the most fascinating experiments with the electric flash are those connected with the analyzing and measuring of its light. The success hitherto has not been great, though sufficiently so to be most interesting and to encourage the hope that farther developments will be made; enough has been accomplished to identify the electric flash with ordinary light; the differences that its spectrum exhibits from that of a Sunbeam are not greater than those between the various flashes, and these differences are readily accounted for. The flash is the product of the pure Electricity derived from the Sun influenced by vapors and gases of a non-solar character, and, hence, we find that, while the principal colors of the pure Sunbeam are always more or less clearly defined, there are unmistakable evidences of the presence of earthy gases and other earthy substances. Professor Knadt, of Zurich, has been the most successful in experiments in this most fascinating field; he has analyzed upwards of fifty flashes by means of a pocket spectroscope. As the scope of this work would not permit a detailed notice of the dark lines that appear on the Solar Spectrum, called "Fraunhofer's Lines" from the eminent Physicist who discovered most about them, we purposely avoided referring to them at all in the chapter on "The True Science of Light," and now we only refer to them to remark that the principal differences between the spectra of the several electric flashes, and between them and that of the Sunbeam, is found in the lines that cross or mark the color-bands; as these lines are attributable in the case of the Sunbeam to atmospheric influences upon the beam in transit, so in the case of each flash they are to be traced to effects produced upon its light by gases that cross its course. The electric flash has a peculiar intensity of action and is proportionately more susceptible to foreign influences than a Sunbeam. As might be anticipated, the various flashes show these influences in greater or less degree in proportion to the length of their journey. As seen by the eye, the light of "straight-lightning" is the purest white, and that of "forked-" and "zigzag-lightning" is purer than that of "sheet-lightning," which has a reddish appearance—occasionally violet and bluish, though the distant "glow-lightning" has specially the violet and bluish aspect; the spectroscope makes the degrees of purity plain. We see in Professor Kundt's discoveries the important fact verified that a cloud discharging into the earth has usually a far greater degree of tension than those discharging into neighboring clouds far up in the air.

But we pass to a brief consideration of the earth's Electricity, Terrestrial Magnetism. We have defined this as "a polar force moving in equilibrium," and have intimated that it is composed of the two forces of Electricity, each being controlled by the other, and the two acting in concert. Before proceeding to notice the character of this harmonious compound and its important agency in every department of Nature's operations, it may not be amiss to mention the origin of the name by which it is designated, though no doubt our reader is already conversant with it:

A Magnet is a substance so charged with Electricity that it attracts certain other substances to itself; a Magnet is *natural* when it exhibits this quality in its natural state, and *artificial* when the quality is developed into action within it, by friction or contact with a natural Magnet. The first natural Magnet discovered was the "Loadstone" which was found in Magnesia, the most easterly division of ancient Thessaly, Greece; the name "Magnet," therefore primarily indicated no more than the place where the wonder was found. Natural Magnets of iron are found in considerable quantities in Sweden and in some districts of New Jersey, and to a more limited extent in other localities. The Magnet contains within itself the dual principles of Electricity, and the points where it shows them chiefly are called respectively its positive and negative poles. Certain substances though they do not naturally show magnetic power, possess it in such a degree that it is readily developed into action—*e. g.*, a piece of iron placed in contact with either pole of a Magnet readily exhibits the same power of attraction, and a piece of steel, though less promptly, is readily converted into a Magnet.

Before considering the special phenomena of Magnetism, let us notice some of the analogous phenomena of Electricity and Magnetism:

In both, there are the two opposite forces, the positive and the negative.

In both, the two forces attract each other and each repels its kind.

In both, there is between the two forces a neutral force, so to speak: in Electricity, as we have seen, the two forces are never present in the same body, and the neutral places itself as a resistant wall between two opposing clouds or a positive cloud and the negative earth; in a Magnet, however, the two forces are always present actively in the one substance, and the neutral appears midway, in the same substance, separating the two and thus preventing their blending and neutralizing each other—the central point where the neutral is placed is called the *equator* of a Magnet; the *equator* shows neither attraction nor repulsion upon bringing near or placing in actual contact with it iron or other magnetic matter, because the attractive power of each ingredient of the neutral is rendered inoperative by the presence of the other.

The presence of this *equator* is the distinctive characteristic of a Magnet; in a magnetic body, the two forces are present, but in a neutral, inactive state. The artificial Magnet is simply a magnetic substance, the two forces in which have been polarized, or fixed apart, with the neutral between; this conversion of a magnetic substance into a Magnet is called magnetizing. The two forces are not separated with equal ease in all substances; in some, as in soft iron, contact with a comparatively weak Magnet separates them instantly, while in others, as in hard steel, they yield only to a powerful Magnet and then only after more or less delay. In the former case, however, the effect is only transient, and in the latter it is permanent.

The one difference between Electricity and Magnetism is that in the former the two forces are never found in one substance, while in the true Magnet they must both be present in an active state but in exact equilibrium, and in a Magnetic body both must be present though neutral and inactive. The forces of Electricity and Magnetism, are however, the same and their source is also one, Light. We have seen that the atmospheric vapors absorb the greater part of the calorific ray, and the actinic ray passes almost entire into the earth; the former becomes charged with the positive, and the latter with the negative, force; thus the negative becomes the characteristic of the earth and the positive of the air. Then the rain, the hail and the snow, fall, bearing the positive with them; the positive upon entering the earth is compelled to come into a state of harmony with the earth's negative, the two poles acting in equilibrium constitute Magnetism. Hence, the Earth itself becomes a powerful Magnet, and everything earthy partakes of its nature in some degree: some substances are natural Magnets, with both poles and the neutral *equator* naturally developed, others are magnetic, containing the two forces in a neutral condition, but more or less susceptible to magnetization, while still others are said to be diamagnetic, because they contain but one force; in consequence of the absence of the second force these substances are always repelled by either pole of a Magnet, which attracts only substances containing both forces. Faraday attempted to prove that all bodies of earthy matter were magnetic; those containing but one force he called diamagnetic. But the presence of both forces in each body is essential to Magnetism, and is the one thing that distinguishes it from Electricity. Hence, we hold that what he called *diamagnetic* bodies were simply bodies containing one *electric* force, and therefore not *magnetic* in any sense.

We have already stated it as our opinion that "Electricity is a peripheral polar force moving *out of equilibrium* (i. e. *independently*) and Magnetism a polar force moving *in equilibrium*"—in other words ELECTRICITY AND MAGNETISM ARE ONE AND THE SAME

THING IN ESSENCE AND POWER: *when either force exists separately it is Electricity, and when the two forces exist together they constitute Magnetism.* Scientists fail to see this unity and therefore even Tyndall is compelled to declare: "The real origin of Magnetism is yet to be revealed."

The Earth, we have stated, is itself a powerful Magnet: it has its positive and negative poles and equator. The Compass consists of a steel needle magnetized and exactly poised on a pivotal point; the positive pole of the Magnet attracts the negative, and repels the positive, pole of the needle, and the negative pole of the Magnet attracts the positive, and repels the negative, pole of the needle. When left free to choose its direction, the negative pole of the needle points towards the North, and the positive towards the South,—hence we know that the North Pole is the positive, and the South Pole is the negative, pole of the earth; as a ship approaches the Equator, the needle becomes more and more erratic in its direction and upon the equatorial line it is as apt to point East and West as North and South.

The Compass is valuable not only to the mariner in navigating his ship, but equally to the Scientist in determining the variations in the Earth's Magnetism:

1st. We find that the needle does not usually point directly North and South—hence we learn that the *Magnetic Meridian* is not coincident with the *Geographical Meridian*; *i. e.* that the Magnetic current does not follow the Earth's line directly North and South, but flows independently or obeys other influences. The angle made by the needle with the geographical line, is called its *angle of declination*; this varies in different localities, and is subject in each locality to the influence of Atmospheric Electricity, as we have shown earlier in this chapter, varying with its diurnal and other variations in tension and volume; at the beginning of the seventeenth century, the normal declination was eastward; in 1660, the normal position was directly North and South; then it gradually declined to the westward, until in 1818 it reached 24° 30'; since that time it has slowly but steadily decreased.

2d. We find that the needle is almost horizontal at the Equator, that in approaching the North Pole the northward point becomes depressed or *dips* in that direction until in lat. 70° 5′ N., long. 96° 46′ E., the needle is almost vertical, and that in approaching the South Pole the same phenomenon is observed, the southward point dipping until the needle is almost vertical at about lat. 73° S., long. 130° E. From this we learn that the electro-magnetic current or circulation passes in at the Poles and out at the Equator, and may be illustrated by the diagram given herewith.

The Compass was known to the Chinese as early as the beginning of the second century and came into use among European navigators about the thirteenth. Invaluable as the Compass unquestionably is, it is but one of many valuable applications of the Magnetic and Electric forces that have made them contribute to the health, wealth and general welfare of mankind.

Just as the atmospheric vapors are the great Storehouse for Electricity, so the earth is the great Storehouse for Magnetism, wherein Light has stored away these mighty dual forces so essential not only to the welfare of the inhabitants of, but to the very life of all things upon and in, the earth.

Everything in Nature has within it one or both of the electric forces—i. e. is either electric or magnetic. As we have said, Faraday classes everything under two heads: paramagnetic or magnetic and diamagnetic; the first class comprises the truly magnetic, and the second the simply electric substances. There is a marked difference in the chemical combination of the atoms in the substances of the two classes. Formerly, only iron, nickel and cobalt were believed to be magnetic, but Faraday has added manganese, chromium, osmium, platinum, palladium, cerium and titanium; a given volume of the three first named contains 230 atoms, and of the others 170. The same volume of an electric metal contains a much smaller number of atoms; for instance, gold and silver, 150; antimony and lead, 85; bismuth, 74—the only two exceptions are: copper, 230, and zinc, 170. Oxygen is the only magnetic gas.

Light is not only the source of the electric forces, it is also the great electro-magnetic polarizer. In the formation of the atom it receives the polar energy that gives it its individuality; its polarity constantly changes in dropping old, and putting on new affinities, but the tendency is to equilibrium or harmony. In inorganic matter the atoms are more angular than in the organic; the spheroidal form being proportioned to the stages of development. Each atom of matter contains one of the electric forces and is surrounded by an ethereal atmosphere of the opposite electricity —thus each atom is a miniature of the earth. Atoms approximate a spherical form; the presence in harmony of the two forces makes the spherical form perfect; the positive force induces an expansion at the poles and contraction at the equatorial diameter, and the negative induces a contraction at the poles and expansion at the equatorial diameter. 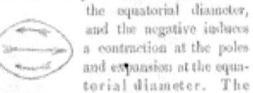 The atomic similarity to the aggregation of atoms, the earth, is most remarkable in the fact that the electric or magnetic force of each atom has a current, like the earth's, passing in at the poles and out at the equator; thus, atoms contain within themselves the elements of their own existence.

He who studies Nature aright, in its minutest atom and in its sublimest wonders, even in Electricity and Magnetism, sees ever the God of Nature, manifesting Himself first in Light and in and through and by Light in the Universe. "Every good and every perfect gift is from above, and cometh down from the Father of Light!" Well, indeed may James call God "the Father of Light" when he ascribes to Him the bestowal of "every good and every perfect gift," for Light is the blessed medium in and through and by which the most precious of physical gifts, even health and life, are given us. But God not only gives the inestimable blessing, he likewise sheds Light into man's intellect and enables him to learn how best to apply it and to reap its highest and greatest benefits. Thus has it ever been, is now and shall ever be until time is engulphed in eternity—His Mercy and Love are even more immeasurable than His universe. Time, as it rolls on is ever bringing to our view fresh, new evidences of His infinite Wisdom to conceive, His infinite Will to decree, His infinite Power to accomplish, and the infinite Love that permeates, influences and controls all the other infinite attributes of the God of Nature, our Father and our God. And now, notwithstanding all that He has permitted man to discover of His Power, Goodness and Love as manifested in Nature, through and by Light, we feel assured that still greater revelations are in store for us. He is even now permitting man to discover new applications of, and consequent new benefits to be derived from, Light—may He bless every right effort to advance and promote these discoveries, and in common with other efforts may He bless this little effort of ours, to the glory of His great Name and the good of suffering humanity!

CHAPTER IV.

MATERIAL FORMS AND VITAL DYNAMICS.

1. The Science of Motion is the Science of Life.
2. The Science of Life teaches how to maintain the just proportions of equilibrated influences.
3. Physical Life is the result of Motion, and can only be preserved and perpetuated by the Evolution and Perfecting of Forms—absolute Rest is Death.
4. Physical Life requires a Physical Form or Body wherein to manifest itself, and the character of its manifestation must be determined by the Form or Body wherein it is required to manifest itself.
5. The Regeneration of Physical Life must be preceded by the decomposition and disintegration of an earlier form or casket—therefore Physical Life is generated in Death.
6. In the Material World, Decomposition and Regeneration are continually going on by the changing of the Polarity of Atoms, the Destruction of Old Affinities and the Creation of New by the action of the Dual Principles of Light.
7. In the Higher Organisms, Physical Life is sustained and perpetuated by the Reciprocal Action of the Subjective and Objective Forces within and without individualized existences.

DEDUCTION.—These axioms lead us to the conclusion of the Ancient Sages that the Universal Basic Principle of Physical Life is a Substantial Motion; that when Motion stops Physical Life ceases—absolute Rest is Death. Light is the Universal Motor and hence the Active Sustainer, Promoter and Renewer of Physical Life—it acts by its Dual Forces, in Disintegrating and Reintegrating, Dissolving and Assimilating, Breaking down and Building up; invisible in its subjective operations, it is manifest in the objective phenomena of Depolarization and Polarization. Everything Physical Dies and undergoes Disintegration that Physical Life may be Improved and Perpetuated—if Forms were Eternalized, there could be No Farther Progress, and the Universe, so far as Development is concerned, would Cease to Move and would be itself Dead.

Thus, in Seven axioms and a deduction therefrom, we state, *in synopse*, the principles underlying the development and progress of Physical Life, the chief product and result of Vital Dynamics. In the course of the discussion of this branch of our theme, in this chapter and the next ensuing, we shall have occasion repeatedly to employ the terms "Evolution," "Progress" and "Development," and must here caution our reader distinctly and steadily to bear in mind that we do not use these terms in the sense in which certain modern theorists use them—we absolutely reject the notion that there has been *evolution*, or *development*, in any sense that can imply that man has descended from any ancestor but man, or a mouse from any but a mouse. The Author of Nature and its laws, by His Will and His Word, commanded the earth to "bring forth the living creature after his kind, cattle, and creeping thing, and beast of the earth after his kind; and it was so." But we define our views of "the Evolution Theory" later, and here only offer a cautionary remark.

"God has not found matter coëternal with Himself, and, like an architect, arranged this to His fancy; but He has, out of His own eternal Omnipotence, by His Will simply, evoked the world out of nothing unto existence. He has thought and spoken, and it was." So writes a learned Mystic, and his statement can scarcely be made stronger by the most astute Theologian of our day, in the way of declaring God's Supremacy and Omnipotence in Creation. Indeed, the Kabbalist, in analyzing and symbolizing the successive stages in Creation, and showing the instrumentality of Light in each stage, just as truly and loyally acknowledges the Supreme Will of God as does the Theologian who iterates the phraseology of Moses. The Kabbalist claims or assigns no power or function for or to Light independently of the great Jehovah; God, manifesting Himself in Light, and working in and by Light as His chosen representative and agent, is the Omnipotent Creator—Light, as His representative and agent, He endowed with His power and might, for the specific purpose of bringing motion and activity into exercise where stillness and inertia had prevailed, and thus to substitute order and life for chaos and death.

Space [who can conceive it?] was filled with an inpalpable, imponderable, invisible *nothing* which the ancients called *hyle* and the moderns call *ether*; there was but one *life* in space, the ONE SELF-EXISTENT LIFE, JEHOVAH. The infinite Wisdom conceived the glorious plan, the infinite Will decreed its accomplishment, the infinite Word issued the mandate, the infinite Power effected the result—"God said, Let there be Light, and Light was." Chaos was no more; darkness fled away before the Light of Life. The plan had been conceived, the decree made, the mandate issued, and the result effected—Light came to manifest the unknowable Supreme, and to represent Him in Creation, Providence, Redemption and Glory. Such is the Kabbalistic Philosophy, and is there anything in it to offend the most sensitive believer in the written word? to militate against a single item of Christian Truth? to antagonise or weaken the most orthodox Faith?

To believe and teach that God effected His own purposes, by an instrumentality of His own choosing, and in conformity with laws of His own decreeing, does not derogate from His Glory, impugn His Majesty or question His Absolute Supremacy. So far from it, such belief and teaching actually intensifies our confidence in, reverence towards and love for God, because it assures us that He who is "the same yesterday, and to-day, and for ever," is still manifesting Himself, and will for ever manifest Himself, in the effecting of His purposes, in and by His chosen instrumentality, and in conformity with His laws, in every portion and department of His Universal Kingdom, to the glory of His great Name and the inestimable advantage of His creatures.

Light, God's first manifestation of Himself as the

Creator, endowed and vivified with Divine Power, and obedient to the Supreme Will, polarizes a portion of the universal *hyle* and fixes a firmament in space to separate between the Celestial World and the proposed Terrestrial Worlds; and now the waters are divided, the "waters above the firmament" being for the refreshment of the inhabitants of the Celestial World [mark, we are not informed when or how the Angels were created, and are not told what they are except that they are God's messengers and servants; doubtless, such information is "too high for us," in our objective state and is reserved to be revealed when we attain the subjective]. But this Light is the Celestial Light, and the next step in the plan and purposes of the Almighty, related to the objective worlds; so now, it focalizes rays from itself into objective Suns, and imparts to each of these the power farther to carry out the purposes of the Almighty. These objective Suns are thus an objective manifestation of the same God who manifested Himself in their Source, the Celestial Sun.

As our present interest is confined to our own Sun and especially to our own world, we shall speak only of these. Observation and experiments now show us how certain results are produced, and it is perfectly legitimate to infer that like results were produced by similar causes in the past, from the beginning of time. Our God changes not, and the laws that regulate and control Nature to-day are the same laws that God enacted when he created our world. As ether is impalpable and imponderable, we cannot experiment with it and demonstrate that Oxygen and Hydrogen were created from it; nor can we decompose either of them and produce other, because we can act upon neither absolutely by itself; but we know their properties—that Oxygen is a magnetic substance of positive power and Hydrogen is a substance of negative power; we know they are opposites, because they readily combine—hence, we conclude that Oxygen is the positive, and Hydrogen the negative, polarization of ether. Farther, we know that a pure Hydrogen flame in pure Oxygen produces steam, and this steam is readily condensed, forming pure water [we have given the proportions in Chapter II.]. We know, too, that earth is contained in pure water, because, as stated in Chapter I., we have precipitated earth from pure Oxygen and Hydrogen in an hermetically sealed vessel, confirming the result by successfully repeating the experiment. From these facts demonstrated by scientific experiments, may we not infer that the Sun's flame of Hydrogen and Oxygen produced water? and that the dual forces of Light precipitated earth from the water, thus making "dry land appear?"

Thus we have: (1) the primordiate manifestation of JEHOVAH, Light, the power or force, the universal motor; (2) the objective Sun and its flame of Oxygen and Hydrogen; (3) water, and (4) "dry land," appearing *out of the water.*

"The Sun and Stars have a perpetual motion, apparently revolving around an unseen centre," says a modern Scientific authority; we have seen what this "unseen centre" is, the great Celestial Sun of the universe, around which the Astral Suns, or "the Sun and Stars, have a perpetual motion," revolving around it as the great Central Orb of the Universal System. The planetary worlds, also, all "have a perpetual motion," revolving around their respective Suns and turning each upon its individual axis. Everything in and upon and about the earth has "a perpetual motion," every molecule and every atom, has its own "perpetual motion." This "perpetual motion" is life—life is "perpetual motion." We see this in our individual existence—when the heart, the Sun of our individual world, stops its beating, the "perpetual motion" that is our physical life stops, and death supervenes, bringing rest from "perpetual motion." As soon as each member of the Universe was created it was endowed with "perpetual motion" dependent upon the central Sun, the heart, of its special system.

The earth in motion, and prepared for inhabitants, according to the Mosaic account upon the "third day" the creation of organic matter commenced: "the earth brought forth grass, and herb yielding seed after his kind, and the tree yielding fruit, whose seed was in itself, after his kind." We see how the dual forces of the Sunlight operate now in the earth and air, decomposing and disintegrating old forms and reüniting the atoms, polarizing and integrating them into renewed forms of their specific types, each type "after his kind." We can then readily understand how the earth "brought forth" the forms of the vegetable orders. And now provision having been made for food for animated beings, the waters "brought forth abundantly great whales and every living creature that moveth, after his kind, and every winged fowl after his kind ;" and "the earth brought forth the living creature after his kind, cattle, and creeping thing, and beast of the earth after his kind." Here, too, we see the same dual forces of Sunlight daily working in the death and decay of old forms, and the creation and development of new forms, and can *realize* the process by which "the waters" and "the earth" obeyed the Divine mandate, just as readily as we see how the later commands to be "fruitful and multiply" have been, and are continuously, obeyed in the waters and the air and the earth.

Perpetual motion is the condition of physical life, and Light with its dual principles is the source of motion, the universal motor, but the "unique law of harmony" is the mainspring and regulator, without which motion would produce death and Light would be eclipsed by, engulphed in, darkness. Perpetual motion, then, is Vital Dynamics, Light is the source and principle of Vital Dynamics, and harmony is the mainspring, the presiding genius.

Creation was not the work of *six days*, or *six periods of time*, as Geologists phrase it, completed and then discontinued; the types or orders of forms were arranged and the laws of Nature enacted, and in accord with these creation is perpetual, to cease only when time ceases. Each new blade of grass, each new-born animated being, is evidence of creation, attests the continued work of a Creator, and proves the continued presence of a creative means or agent. The blade of grass is not the spontaneous product of the earth, or of the seed, separately or jointly—the seed and the earth are essentials, but there is a vital energy even more essential to make the seed germinate in the earth; we say this vital energy is more essential because it is conceivable that the vital energy could form a seed or earth as at the first from the original elements, but neither seed nor earth nor both coöperating could create a vital energy—this vital energy must be a manifestation of the Divine Vitality. But what is the vital energy that produces the blade of grass from the seed placed in the earth? It is the same that at the first of time enabled the earth to "bring forth grass:" it is Light. It required no other power to create the world, and no more power, than it requires to perpetuate and renew continually the work of the first "six days." Those first "six days," are repeated perpetually, and must continue to be repeated, or the universe must return to chaos and to darkness. God is the Almighty Creator to-day as truly as "in the beginning," and Light is His active Representative, His Manifester, in creation to-day as it was when he said "Let there be Light, and Light was." But not only is the work of creation a continuous, perpetual work in our world, it is so in the universe beyond our world: what are the nebulæ ever present in the vicinity of the Sun, if they are not nuclei of planetary worlds in course of creation; development (for creation is development), to be assigned their places in space and their orbital and axial motions in due time—when their respective "six days" are accomplished?

The Celestial Sunlight is the original, perpetual source of Vital Dynamics for the universe of Solar Systems as well as for the Celestial World, and the Astral Suns are the subordinate perpetual sources of

Vital Dynamics for their respective Systems, each for its own System, and for each world of its System. Hence, our Sun is the perpetual source of Vital Dynamics for our Solar System and for each world thereof.

The limit of the vital or creative energy of the Sun is the periphery of the space comprised in its system, and throughout that space its light perpetually exerts its dual principles, imparting to each atom of every created thing the motion that constitutes its vital power; the forces of attraction and repulsion, of integration and disintegration, are implanted and sustained by light within each atom, and from time to time, when Nature would regenerate and renew vitality, and produce a higher development, the same light destroys old affinities and creates new, and the atoms of an old form assume a new. Now, note that this change is the direct result of deviation from and return to equilibrium between the dual forces in the atom: while harmony continues and the equilibrium is maintained between attraction and repulsion, there can be no change—no decay or renewal. It is seen by this what is meant by the statement that there is no death or decay in Heaven: harmony is always absolute there, and death and decay can only result from disharmony. When Nature would regenerate and renew vitality, then, to repeat what we have said in other words, the negative or chemical force of light assumes the reins, increases the force of repulsion within the atom so that it subdues its opponent, attraction, and the atom repels and separates from its neighbor atoms; the positive or polar force of light then asserting its power, increases the force of attraction, the atom seeks fellowship, acquires new affinities, a new substance is formed, or the old affinities are revived and the old substance is reformed—when equilibrium is reëstablished. This is a plain statement of what we see every day and fail to understand: the processes of decomposition and composition, of disintegration and integration, of depolarization and polarization, the opposite action of the chemical or actinic rays and the polar ray of light. Thus light is the vital energy that destroys and creates.

We have said "creation is development," and is it not so? We are wont to speak without realizing what our words mean—to utter great truths in commonplace phrases, without even a faint conception of the grand scope of our expressions: *e. g.*, we see that a rose by *cultivation* may be made to improve in the number and excellence of its flowers, or in other particulars; that a pear- or a peach-tree, the natural fruit of which is scarcely fit to eat, may be made to produce most delicious fruit; that almost worthless breeds of cattle may be made exceedingly valuable; that a weak, feeble animal frame may be made vigorous and powerful; that our own physical or mental powers may be improved—we see all this and comment on it and in the next breath denounce the doctrine of development, never realizing that all these evidences of improvement are overwhelming evidences that the *true doctrine of development or evolution is correct*. If man, with his comparatively limited faculties and functions, can effect such developments as those we have noticed, who dares to deny or circumscribe the power of Nature, of Light, or of the God of Nature, in the same direction? Mark: man cannot develope a rose out of lily—a pear-tree out of a peach-tree—an ox or a cow out of a sheep—an animal frame out of a mineral or a vegetable form—an arm out of a finger! man *cannot effect any such developments or evolutions*, and Nature, or Nature's God, *does not*, because He has enacted laws that determine the types; GOD *does nothing that He does not permit man to imitate to the extent of his power and ability!*

Nature, to develope mental and spiritual qualities, must have a form suited to their unfoldment. Those who endeavor to demonstrate an evolution passing from type to type of forms, making an inferior the parent or ancestor of a higher type, appear to conceive that perfection in material forms was the Almighty's highest aim in creation, while the enlightened student of Nature should realize that the unfoldment of Soul-life—the making of man "in His own image, after His own likeness" was the grand sum of God's original purposes in creating "the world and all things therein." Nature and the Bible alike teach that the successive stages of creation, from the command "Let there be Light," until He "saw everything that He had made, and, behold, it was very good," were designed to prepare the earth, and provide food and all things requisite, for man. The development of material forms was only to provide one suitable for the complete unfoldment of the Soul, Spirit and Mind into the image of the Supreme. God is a Spirit, and a physical form, however perfect, could not be "in His image or after His likeness"—only a complete development and unfoldment of the subjective faculties of his soul can constitute man in God's image or elevate him to be after God's likeness—"likeness" to God can only be found in a Godlike Soul!

There is another thought that suggests itself here: If perfect development of body were the high purpose of Nature and of Nature's God, man, the highest type, would be distinguished by physical strength, for that is the highest physical quality, whereas there are numerous orders of inferior animals vastly stronger than man; indeed, man in proportion to size, is almost the weakest physically.

Evolution is development and development is creation or regeneration; but the progressive creation of forms is only the process by which Nature provides a form adapted to the highest unfoldment of the Soul. There is no subject so worthy of study as Nature, and the most interesting study in Nature is the process by which she provides a suitable temple for the Soul; in prosecuting this study we perceive in each order and type of material form, the grand life-principle attaining the fullest unfoldment possible therein; we note exceptional cases in each order or type of forms, in which physical defect or disease impairs the casket, and in these the life-principle goes only so far as the defect or disease will allow, though frequently it repairs the defect or disease to secure a fuller unfoldment. We shall see, hereafter, that man alone, by the unholy exercise of his superior will-power, seeks to baffle this principle in attaining complete unfoldment; man is required to assist in the unfoldment of the faculties of his Soul, and far too often cultivates only the objective faculties, utterly neglecting the subjective. But of this we must speak in a later chapter.

He who thoughtfully studies Nature must be impressed with the fact that there is a principle therein that is progressively unfolding in organic forms. In man this principle becomes individualized and is called the Soul—the Soul being, as we have seen, a manifestation of Light in both its subjective and objective qualities. This principle is Light, in whose operations we observe, besides the dual objective forces of polarization and depolarization, a subjective power that controls the objective directing the dissolution and creation of material forms. Unless we recognize this principle as directing, we must, with the materialistic evolutionist, ascribe to matter itself a quality which implies intelligence, and believe that matter chooses successive forms in which to appear and then controls its own reconstruction—for this is the logical deduction from the ordinary evolution theory; or, on the other hand, we must deny what Scripture and Nature clearly teach, i. e. that God invariably employs agents to accomplish what He wills, and believe that He personally directs in each case, the dissolution of the old, and the creation of the new, form. We must believe that God has designated Light as His active agent in Nature, and that Light is the principle in Nature that by its subjective power directs and controls, and by its objective forces executes, the processes of disintegration and integration, and thus carries on the work of creation throughout time. As we have before distinctly affirmed, this recognition of Light as the power or force in and of Nature, does not seek to elevate Light into a God, or otherwise derogate from God's absolute Supremacy: God manifests Himself in Light, and Light exercises, not independent, but God-given power in fulfilling its God-given mission.

But let us now briefly observe the operations of this "principle in Nature" in its objective processes, and through these we may also profitably seek to comprehend the unseen subjective influence; when the chemist would produce water, he must employ both the decomposing and combining forces of light—the first to obtain the hydrogen and oxygen and the second to make water out of them; but, in both processes we see an intelligence directing, as well as the two forces acting: the first cannot produce the water without the two forces, nor can they without the intelligence to direct. And so, in studying the operations of the two forces in Nature we must realize the important influence of the unseen subjective principle that directs them.

Bearing in mind that material forms are but convenient objective media in which that unseen mysterious something we call life must unfold itself, and through which it must manifest its unfoldment, we observe in Nature an infinite variety of forms, and consequently see manifestations of an infinite variety of life-developments; and the life-development we find in each case, depends upon the nature of the forms within which the life-principle must unfold itself.

Nature is divided into three distinct "kingdoms," the first of which comprises only inorganic matter, and the other two comprehend organic forms, endued

the one with *still life* and the other with *active life*. In
studying these three kingdoms we shall discover that
Nature adapts material from the first in creating the
forms of the second, and from both in creating bodies
for the third; we shall find, too, that in the inorganic
mineral kingdom, though there is no life, there is
constant testimony to the influence of the directing
"principle" of which we have been speaking, in the
production of innumerable simples and compounds
that are indispensably essential to the life of both the
other kingdoms; and farther, we shall doubtless discover a *wonderful* adaptation of forms to every conceivable kind and degree of life-development, and still
more we shall marvel if we study aright the mysteries
of life, at the wonderful system that pervades the two
life-kingdoms: *e. g.*, we cannot but marvel when we observe that, under the guidance and control of the sublime life-principle, there are ever present in each form
the two antagonistic forces, one destroying, the other repairing and restoring; the latter sustained by the life-
principle, more than repairing and restoring, actually
adds to and increases the vigor of the form until the
life within has attained the fullest development that the
form will permit, and from this point we notice a decline, the life-principle is no longer interested in preserving the form, the repairs and restorations no longer
keep pace with the decay, and the form passes away, and
then a new form is reared with capacity for a higher
life-unfoldment—this upbuilding, sustaining, decay and
reconstruction are repeated again and again, until the
type or class of forms has attained its acme. Then,
we find a type or class commencing at a higher min-

imum and attaining a higher maximum, and then a
still higher scale, until life-unfoldment within the
kingdom has attained the highest state to which it is
capable of being brought. Whereupon we discover
that Nature's resources are not yet exhausted: another
kingdom is created with capacity for a far higher
state of life-unfoldment. In this kingdom, we find,
as in the one preceding, a series of types or classes
comprising a vast number of distinct forms. The
lowest type is but little, if any, above the lowest of
the former kingdom, but this second life-kingdom
soon shows that it was created to provide forms that
would admit of far higher life-development, for the
successive types of forms ascend, like the rounds of a
ladder, steadily upward, until in man the zenith of
material forms is reached. Physical life can attain no
higher unfoldment than in the form of man, and Nature
has reached its ultimate power of developing life;
but the God of Nature would have a still higher development,
and He implants within this form the
germ of a higher life, which may be unfolded to some
extent within the material body, but attains its full
unfoldment only when transplanted to the Celestial
World. But of this in a later chapter.

We cannot do more, in this work, than in the briefest
manner to glance at the several kingdoms, and
note their most conspicuous characteristics, scarcely
more than suggesting lines of study, but hoping that
our readers will become sufficiently interested to pursue
the study of Nature in the light of truth. Our purpose
is only to show how Light is the universal motor,
the Source of Vital Dynamics, and we can only dis-

cuss the distinctive features of the three kingdoms in
so far as they are produced by Light. In the present
chapter, we shall speak generally of the three kingdoms, noticing the peculiarities in material constitution of each, the nature of the life and character and
extent of the life-development in the two life-kingdoms, reserving the specific investigation of human
life, and of the human organism, for the next chapter.

To the Mineral Kingdom belong the air we breathe
and the water we drink and the earth upon which we
dwell, and thousands of substances that contribute
directly and indirectly to our pleasure, wealth, health
and general well-being, even if we ignore their combination by Nature with the food we eat, both
vegetable and animal, and with every part of our
physical organism. None who appreciate the metals
that enter so largely into the utensils of the house-
hold, the tools of the workshop, the implements of the
farm, the machinery of the factory, the apparatus of
Science, and into the millions of useful appliances of
every walk of life, to say nothing of those that supply us with coin, or of the gems and precious stones
that are far from being the most precious of Nature's
inorganic treasures, will undervalue the Mineral
Kingdom. But we must not ignore the important
ingredients Nature obtains from this first of her kingdoms in the creation of the forms wherein to unfold
the life-principle in her two life-kingdoms; even in
man, the highest form she rears, inorganic matter
supplies the bulk of her materials, as we shall see
when we come to consider man in detail. Notwithstanding the value to us of the substances of the Min-

eral Kingdom, however, they have not the smallest trace of that most precious of all natural gifts, that mystery, life. We find, indeed, the two objective forces of Light in the forces of attraction and repulsion that have been imparted to each atom, but the subjective principle must work from without.

We have before, more than once, mentioned an intrinsic difference between this and the other kingdoms, which we repeat because it is peculiarly worthy of consideration in this connection: the atoms of inorganic matter are angular, while those of organic bodies are spheroidal in the lower forms and becoming spherical as they advance in the scale of development; this clearly shows that Nature, in developing forms, adapts her materials to the requirements of each case: the atoms of an inorganic substance being required, she unhesitatingly appropriates them to a higher purpose, but first she trims off the objectionable corners, or otherwise modifies them; then having adapted them to their new use, she obtains or creates other desired ingredients and fitting each atom to the place it is designed to occupy in the new structure, she puts them together, fixing or polarizing them in the exact form she desires; meanwhile to each atom she has imparted the dual forces that, maintained in equilibrium, will keep them in their places and thus preserve the form of the aggregate substance, until she shall require their atoms for still higher and more excellent forms, when, as we have seen, she suspends or destroys the equilibrium, and they part asunder, to be again subjected to suitable changes and modifications, readjusted to new forms, have additional ingredients brought into ties of affinity with them, and become parts of new structures. In each and all of these processes Light is the operator.

The first of the two life-kingdoms is, of course, the Vegetable, and the second the Animal, Kingdom. That the elementary ingredients in the forms of both are essentially the same, Chemistry sufficiently attests, and both derive their vitality from the one source, Light. Yet we see that their forms are utterly and entirely different and the life of one is in no one respect like that of the other—the one we have designated *still life*, the other *active life*, and the correctness of these designations will soon be seen:

In both the Vegetable and Animal Kingdoms, the commencement of life-forms consists of simple cells. The lowest form of the former is found in the *Protococcus pernacinus;* these comprise microscopic spherical globules having a transparent covering, filled with a red, oily substance. They are species of Algæ, and are of various colors. These minute organisms give to the snow in northern latitudes, at times, a peculiar red color. Ehrenberg who has observed these strange little *vegetables* very closely, has found with them certain microscopic *animalcula* which he has called *Philodina roseola*. How this low form of vegetable life can exist upon the top of snow is a mystery Ehrenberg has not solved. The lowest life-form of the Animal Kingdom are the *Protozoa*, most of which are microscopic; they consist of a jelly-like substance, which has associated with it inorganic constituents in the higher forms, chiefly carbonate of lime. They have no digestive organs but live by imbibition; they

possess pulsation, show sensibility and are guided in
their movements by instinct. Thus, a simple cell appears to be the starting-point in life-forms in both of
the organic kingdoms, and in both we find that, as
we advance in development, the cells unite and form
tissues. But soon we find a marked difference apparent in the forms of the two species of physical life:
Organs essential for a higher state of development
begin to show themselves in the animal forms that
never occur in the vegetable kingdom; in this branch
of Nature, the vital forces that sustain and develop
life are purely objective, derived entirely from without; there is within no soul or responsive centre of
vitality; and, besides the life-forces of plants are more
or less intermittent, depending in considerable degree
upon the seasons, and even upon thermometric, barometric and electric variations; while animal life is, especially in the lower forms, also somewhat subject to
these external influences, the something within that
serves as a reservoir of vitality acts as a regulator.
The tissues in the plant are directly worked up into
the various forms of body, while in the animal they
are united to form organs which in turn are united to
form bodies. There is not a tissue in the animal form,
from the humblest type to man, but what consists of
cells—even the hair and the nails are aggregations of
cells.

The plant has a circulatory system, but no beating
heart or pulsating arteries; it is said to exhale and
inhale, but it has no lungs, and its so-called respiration is simply the direct action of the Sunlight driving
in and drawing out certain gases or vapors; it is said

to feed, but here again the term expresses too much—with the exception of two or three species to be noticed later, plants bear no part in receiving or digesting or assimilating the substances that sustain their life and with the same exceptions, plants have no perception, consciousness, instinct, or volition; they have certain sexual properties that resemble the sexual organs of the animal in their functions, but they are dependent for copulation upon birds, insects, the wind or other foreign aid; and in the germination of their seed they bear no part. In short, plant-life is a receptive, inactive, still life; Light acts in and for it, in a special sense in which it does not act in and for animal-life: it must not only prepare its food, but must feed it and then assimilate the food and convert it into cells, adjust the cells and fix them into tissues, and so throughout completing the process; even the circulatory system ceases to act as soon as the genial warmth of the Sunlight is withdrawn or the approaching winter abates its power; plants are largely composed of carbon and hydrogen, but the chemical force of Light must draw the former from the earth and the latter from the water for it, and the polar force must apply them to the plant; under the Sunlight, the plant is said to exhale oxygen, and in the dark to exhale in the form of carbonic acid, part of the carbon given to it by the Light. Speaking of the carbonic acid exhalation, suggests a word upon the beautiful process by which Light applies a constituent of the earth to the formation of plant-structure: it extracts carbon from the soil, forms it into carbonic acid with the help of some oxygen, introduces it to the cells of a leaf, by which it is absorbed, meeting in the pores water, salts and the organic matter of the sap. A microscope now shows an immediate vibratory movement by which molecules are formed, and as soon as these have attained their growth the vibratory motion ceases; other quantities of the same materials are sent in, go through the same vibratory motion and the molecules attach themselves to the previous number, and so little masses are formed which chemists call granules of starch; in the same manner the most complex substances in the vegetable forms are created.

It is noteworthy that the processes by which vegetable and animal life are sustained are chiefly opposite: the first is one of deöxidation, the other of oxidation—the one throws off oxygen, the other seeks it. Also, that wherever vegetable life is abundant, animal life is usually equally so; this no doubt is due in a measure to the fact that the one furnishes food for the other—but it is no less due to the fact we have just remarked on, that the life-process of the one is opposed to that of the other, and thus the one prepares the atmosphere for the other; it requires no argument to show that the latter reciprocates favors received. Indeed, we may almost consider the two sorts of life as representing the opposite principles of Nature, the passive and active, or feminine and masculine.

We do not deem it necessary to trace the development of life and forms in the Vegetable Kingdom from the *Protococcus* to the *Droseraceæ*, the highest life-development reached therein; it will suffice for our present purpose to notice the three types, or the three species of one type, which show a kind of sensibility and instinct together with something resembling the digestive organ of the animal: The "Pitcher-plant," "Venus's Fly-trap," and the "Sundew" are the plants to which we refer: the Fly-trap and the Sundew are dissimilar and yet are certainly species of one class or type, the *Droseraceæ*, and probably the Pitcher is related to them. At any rate, they are alike in voracity: if a fly or any other insect alight within reach of their tentacles or bristles, they promptly capture and eat it; they are provided with a juice similar to the gastric juice of animals, and actually digest not only insects but small pieces of meat that may be given to them, and the product goes to the nourishment of the plant.

In the animal kingdom, the next type above the *Protozoa* are the *Radiata*, the lowest order of the *Invertebrata*. The highest forms of these have a mouth or opening, around which there is a circular row of ganglia connected by commissural bands of nerve-fibres and nerves leading off from the ganglia to the digestive canal and the reproductive organs. Their nervous system is adapted to simple requirements of their life. They live in water. They have sensibility and evince a trace of instinct not exceeding that of the *Droseraceæ*.

The next step brings us to the *Articulata* and *Mollusca*, where we find ganglionic centres set apart or developed to meet the wants of a higher life. These have organs of locomotion, deglutition and respiration, with a nervous system attached to each. We do not find consciousness developed until we come to that stage where organs of special sense appear, though, as we have seen sensibility and a low order of instinct exist below. As the seat of consciousness is at the base of the brain and there is no indication of brain in the *Invertebrata*, such as appears in the *Vertebrata*, the inference has been that none of the former have consciousness; this is a mistake, surely; their nervous system is ample for their requirements, and where we find organs of special sense there must be consciousness or the organs would be valueless.

We must remark in the *Vertebrata* a still higher form, with a complete nervous system clearly defined; even among the lower types of this general division, we see a spinal cord consisting of linear aggregations of ganglia, at the upper end of which there is a rudimentary brain, wherein are located the organs of special sense and the seat of consciousness. Among the most conspicuous features of this type are a more pronounced sensibility, instinct and consciousness than in those below, and in the higher forms (below man) is seen a low order of intelligence, with passions and emotions. We do not use the term consciousness in the sense in which it is ordinarily used—as we understand the term it signifies purely an objective power of discerning and understanding external things. The instinct of the higher types of the *Vertebrata* is itself almost intelligence, but they have actually a species and degree of intelligence scarcely surpassed by that of men the objective faculties of whose souls are developed to the suppression of the subjective, and exceeding that of men whose souls are entirely uncultivated. The horse affords a ready illustration of this; some horses show a capacity for learning, for development of intellect that well-nigh entitles them to be credited with reason.

And now we have reached the zenith of physical perfection, MAN, the highest form of created bodies, who may attain the high privilege of being God's image and likeness, if he but cultivate the faculties within his Soul.

Thus we see a unity with diversity throughout the wonderful aggregation of wonders we call Nature—one source of materials for the forms, and diversity in their combination; one source of vital forces, with diversity in the manner and degree of the life-unfoldments. Nay, we see more: we see in the diversity not only the infinite Wisdom, Beneficence and Power of the Author and Creator of Nature, but the marvelous unity of purposes, that, constituting Light His sole representative and agent, created by and through its agency, forms adapted to every kind and degree of life-unfoldment up to man, the Synthesis, with capacities for a degree of unfoldment that, if accomplished, will make him so Godlike that he will be "in the image" and "after the likeness" of Jehovah Himself, which it is evident throughout was the grand sum of His purposes.

In the next chapter we propose to discuss "The Human Organism and its Vital Dynamics," and a grander theme pen cannot essay. Man's physical frame, with its nervous and arterial systems and its centres of force, is unquestionably the most complicated mass of mechanism, and the most perfect, ever created, and is moved by a dual vital power within that mere human intelligence can never comprehend—he who would understand it aright must be illuminated by the same Celestial Sun of Suns which is its original source. Marvelous, indeed, is this dual vital motor that, if allowed full scope, will elevate man to so high a plane of excellence that he will be "in the image" and "after the likeness" of the Creator Himself and a worthy citizen of the Celestial World. We hope to make plain the stupendous purposes of "the Father of Light" in creating "the world and all things therein," and especially in creating man, the Synthesis of the Universe, the perfection of material form.

Meanwhile, in closing this chapter, let us take a reviewing glance over the ground we have traversed in our investigations thus far, summarizing what we have learned about Light as the power or force in and of Nature, the universal motor, the sole source of vital dynamics:

Walker defines the word Science thus: "Knowledge; certainty grounded on demonstration," and the etymology of the word sustains the definition, but it certainly will not do to be so restrictive in the use of the term, or we shall have to conclude that Science is a very limited field for study. "Ganot's Popular Physics" offers us the following: "Science is a *knowledge* of the laws that govern the Universe,"—this is scarcely more favorable to the *Science* or *Scientists* of modern times; we are afraid that Ganot, under *his* definition, would scarcely take high rank as a genuine Scientific scholar, and all the great authorities of our day would hesitate in accepting a definition that would exclude their theories. Were we to insist on Walker's or even Ganot's definition, we scarcely know where we should look for a modern Scientist in the field of Light.

We have not found an approximately correct answer to the initial, fundamental question: What is Light? We have seen that an authority of no mean rank tells us it is "that force in Nature which, acting on the retina, produces the sensation of vision," and a higher authority tells us it is "the vibration of a substance," while Tyndall and others are content to tell us what it is not. Ganot defines "Optics" as "that branch of Physics which treats of the phenomena of light," and then informs us that "Light is that physical agent which, acting on the eye, produces the sensation of sight." Now, of course, our reader is aware that "*Optics*" is *the smallest fragment of the Science of Light*. Then, when we pass the initial question and the most unsatisfactory answers, we find in modern treatises on Light chapters of theories with an occasional item of *Science*, according to Walker.

We do not realize fully, however, how little modern "Scientists" know of Light, until we look into the popular treatises on Physics and find extended disquisitions upon and attempted definitions of "Physical Agents," "Forces of Attraction and Repulsion," "Motion and Rest," "Accelerating and Retarding Forces," "Centrifugal and Centripetal Forces," etc. etc., and, throughout, not a word to indicate a suspicion on the part of their authors that Light has aught to do with these agents, forces, etc. Light to them is no more than something that "excites the sensation of vision," and permits objects, by the exercise of a caprice called *selective absorption*, to paint themselves with its colors [see pages 73, 74 and 76].

But if modern *Science* knows little of *the True Science of Light*, the ancient Philosophy knew much—nay, knew all—about Light in its subjective power, and thence we have learned that the Science of Light actually comprehends all other Sciences, Physical, Metaphysical and Psychical; that Light is the original of all forces, the universal motor, the centre and source of vital dynamics [see pages 23, 56 to 63, 68, 96, 97, 100, 102, and the present chapter especially].

We have learned that Light was, "in the beginning," has been ever since, and will continue to be until the end of time, God's special, peculiar manifestation of Himself in creation; that the Celestial Sun is the great Central Orb of the Universe, the source of the Astral Suns (or the Sun and Stars), and the centre around which they revolve; that the law of harmony, which we have seen pervades all the universe, is absolute in the Celestial Light and relaxed in the objective Suns in order to adapt their light to the necessities of the inhabitants of the several worlds in their respective systems; that in consequence of this relaxing of that unique law, Nature applies the light and heat separately, and even employs single rays in special operations, and man, too, is thus enabled to analyze the objective light and employ its rays in various ways; that, though relaxed, this law is not abrogated, the Almighty still enforces it when man presumes to disregard it, physically, mentally or morally; that, in proportion as any one of God's creatures disregards His laws, He enforces the penalty—

for instance, a disregard of the laws of health destroys the equilibrium within, and the penalty, disease, is proportionate to the infraction, but He permits us, by restoring the equilibrium, to escape the penalty and recover health; that He places in our reach means for restoring the equilibrium of health and, if we seek aright to learn, enlightens us as to the mode of applying the means.

Later chapters will specially be devoted to the elucidation of the laws of health, the ascertaining of what is health and what disease, and the discovery of the best means and methods for expelling disease and restoring health.

We have learned that in the mental world, as in the physical, disregard of the law of harmony entails disorders of the mind, and in the moral world sin is disregard of that law and its penalty is the withdrawal of Light, and, if persisted in, the penalty becomes the darkness of hell. That the happiness and glory of Heaven are due to the one fact that absolute and uniform harmony reigns therein at all times forever, and sorrow and sighing, pain and sickness, decay and death, consequently cannot enter there; that this world is the world of darkness solely because man disobeyed God and defied His law, thus entailing not only upon his posterity, but upon the entire world, a condition of inharmony in which the true Light cannot shine, and the withdrawal of Celestial Light constitutes Spiritual Darkness; that, as ordinary darkness favors disease and ordinary light promotes health, so in an infinitely greater degree Spiritual Darkness produces sorrow, pain and death, and Celestial Light produces happiness, health and life; that, as the natural world is in a state of profound spiritual darkness, so the natural man is in a state of spiritual blindness and death; that, in Christ, "the Sun of Righteousness," the true Light was gloriously manifested, and those who receive that Light into their Souls no longer "walk in darkness," but become "new creatures," are "born again," and are transformed into "children of Light;" that " whosoever will," may be enlightened by that glorious Light, if he will but seek that enlightenment by earnest self-denial and devotion; that he who cultivates the subjective faculties of his Soul, even while yet in this world of darkness, is not of it, but is a "child of Light," a citizen of Heaven, and to him death is but a more complete realization of the eternal blessedness of Light; that the "child of Light" cannot "hide his Light under a bushel," but must "set it on a hill to give Light to the world," and thus become a "Light of the world;" that, when Christ was in the world corporeally manifesting Celestial Light, men could not "see the Light," because they "loved darkness rather than Light," and, even were it possible for a dark Soul to attain Heaven, it could not be happy there, because, to enjoy the Light and consequent delights of the Celestial World, the Soul must be in harmony with that Light, and, hence, that he who would reach Heaven and be forever happy there, must cultivate the spiritual part of his Soul, and bring it into a state of harmony with God and Heaven by becoming a "new creature," a "child of Light;" that the "natural man," even if he be an Astronomer, "cannot see the Kingdom of God," while the humblest "child of Light," shall have a foretaste of its joys and glories in this life, and at the last abide therein " forever blest."

HARMONY *is the sublime law of physical, mental and moral health and life*—the law of God, and of Heaven! May we then seek to understand and obey it aright in body, mind, Soul and Spirit.

CHAPTER V.

THE HUMAN ORGANISM AND ITS VITAL DYNAMICS.

"I WILL praise thee; for I am fearfully [incomprehensibly?] and wonderfully made;" "Thou hast made him [Man] a little lower than the angels, and hast crowned him with glory and honour." David, "the sweet singer of Israel," illuminated by Celestial Light, had a high estimate of the human organism and a still higher conception of its crowning glory and honor, the Soul! and the Man who *knows himself* aright can scarcely refuse or neglect to praise the Almighty, or refuse or neglect to perform the part assigned him by God in the care of his body and the cultivation of his Soul—he who *knows himself* must realize that God has not merely created a marvelous frame and placed within it a still more stupendous system of machinery to move the frame, but has provided a sublime centre of vital force, capable not only of keeping the machinery in action and impelling the form through earthly life, but of elevating the higher nature within, fitting it for eternal life and carrying it in safety through the world of darkness to the realms of ineffable light and joy and glory! but, realizing all this that God has done, he will learn that the frame must be kept in repair, the machinery in running order and the Soul in active exercise.

Man, physically considered, is the masterpiece of creative skill! the highest type of material forms! the noblest creature that matter is capable of being moulded, created or developed into. Considered as a *living* creature, Man's superiority over all animated beings is still more evident, and is so great that the most thoughtless perceive it. But we cannot begin to estimate how "fearfully and wonderfully" we are made, until we study the vital forces within; nor can we fully realize the entire "glory and honor" of Man's organization until we attempt to understand and define that incomprehensible fountain of objective and subjective life, whence all the vital forces derive their vitality, the Sun of the human system, the Soul! The inferior animals, as we designate all animated creatures below Man, are only less wonderfully made, are provided with systems of vitality within, and have each a centre of vital energy, a Soul, but the highest of them all is so far below Man that the most ignorant and unthinking perceive, if they do not conceive, the difference.

Man has been called the Synthesis of the Universe, because he has within him the subjective principles of the Universe, the Soul and Spirit, together with the objective factor of the Soul; but he is also the Synthesis of the material creation, for in his physical composition we find elements of the Mineral and of the Vegetable and Animal kingdoms of Nature. "In the beginning," while space was filled with *Ayte*, or *ether*, unpolarized, inert, black, "without form and void," the Almighty "Father of Light" conceived the marvelous plan of manifesting Himself in Light, and through Light in Creation; the grand object being to develope in corporeal form a Soul of Light "in His own image and after His own likeness," a complementary, complete manifestation of Himself in Nature. To this end, the *Rouach Elohim* brooded over the waters; God said "Let there be Light, and Light was"—His first manifestation, but not corporeal. Darkness fled, chaos ceased, Light prevailed and order and beauty were developed. Creation was not completed, however, until its Synthesis, Man, "became a living Soul."

Now, alas! Man forfeited his "likeness" to the Creator by disobedience, and Spiritual Darkness, Spiritual Chaos, came upon the world; but the Almighty would not be baffled in His sublime purpose, and, even in the hour of punishing fallen man, announced the accomplishment of that purpose in Christ, the perfect realization of the Divine essence manifested in the human form—" No man hath seen God at any time; the only begotten Son, which is in the bosom of the Father, He hath manifested Him;" "Without controversy, great is the mystery of godliness [God-likeness]; God was manifest in the flesh." "The seed of the woman," Christ, was "in all points tempted like as we are, yet without sin"—the objective faculties of His Soul could not lead Him astray because the subjective were completely developed and perfectly unfolded, and He was "the Sun of Righteousness," the Celestial Sun—absolutely the Almighty JEHOVAH "manifested in the flesh," and could truthfully say "I and my Father are one!" He it was of whom Isaiah spoke when he exclaimed to "Zion," the church of the Living God: "Arise, be enlightened, for thy Light is come, and the Glory of JEHOVAH is risen upon thee. . . . The Sun shall be no more thy light by day; neither for brightness shall the moon give light unto thee: but JEHOVAH shall be unto thee an everlasting Light, and thy God thy Glory. Thy Sun shall no more go down; neither shall thy Moon withdraw itself: for JEHOVAH shall be thine everlasting Light." Then he adds the assurance: "Thy people also shall be all righteous"—but the millennium has not yet come, and we await the fulfilment of this promised result of the Messiah's coming, which will occur when the world receives "the Sun of Righteousness" and ceases to "love darkness rather than Light." Meanwhile, though no man can, in this world of darkness, attain to so perfect a "likeness" to God as did our "elder brother and exemplar," we may, by "taking up our cross and following" Christ, in holy living and good works, become "children of Light" and we have the encouraging promise that "we shall be like Him" when "we see Him as He is."

We opened this chapter with a quotation from Psalm 139, and we quote a few more words from the same passage, which show that the Psalmist knew whereof Man is made: "My substance was not hid from thee, when I was made in secret, and curiously wrought in the lowest parts of the earth. Thine eyes did see my substance, yet being unperfect; and in thy book all my members were written, which in continuance were fashioned, when as yet there was none of them." Is not this a striking picture of the Psalmist's view of

God's care and forethought in Man's creation? his idea appears to be that God, like a careful workman, set down in a book the details of the human form, each member, or part, with the materials to be used in its construction. But it is more: it is a recognition of the fact that, in the act of creating inorganic matter, even "in the lowest parts of the earth," the ultimate design of using it in producing Man was borne in mind. Chemical analysis shows that the Psalmist was correct in his view that the *members* of the body were developed, or at least the materials prepared, "in secret, and curiously wrought in the lowest parts of the earth;" for it demonstrates that a very large percentage of the materials that enter into, not only the members, nor only into the bones and flesh, but actually into the life-centres and -tissues, even into the brain, consists of inorganic matter, sometimes modified, adapted and worked-up into special forms or compounds, but often without change, precisely as it occurs in the earth. But let us note some of the more important of these inorganic constituents of the human organism:

WATER.—We have before alluded to the large proportion of water in the material form not only of man, but of all organic things. Water is the most important of all substances in Nature,—nay, there is water in Heaven: the "water above the firmament," and the globe of the objective Sun, we have seen, is chiefly composed of water; but for water, in the form of vapor, in our atmosphere, warmed by the calorific element of Light, there could be no life upon our planet; while its importance in the springs, rivulets, rivers, lakes, seas and ocean, is obvious to the child when first he begins to exercise his reason; and without water no substance could exist—even the flinty rock contains water. The importance of water to vegetable life requires no demonstration; those who think not why, recognize it, when they water the garden or the pot-plant. From 20 to 99 per cent. of vegetable forms is water, and of animal forms it is the chief ingredient: just as the plant shrivels and withers and dies in proportion as the needful water is withheld, so the man or beast could not sustain life within his body without water. Water is the only liquid God has created, and man can devise nothing to take its place even in the smallest proportion (hence the ancients regarded Water as one of the four primary elements); water alone supplies moisture to the atmosphere, the earth, the plant and the animal, and nothing can be made to supplant it or do its important work; other liquids may have their uses (for instance, alcohol as a solvent for certain substances not soluble in water), but their field of usefulness is not in man's body any more than in the vegetable body.

The human organism contains nearly four parts water to one of all other ingredients combined—*i. e.*, a man weighing 150 pounds contains 116 pounds of water. This is distributed through the system as follows:

	Percentage of Water.
Bone	10 to 20
Hair	40
Cuticle	50
Nerve	57
Skin	60 to 70
Fibrous Textures	65 to 70

	Percentage of Water
Artery	70 to 75
Cartilage } Muscle } Glands	72 to 77
Blood	77 to 80
Wall of Intestine	82
Brain	80 to 84
Fat	

The purposes which water subserves are different according to the matter with which it is connected; 1. It imparts to the tissues the necessary suppleness and extensibility—e. g., a piece of tendon desiccated shrinks into a nearly inflexible rod, resembling dried glue, but, if macerated in water, recovers its original pliancy. Even to the harder bones it imparts strength. It will be observed that the amount of water in the various parts, is proportionate to their relation to vitality—thus, the bones have the least, hair but little more, and so on, until the artery has an average of 73 per cent., the muscles of 75 per cent., and the brain has the most, more than four-fifths being water.

2. Water is invaluable, indispensable to the system as a solvent to prepare the way for all the chemico-vital processes by which the integrity of the living body is maintained; and a deficiency in the water-supply is soon apparent in a derangement of these operations even before the constitution of the tissues is sensibly affected. It is well known that chemical action is impossible between the atoms of solid substances; a solid must be vaporized or dissolved before its atoms can be freely attacked by the chemical force. Alimentary material for the uses of the Organism must

be dissolved ere it can be applied; food received into the stomach would produce evil rather than benefit but for water to dissolve it. It is water, too, that continues to act as solvent for the nutritive matter after it has found its way into the current of the circulation, and has undergone that assimilating process that prepares it for application to the renovation of the solid tissues: water forms an average of nearly four-fifths of the "vital fluid" which courses in minute streams throughout the body, imparting the vigor of life to the tissues it traverses. But, the water of the blood not only brings to the living tissues the materials for repair and development, it also takes up the products of their decay and disintegration and conveys them, by a complicated but perfect system of sewerage, out of the body.

LIME, PHOSPHATE AND CARBONATE OF.—1. The Phosphate of Lime, or "bone-earth," is second to none of the *solid* inorganic components of the human body either in amount or the important mechanical purposes it directly serves, while eminent investigators ascribe to it an equal importance as contributing to the chemico-vital processes of the economy. Healthy bones contain an average of from 48 to 59 per cent., those containing most that are specially required to possess power of resistance—of the *Dentine* of teeth it forms 66, and of the *Enamel* nearly 90 per cent. This calcareous salt is, however, by no means confined to the bony frame, it is present in all the soft tissues, and in solution, or suspension, in all the fluids of the system, those conveying in nutriment and those conveying out excrement. 2. The Carbonate of Lime is always present, though in much smaller proportions than the Phosphate.

CHLORIDE OF SODIUM occurs in nearly every part of the Organism of Man, both solid and fluid, in close and intimate relations to the organic constituents, the chemical and physical properties of which are materially affected by it; it is second only to water in importance of the inorganic components in a chemical point of view. In a state of health, the proportions of salt in the tissues and fluids are definite and constant, the variations being very slightly perceptible after even an excessive eating of salt food; all in excess of the normal amount appears to be rejected and passes off chiefly by the kidneys. In some diseases the quantity of salt in the blood is liable to great variations. The proportion, however, in health, differs greatly in the several tissues, and in the same tissue at the different stages of its development.

Besides these, there are: *Phosphate of Magnesia*, *Flouride of Calcium*, *Silica* (only in the hair as a normal constituent), *Hydrochloric Acid* (an important chemical agent, especially in the gastric fluid), *Alkaline Carbonates* (these, according to Professor Liebig, keep the chief solid constituents of the blood in a fluid state; but for alkali the water could not dissolve the oxides of iron or other metallic oxides, and further they promote the metamorphosis of the oxalic, citric, tartaric and other organic acids that pass into the body with the food), and *Alkaline Phosphates*. Though *Soda* is the chief base of the Alkaline Carbonates and Phosphates, *Potash* is also present in appreciable quantities. IRON is, of course, a constituent of the human body, but it is chiefly as an element of *Hæmatin*, which we shall mention among the organic constituents. *Sulphur* and *Phosphorus*, like Iron, must be noticed among organic ingredients, because though themselves inorganic, they appear chiefly in intimate relations to organic compounds. It was at one time claimed that *Arsenic* was constantly met with in the bones, but subsequent researches show that it is never present as an ingredient, and its presence must always be attributed to some exceptional introduction. *Copper* and *Lead* are found, the former in the bile and biliary concretions, and the latter in the tissues and fluids of the body, but neither of them is a constituent (it is noteworthy that Copper appears to replace Iron in the blood of some marine animals, both Molluscous and Articulated). A peculiar *cumulative* property of Lead causes it, when received into the circulatory system, to attach itself to certain tissues in considerable quantities, often occasioning paralysis of certain muscles or groups of muscles, or other serious evils.

Notwithstanding the large amount and importance of the inorganic components of the human organism, however, its organic constituents claim a higher rank; while it is difficult, where each ingredient has its part to contribute, which no other can supply so well, to pronounce one more important than another, it is not amiss to recognize a higher rank for those that enter specially into the life-centres and vivaducts of the system, as do the principal organic compounds in the body. These come from the earlier inorganic kingdom, but by way of an organic go-between, wherein they have once undergone Nature's developing manipulation, and are therefore the better fitted for use in the more delicate and essential works of the grand machine, requiring less to adapt them to the important functions now to devolve upon them. The chief organic components of the body are:

I. THE HISTOGENETIC SUBSTANCES, or *the Tissue-Creators*. These substances have either been introduced into the system, or generated from organic and inorganic matter otherwise introduced, as the materials of its fabrics, undergoing needful progressive metamorphoses. The organic matter of the Histogenetic group, with the exception of the fatty substance, is of the *azotized* or *nitrogenous* class.

II. THE CALORIFIC SUBSTANCES, or *the Heat-producers*. These, too, either enter the system as components of the food or are formed within by the metamorphosis of portions of the Histogenetic substances or of components of the tissues themselves. They are all of the *saccharine* and *oleaginous* classes.

III. THE CONSTITUENTS OF THE ACTUAL LIVING TISSUES, and

IV. THE EXCREMENTITIOUS SUBSTANCES, or *the products of the Disintegration and Retrograde Metamorphosis of the Tissues*.

Of course, this classification is only general or relative, as it is obviously impossible to make an absolute classification where the several classes are so closely connected materially, as well as in their functional work, that they cannot be isolated. Thus, fatty substances must be regarded as Histogenetic, because they seem essential to the production of all the tissues, and form an important constituent of the adipose and nervous; yet they as clearly must be considered Calorific, since their production within the body contributes largely to the combustive process, in which a much larger proportion is daily consumed than can be demanded for the repair and renewal of the organized fabric; and, again, fat belongs also to the third class, being an essential component of the living tissues. Still we must not imagine that it, like the Histogenetic substances proper, undergoes actual organization, as it simply combines mechanically with the other ingredients, and that so loosely that it is readily separated when the system demands the separation.

A thoughtless reading of the classifications would lead to the conclusion that the third must be almost identical with the first class, and *chemically* no doubt it is, but the molecular character of their components is very different; indeed, the properties of the living tissues can only be chemically examined by first reducing them back to the forms or the state in which they entered the body. Then, here we meet another transition link: *Fibrin*, one of the Histogenetic compounds, so exactly resembles "liquid flesh" that it claims a place in the third class.

The close connection between the fourth and third classes presents another difficulty: Excrementitious substances are separated from the blood into which they have been received back by the agency of glandular structures of whose organized tissues they form part for a time. This difficulty is augmented by the relation of the fourth to the second, a material part of the products of disintegration being utilized in the calorific process, undergoing metamorphosis within the body into saccharine and oleaginous matter little differing from those received as food.

Hence, as the foregoing classification, though the only one physiologically practicable, is yet not exact, we shall not adhere to it tenaciously, but shall permit the chemical nature of substances to influence our brief notice of the organic constituents of the "fearful and wonderful" machine called man; and in doing so we must make a partial re-classification, treating: 1. The compounds of the *Albuminous* type, or "protein-compounds," both as the materials for, and the metamorphosed components of, the living tissues; 2. those of the *Gelatinous* type under the same progressive forms; 3. the *Oleaginous* compounds, as related to the first and second, and measurably to the fourth of the physiological classes; and 4. the *Saccharine* substances, under the second and fourth classes:

1. The Albuminous Compounds comprise a series of constituents of primary importance in histogenesis, or the formation of tissue, as the tissue of all natural forms, vegetable no less than animal, is largely composed of albumen. Albumen, the nominal is also the actual base of this group, with which we find Casein, Globulin and Fibrin—these are what are called "protein-compounds," a name first applied to them under a mistaken notion that they contained a certain organic base, free from sulphur and phosphorus, which was called *Protein*. These compounds cannot be resolved by analysis, like complex inorganic matter, into two or more compounds that may be resynthesized into their original; and therefore no exact clue has been

obtained to their very complex composition. The protein-compounds are, however, extremely susceptible to the air at ordinary temperatures, decomposing spontaneously with great rapidity; this decomposition ultimately resolves them, with oxygen from the atmosphere, into water, carbonic acid and ammonia, and various organic compounds may be formed by a less complete disintegration; again, by the help of oxidizing agents, the formic, acetic, butyric, caproic, and other organic acids of the same type, that occur naturally in the body, and the ordinary fatty acids, may doubtless be produced in the same way. The ready spontaneous disintegration of these substances affects other substances in the body, and thus adapts them to extensive usefulness in the organism; it is found, *e. g.*, that at a certain stage of decomposition, a protein-compound converts starch into sugar; at a later stage converts the sugar into lactic acid, mannite and vegetable mucus; and at a still later stage, lactic acid becomes butyric acid, hydrogen and carbonic acid. This property of influencing changes in other substances, whilst themselves in process of decay, obviously augments their value, by adding a value as *ferments* to their histogenetic importance; this action also shows their right to a place in the calorific class.

Of all the protein-compounds, Albumen is the special *pabulum* of the tissues; indeed, the other histogenetic materials must be reduced to the condition of Albumen before they can be appropriated by the living system. A convenient illustration of the latent energy in still Albumen, as well as of its nutritive quality, is presented by the ordinary hen's egg, of which it is the main ingredient. Just as the store of material in the egg, under a steady, gentle warmth, developes into bones, muscles, nerves, tendons, ligaments, membranes, skin, bill, feathers, etc. of the chick, so the like tissues of the human body are formed and repaired from the albumen of the human blood. According to Mulder, Albumen is composed as follows:

Carbon	53.5	per cent.
Oxygen	22.0	do.
Hydrogen	7.0	do.
Nitrogen	15.5	do.
Sulphur	1.6	do.
Phosphorus	0.4	do.

Professor Liebig denies the presence of Phosphorus as a constituent, and claims that it has no existence in any article of food, or in any tissue of the body except in combination as Phosphoric Acid.

As a rule, Albumen is a constituent of all the *nutritive* fluids of the body, as the blood, the chyle, the lymph, and the serous exudation that percolates through the interstices of the tissues; it is also found in considerable abundance in the tissues themselves, but may not always be a constituent. The presence of Albumen in excretory matter indicates either disease of the excreting organ, or a marked alteration in the composition of the blood or in the mode of its circulation.

Casein replaces Albumen in the milk; the two differ chiefly in chemical properties; the only positive difference appears to be that the former contains less Sulphur than the latter, and it certainly contains no

Phosphorus which Albumen possibly does. It is the Casein in the milk that coagulates when "rennet" comes in contact with it—Albumen, on the other hand, is insensible to the influence of "rennet." Casein, like Albumen, is always intimately associated with other substances; it has a special affinity for Phosphate of Lime.

Another of the Albumen family is *Globulin*, which is found, as a constituent, in the red blood-corpuscles and in the cells of the crystalline lens; it is so nearly identical with Albumen proper that it is regarded by chemists as Albumen modified by its combinations.

But the most important compound of the Albumen group is perhaps that known as *Fibrin*, chemically almost one with Albumen but physiologically very different; indeed, so marked is this difference, in view of the chemical similarity, between the two that Fibrin must be credited with the distinctive presence of the *vital* principle. It is the only one of the protein-compounds that evinces an independent, spontaneous action, in the direction of organized structure: *e. g.*, while retained in the living body it exists in solution in certain fluids, but upon escaping from vital control, as when withdrawn from the body or when the body dies, it coagulates spontaneously, and the coagulum, when formed under favorable circumstances, exhibits a definite organic structure, simple indeed, but closely resembling that of the tissues that form a large part of the human fabric. Fibrin is, therefore, a substance of the highest physiological importance. It is found in all fluids that are being applied to the nutrition of living tissues, or are in course of preparation for that purpose; it is one of the most characteristic constituents of the blood, is found as an important ingredient of chyle and lymph, and is a component of the "plastic" exudations. On the other hand, it is never found in the *secreted* fluids. *Fibrin is a Histogenetic substance in the act of conversion into living tissue,* its molecules showing a tendency to assume spontaneously one of the arrangements characteristic of organization. As we have said, the chemical composition of Fibrin does not appreciably differ from that of Albumen, and we will not pause to speak of it in this light.

Hæmatin next demands a short notice: it differs very considerably from the protein-compounds in its chemical constitution, though four of its five ingredients are the same as theirs—Iron being the fifth and Sulphur and Phosphorus being absent; but Mulder's analysis shows a marked difference in the proportions as compared with Albumen:

    Carbon... 65.3 per cent.
    Oxygen.. 11.9   do.
    Hydrogen.. 5.4   do.
    Nitrogen.. 10.4   do.
    Iron.. 7.0   do.

We see here a large increase in the amount of Carbon, while the Oxygen falls off nearly one-half, and Hydrogen and Nitrogen each falls off nearly one-third, while a considerable proportion of Iron makes its presence felt. It was thought that the Red color of the blood was due to the Iron, but experiments have shown that the Iron may be withdrawn without affecting the color—we shall not here attempt to account for the color, but shall do so in due time. It has not been satisfactorily ascertained how Hæmatin is produced, but it is doubtless generated by the vital force in the blood-cells from the Albumen of the fluid in which they float, the Iron being introduced into the system by many articles of food. Hæmatin is the color-constituent of the red corpuscles of the blood, and is not normally present in any other fluid or solid of the body. *Hæmatoidin*, found in sanguineous effusions, such as those in the substance of the brain or skin, and elsewhere, is Hæmatin in a state of retrograde metamorphosis. We cannot take space to state the grounds upon which we base the hypothesis, but must be content to affirm, that Hæmatin is Albumen in course of preparation for the nutrition, strengthening and vivifying of the *muscular* and *nervous* tissues; a single well-known fact is worthy of note here, as strongly confirmatory of this statement: the nervo-muscular power of an animal always bears specific proportion to the number of red corpuscles in its blood.

Doubtless, the color, Red, carries with it the vital polar energy of the ray of Sunlight that gives it birth, and HÆMATIN *is the representative of the polar-force of* LIGHT!

2. *The Gelatinous Compounds* form a large proportion, perhaps fully one-half, of the tissues of the human organism. Their principal physical characteristic consists in their ready solution in boiling water, and their becoming a jelly when cooled. Some tissues dissolve more readily, and leave much less residue, than others. Gelatin is thus discovered to be a considerable constituent, often the chief one, of bones, car-

tilages, tendons, ligaments, skin, mucous and serous membranes, etc., and in some instances it appears almost alone. Gelatin is found in two forms, *Glutin*, or Gelatin proper, and *Chondrin*. They differ in their chemical constitution and in some minor points, but agree in their very slight solubility in cold, and prompt solubility in hot water, and in forming a jelly upon cooling.

Glutin is the form yielded by the white fibrous tissue wherever found and by the animal basis of bone; it is so decidedly glutinous that 1 part to 100 of water forms a jelly of evident consistency on cooling. Tannic acid is its most active reagent, contact with which in solution produces a white cheesy precipitate that is so pronounced that it is visible in 1 part of Glutin to 5000 of water; this is the only acid that throws down Glutin from its aqueous solution, and alkalies only precipitate a small quantity of bone-earth. Care must be exercised in boiling, for boiling too long deprives it of the glutinizing property, and causes it to part with Phosphate of Lime; the same effect is produced by repeated dissolving with exposure to air. According to Gasmal, the Gelatigenous tissues are always the first of solid animal structures to putrefy; Glutin shows a much greater tendency to putrefaction than Fibrin under similar circumstances. There is no Phosphorus and only 0.50 per cent. of Sulphur in Glutin, and it exhibits a decided partiality for forming definite chemical combinations with the Phosphate and Carbonate of Lime. Boiling in Caustic Potash for some time decomposes Glutin, and throws off Ammonia, producing two new compounds: *Leucine* and *Glycine*; the latter is simply Gelatin-sugar, which is an organic base of certain excrementitious substances.

Chondrin in its general properties differs little from Glutin, but it is obtained from cartilages alone, and then only after long-continued boiling, and it is easily precipitated by certain reagents which do not affect Glutin. The difference in composition between Glutin and Chondrin, and between them and Albumen and Hæmatin, may be seen by comparison of the following with the tables of the two named; like the former tables, this is from Mulder:

	Glutin.	Chondrin.
Carbon	50.4	50.0
Hydrogen	6.7	6.6
Nitrogen	18.3	14.4
Oxygen) Sulphur)	24.6	29.0

It is very remarkable that though nearly, if not quite, one-half of the human tissues are Gelatigenous, not an atom of Gelatin is found in the blood or in any of the healthy fluids. This clearly indicates that the Gelatinous form is never assumed until the Albumen is ready for immediate conversion into fibrous tissue, and, therefore, Gelatin never belongs to the first of the physiological classes, and it does as clearly belong to both the second and third, and in a measure to the fourth, though when it reaches the excrementitious fluids it quickly loses its peculiarities. The most striking difference between the Gelatinous and Protein-compounds is, therefore, to be found in their physiological characteristics: the functions of Gelatin in the system are purely *mechanical*, the Gelatigenous tissues being notably those that bind parts together, resist tension and antagonize pressure; on the other hand, the properly *vital* tissues are largely Albuminous.

3. *Margarin* and *Olein* are the two forms which the *Oleaginous Compounds* assume in the human fabric; the latter is a permanent, fixed oil, or fluid fat, retaining its fluidity even below the Fahrenheit zero, while the former is solid when separate from Olein, but in the body it is dissolved when it enters the latter. Margarin is a spermaceti-like fat, melts at 118° F., and may be specifically designated *human* fat, as it is not found in most animals, being replaced in them by *Stearin*; it is, however, the principal solid constituent of vegetable fats.

The Oleaginous substances serve important purposes throughout the system and claim a place in all four of the physiological departments. Of course much of the fat required for its uses is introduced into the body with the food, but a large proportion is created or generated within from the Albuminous, Gelatinous and Saccharine contents of the organism, the Liver being the chief fat factory of the complex machine. It would be interesting to notice the processes of healthy fat-making, and no less that by which "fatty degeneration" is produced, in the living system, and possibly still more interesting to remark the very peculiar, if not mysterious, production of "adipocere" in dead bodies—but we have not the space to spare, as these processes have no place in the scope of our present work.

The importance of the Oleaginous Compounds to the human economy cannot be measured by the proportions of the adipose tissues, for they furnish a most considerable portion of the nutriment and material for repair of the nervous tissue, and their presence in the blood and chyle indicate a still wider range of usefulness in promoting the general nutrition and maintenance of the physical and vital portions of the organism. Then, again, it must be borne in mind that the remarkable process, resembling combustion, upon which the needful warmth of the body depends, is due more to this class, than any other, of the compounds that Nature introduces into and produces within, the animated fabrics of "warm-blooded" animals.

There are two forms of non-saponifiable fat, called "lipoids," which appear to be normal constituents of the blood; these are *Cholesterin*, or "biliary fat," and *Serolin*, but they are probably only excrementitious products.

4. The *Saccharine Compounds* belong more exclusively to one physiological class, the second, than any other of the organic constituents of the body. *Glucose*, or "grape-sugar," is the form in which Saccharine matter is normally present in the blood and chyle. We shall not dwell upon this class of compounds, beyond remarking upon two or three facts specially noteworthy: Cane-sugar when introduced into the system, passing into the circulatory currents, is neither assimilated nor removed by combustion, but finds its way out of the system, unchanged essentially, by way of the Kidneys; on the other hand, Glucose, even when introduced into the system in much larger quan-

tities, is entirely appropriated to useful purposes, not a trace of it being discoverable in the excrements. Indeed, when an insufficient quantity of the required sugar is received in food, the Liver generates liberal supplies from starch and other sources. The Liver is the chief sugar-creating organ, but we have seen that the protein-compounds, in certain stages of decomposition work in the same direction. The Saccharine product, *Lactic acid*, is recognized as one of the most important agents in the combustive processes of Nature in the human organism, although it distinctly identifies itself with the fourth physiological class.

Lactic acid is a constant constituent of the gastric juice, and though its presence in healthy blood cannot be demonstrated by direct experiment, its certain presence in the gastric, urinary, cutaneous and other secretions, prove by induction that it must exist in the blood, even if only long enough to pass through. In a healthy condition of the system, Lactic acid is decomposed by the respiratory process, or eliminated from the blood by the secretory operations, as fast as it enters the circulation: its evident presence in unhealthy blood is due to excessive introduction or to the checking of the eliminating processes.

A very brief notice of the *Excrementitious Substances* will suffice here: these are the products of the disintegration of the tissues and of superfluous alimentary matter. The Sewerage system of the animal organism is no less wonderful than the Circulatory, and is equally essential to the welfare of Man. And in this light, this class of substances appears no less important than the Histogenetic or Calorific class.

Still, as they are produced from the substances already noticed, a mere recognition of them is all that we deem requisite here.

We have now, briefly it is true, only in *epitome* indeed, but as fully as the scope and design of our work demand or justify, noticed the principal constituents and ingredients of the material form of Man. Wonderful, as unquestionably is the fact that so many and such various materials have been employed in creating a casket for the Soul, *far more wonderful* is the manner in which these materials have been progressively created and developed, until exactly adapted, each for its special place in the stupendous fabric; *still more wonderful* is the manner in which the prepared materials have been brought together, adjusted, combined, assimilated, and unified into a form that is simply perfect in every light in which it can be viewed; *still far more wonderful* is the provision made for the continuous development and repair of this perfect form; and this brings before us the absolute *wonder of wonders*, the invisible, imponderable, impalpable, and yet mighty, something within that we call LIFE, which is the manifestation of an incomprehensible Divine principle that we call the SOUL, an emanation direct from the LIGHT OF LIFE, the Celestial Light!

As we have said, the prime object in Creation was the providing of a form adapted to the highest possible unfoldment of that principle in Nature called LIFE that in Man is individualized into the SOUL; when the successive creative evolutions had produced forms adapted to *active life*, each form was endued with the Life-principle which developed the form, and itself within, to the extent to which the character and capacity of the form would permit. When the highest type was reached, we are told by Moses, "*Man become a* LIVING SOUL!" Hence, the material form is not *Man*—it is but the casket within which Man may be unfolded—MAN *is* A LIVING SOUL! The SOUL could not be fully unfolded without a suitable body, and the body was provided. This body consists of Bones, Teeth, and Cartilages, which form its solid frame, with the Ligaments which unite them, and the Tendons which communicate motion to them from the Muscles; the Skin, with its appendages, which envelopes the exterior of the frame, the Mucous Membranes extending into all the cavities, and the Serous Membranes lining the shut sacs; the Blood-vessels and Absorbents, which distribute the nutritive fluids, and the Glands to eliminate unnecessary or exhausted substances from these; the Muscles which communicate motion by way of the Tendons to the osseous framework and to the contents of the canals and tubules that convey alimentary and other substances through the system; the Nerves which excite the Muscles and serve as the instruments for the reception of sensations and for the operations of the Mind; the Areolar tissue which connects together the preceding, and the Adipose which is commonly diffused more or less through this—each of these having a structure and a mode of vital action in some degree peculiar to itself, and hence possessing distinctive vital endowments. Thus, we find but one Vital Force, and more than one Vital Reservoir or Centre—one original Life-principle concentrating its energies in suitable centres, each of which has the peculiar power to disseminate its portion of vitality in the channels provided for it. We propose now to consider, in the ensuing chapter, the Centres and Original Source of Vital Dynamics within the Human Organism, and the great Actual Source.

CHAPTER VI.

THE CENTRES AND ORIGINAL SOURCE OF VITAL DYNAMICS WITHIN THE HUMAN ORGANISM, AND THE GREAT ACTUAL SOURCE.

THE *simple* CELL *is the Type and the Base of* ORGANIZATION, *and Organization is* LIFE! The humblest Plant and the perfected Human Organism have a common starting-point—a simple Cell. Each Cell is an Organism, and therefore each Cell has within it the principle we call Life, in its *essence* the same—in its *source* the same—in its *dependence* the same, as the Life of the most complex Organism. In other words: there is but one Actual Independent Life, JEHOVAH, manifesting Himself in the Celestial Sun, which thus becomes the Centre and Source of Creative Energy, or of Life-unfoldment; for Life unfolding is generation and generation is creation—organic forms are manifestations of Life, the successive types, from the simple Cell to the complex Human Organism, being *progressive* manifestations of the *one principle*, LIFE, in higher and higher degrees of unfoldment, from mere existence to individualization in the Human Soul, and in the individualized Soul appears the germ of a still higher Life—Subjective Faculties which, in proportion as they are carefully cultivated by self-denial, holiness and devotion, impart to the Soul the image and like-uses of the Author of Life, and thus accomplish the original purpose of the Creator.

Perhaps the most interesting study in Nature consists in tracing the unfoldment of the Life-principle from the Cell upwards, and the necessarily correspondent development of forms from the minute Cell to the perfect Human body. We have, in an earlier chapter, skeletonized the study, and our space and the character and scope of our present work forbid more, however much pleasure and profit we might derive from presenting, and our reader from studying, Nature in this aspect.

A careful prosecution of this study shows that, though each Cell has Life, and possesses within itself the germ of development, an aggregation of Cells in any number at once destroys the independence of cell-life and produces mutual dependence—each cell of an aggregate body is necessarily dependent upon each and all other cells of that body. The cell no longer lives *by itself*, and can no longer live *for itself*; it must now live *for the body* of which it constitutes a part. An aggregation of cells must have, not a number of independent lives, but *one life*—the two, or the hundred, or the thousand, or the millions, of cell-lives must be so intimately combined and blended, so actually *unified* as to become *one life!* The hitherto separate organisms must be reorganized into *one*. Of course, this complex Organism possesses all the powers and functions of its component organisms, but they must be not simply brought together, they must be united—there must be ever present an equilibrium, a *harmony*, for antagonism between cells within a body must produce death. To produce this *harmony*, there must be developed a Centre of Vitality, to regulate the equilibration of life throughout the Organism, apportioning its needed portion of the aggregate vitality to each cell. Thus, in the first aggregations of cells into animated bodies, the combined lives were harmonized into one; and in later forms, as a larger number of cell-lives were embodied, a Centre of Vitality was developed to insure harmony; in still later forms, wherein the number of cell-lives demanded more than one centre, harmony was insured by the development of a centre of centres, a Soul, as in the higher types of animals. At last, in Man, the main centre became individualized into a self-conscious Soul, with certain attributes and powers not found in any other aggregation of Life, and with a consequent authority and responsibility of which we shall speak hereafter.

Of course, two Cell-lives *combined* possess a greater and higher power than one, or even than the two separately, could attain, and so we find, from step to step, as higher organizations are reached, still greater and higher powers and functions appear—each successive step is a step forwards and upwards. Each successive advance in Life-development we see manifested in an improved type of material form, and conversely in each progressively improved type of form we look for and discover a higher Life-unfoldment. We cannot see Life, but can see its manifestation in material forms, and hence can realize that in a horse Life is vastly higher and developed in a far greater degree than in an insect or even in a reptile. So, likewise, we can see that in Man the character and degree of

Life-unfoldment is immeasurably higher and grander than in the horse. The Life-principle is the same in insect, reptile, horse and Man—but how different the manifestations!

We have here, however, to consider Life as manifested in MAN, whose material form, we have seen, is "fearfully and wonderfully made," even if we consider only the nature, number and variety of its ingredients and constituents. We come now to consider it as a stupendous complex Organism, comprising nine distinct systems, with each its own Centre or Organ of Vital Force, all controlled, directed, regulated, and harmonised by the Soul, Divinely constituted and assigned the post of authority—at once the Pilot, Captain and Engineer of the mighty, though delicate and fragile, Human Machine, over the troubled seas, and through the trying tempests of the probationary earthly voyage.

The Nine Organic Systems are:

1. The System of Organs for the Digestion and Assimilating of Food, thus Preparing Materials for Development and Repair.

2. The System of Organs for Eliminating Disintegrated and Morbid Products, and Casting them out of the Body — the Excrementory System.

3. The System of Organs for Distributing and Supplying to each and all parts of the Organism the Materials prepared for Development and Repair — the Circulatory System.

4. The System of Organs of Reproduction.

5. The System of Organs of Locomotion.

6. The System of Organs of Special Sense.

7. The System of Organs for Distributing Vital Energy through the Organism = the Nervous System.
8. The System of Organs of Intellect and Consciousness.

These eight Systems are recognized by Physiologists universally; there is a ninth system, not so recognized, yet of as much higher rank than the eighth of the above as that is higher than the seventh, sixth and fifth, and these than the other four—we mean the System of Subjective Organs, the Organs that represent most especially the Subjective portion of the Soul, and elevate Man above the Chimpanzee, the Horse, etc.—the Organs that make him a Responsible Being, and gain for him Immortality—the Organs of Self-Consciousness, of Conscience, and of Intuition.

It must be observed that the first four classes of Organs are possessed in common by both kinds of organic Nature, though modified in character, functions and mode of exercise by the addition of successive classes; just as the combining of cells modifies or changes Cell-life, so the successive development of new Organs necessarily modifies or changes the functions of the earlier ones. This is readily understood by any who will but think : The first three are essential to the maintenance of Life, the fourth to the propagation of forms of any one type—hence, Vegetable Life must have them in some degree. But, we have seen that Vegetable Life is *still life*—it has no power of locomotion, and cannot seek its food; and, farther, except in three exceptional instances which we have mentioned, Plants cannot be said actually to possess the first three of the organic functions enume-

rated above; they are directly fed and cared for by the
Sun, and in the exercise of the fourth, they are dependent upon the wind, birds, insects, etc. But when,
in animated life, powers of locomotion are developed,
of course all is changed—the animal must now seek
his food and minister to the necessities of his higher
system. And so, too, when the sixth sort or class of
Organs are unfolded, the fifth as well as the former
four are more or less modified and adapted to the new
order of life. The Organs of Special Sense succeeded
the Sensibility of the lower animal. Then, the Instinct that accompanied Sensibility was of a very low
order, because more pronounced as Sensibility gave
place to Special Sense, and developed into a low order
of Intellect, which in turn continued to develope until
in Man it attained a high degree of unfoldment, and,
meanwhile, the Consciousness, that first attended the
Organs of Special Sense, and was then of the very
lowest, grew in strength and functional power, until,
when the Organs of Intellect were unfolded and
necessitated the creation of a habitation for it, Consciousness took its seat with Intellect at the base of
the newly-developed brain.

With the development of Intellect and Consciousness, mere animal Life would attain its highest possible unfoldment; but these could not be fully unfolded
in a mere animal form. Throughout the successive
types, no one Organic System attained its complete,
ultimate extent of unfoldment until a higher System
of Organs was developed with a higher type of form
to afford greater scope, and so now, to secure the complete, ultimate unfoldment of Intellect and Conscious-

ness, the Subjective Organs of Self-Consciousness and Conscience were developed with the highest possible type of material form to afford scope for the highest unfoldment possible in mortal guise; to secure the complete, ultimate unfoldment of these Subjective Faculties the Immortality of Celestial Life was promised to Man, opened out to his Subjective Sight, and, to encourage and assist Man in unfolding these high and holy endowments One was sent in whom the Subjective Faculties were so gloriously unfolded that He was the Living Embodiment of Light, the Personal Manifestation of Jehovah, as a Son is of his Father—"the Word made flesh," "the Sun of Righteousness," "the Light of the World," "the Light of Life," "the Author and Giver of Life," "the Elder Brother" of "the children of Light," and "the Everlasting Light" of His true followers, in this life and in the Eternal Life beyond, for he is "the Light of Heaven."

Just as we have seen the successive development of each new class of Organs modified those preceding by increasing their capacities for unfoldment, so the development of the Subjective Organs has modified all the others and increased their capacity for unfoldment, and this is seen in some measure even in some intellectual and scientific giants whose Subjective Faculties were themselves not cultivated. But of this we shall speak more fully later. In the preceding chapter, in making a physiological classification of the ingredients and constituents of the human body, we found it impossible to secure exactness, because some of the compounds and simples naturally belonged to two or more classes—so, in classifying the Organs we meet the same difficulty only in a greater measure. The Human Organism is one comprising nine classes of vital functions, and the Organs necessarily have a mutual dependence upon each other, and exhibit a mutual coöperation in the general economy; some of the Organs possess more than one class of functions; e. g., the Liver is an important Assimilating Organ, as well as the leading Excrementory Organ, the Bloodvessels are constantly performing the two-fold work of supplying materials for repair and eliminating needless or pernicious substances and morbid products, etc., etc. Nevertheless, we find that, in a state of health, all the processes go on in the entire Organism in an orderly and regular manner, disintegration and integration, decay and generation, depolarization and polarization—the workings of the two forces of Light with whose operations we are familiar in every phase of Nature—because the grand, unique law of God, the law of harmony, enforced in the Universe by the Celestial Sun, in the Solar System by the Astral Sun, is enforced in the Human Organism by its Sun, the Soul. In obedience to that law, under the control of the Soul, each Organ performs every duty assigned it, whether it be to disintegrate or renew, to remove effete matter or generate new, to bear away the products of decay or bring the materials for repair. In exact proportion as this law of harmony is regarded, health is maintained, and the slightest disregard of it, as well as more flagrant disobedience, entails a proportionate penalty in the shape of disease. The office of the physician is simply to endeavor to remove the penalty by seeking to restore to the law its due observance, and if he cannot do this the ultimate penalty must ensue in death.

The difficulty we have stated in making an exact classification of Organs, is even greater when we attempt to describe and define their functional operations in and for the Organism; and it seems best to make a general classification into three classes: (1) The Organs essential to Organic Life in General; (2) The Organs peculiar to Animal Life; and (3) the Organs that distinguish Man from all other creatures. We shall find it impossible to adhere rigidly even to this general classification, because, as we have seen, each successively developed Organ or System of Organs modifies all that have preceded it, changes their functional powers and the mode of their exercise, in some measure. Thus, the processes of Digestion, Elimination, Nutrition and Excretion are essential to Organic Life, for all healthy life comprises continuous decay and renewal, and these demand the removal of the products of decay, the reception of food, its conversion by digestion, assimilation and elimination into suitable nutritive material, the carrying of this to the several points of demand and its application to its purpose—these operations demand similar apparatus in both *still* and *active* life; but we find that in the one the Sun is the actor and the plant the quiet recipient of the action, while in the animal the feeling of hunger produces the consciousness of the want of food, the will impels, and the power of locomotion enables him to seek it, when found the consciousness and will call in the aid of the nervo-muscular forces in securing and devouring it. Then, in the exercise of the fourth class of Organs essential to life, those of reproduction, the reader can trace like differences in the two sorts of life. So, too, when we come to consider the Organs peculiar to animal life, we readily discover in each successive type the influence of higher in the operations of the lower functions—*e. g.*, the Lion, in quest of food, is conscious only of hunger, knows nothing of the processes within his body that produce that consciousness, nor does he recognize any questions of right or wrong in seizing and devouring whatever he can, he knows nothing of theft or murder, he knows only that he is hungry and the prey suits his taste; but Man has higher Organs to control his animal propensities and direct his animal functions.

This general classification suggests a thought the expression of which we do not deem out of place here: Man is called the Synthesis of creation, and we see not only in his material form materials from each of the kingdoms of Nature beneath him, but his Organism brings before us the inferior Organic systems, with a higher, nobler System of Organs to elevate and ennoble them! He is called the Synthesis of the Universe, and we find in him an aggregation of Systems each with its centre of Vital Force, and a Subjectively Individualized Soul to control and direct them, just as in the Universe we find an aggregation of Systems each with its Objective Sun, and a Mighty Subjective Sun to control and direct them.

Bearing in mind, then, the influence of his higher Organs in the exercise of the lower, let us briefly consider Man under the three heads indicated above; we shall be compelled to note influences of the second or third class upon the first, and of the third upon the second, but shall endeavor to make clear the peculiar character and functions of each class of Organs under its special head:

1. THE ORGANS ESSENTIAL TO LIFE IN GENERAL.—In the Human Organism, as in all organized forms, Vitality must be equally sustained throughout to maintain the integrity of the complex whole; and, conversely, the integrity must be maintained to sustain the Vitality. So soon as Vitality ceases within, the body dies, and so, in the case of any part thereof, an arm or a leg, for example, whenever Vitality deserts it death ensues, in that part at least, and the whole body sympathizes with the dead part—if it be a *vital* part, the whole body dies; and, conversely, Vitality cannot be sustained in a dead body, or a dead part of a body. Just as Life requires a material form wherein to manifest itself, so the form must be kept in healthful repair to insure vigorous Life. Now, every exercise of Vital Force within a material form is a strain upon it and exhausts it in proportion to the extent or violence of the strain; Vital Force is constantly in exercise, except in the hours of sleep (and even then it does not loose the reins, it only slackens them), hence there is a constant exhausting of the material form; as each cell of the Organism contributes its share of Vitality to the entire mass, so each cell receives its share of Vitality from the common centres, and thus each cell throughout the Organism undergoes its share of the exhaustion, if this be general. Complete exhaustion entails loss of Vitality

and loss of Vitality is death. Were an entire part of the Organism to become completely exhausted at one time, the entire part would die—so, necessarily the body would die if entirely exhausted. But, the human body, though one, is an aggregation of cells, each cell an aggregation of particles—and the God of Nature has, in His infinite Wisdom, so ordered that, although the exhaustion is constant, it is complete only in particle by particle—and thus particle after particle dies, its polarity ceases with its Vitality and it falls away from its fellow-particles, to be immediately replaced by a new one. In this way, by a continuous disintegration of exhausted, and integration of new, particles, the Organism is kept in repair and Vitality is sustained. The opposite processes must be performed in exact equilibrium—a single new, must always instantly replace a single dead, particle. Of course, the exhaustion will be always proportionate to the strain and that in turn will necessarily depend upon the measure of the exercise of the Vital Energy—hence, the number of particles dying and falling away is greater or less at different times, and the supply must always be exactly equal to the demand. But, observe farther, the new particles must invariably be identical with those they replace—an Albuminous particle cannot be replaced by a Gelatinous, nor a Gelatinous by one of Hæmatin, although these are nearly allied.

Now, the materials from which the new particles are made must come from without, and Man himself must procure and introduce them into his body. The demand for solid matter is made known to his consciousness by the feeling of hunger, and for liquids by that of thirst; his intellect, influenced by his taste in some measure, selects the article or articles of food, his will determines upon their procurement, and the necessary Organs aid in procuring what he desires; the sensori-motor nerves now induce the reception of the food into the mouth, and its mastication and insalivation; the food, coming in reach of the pharyngeal muscles, is propelled down the œsophagus, the muscular coat of the œsophagus responds bearing it into the stomach. The Saliva has already modified the food somewhat, and upon entering the Stomach, another secretion, the Gastric Juice, farther modifies it, and, by the assistance of the high temperature maintained in the Stomach, the continual agitation produced by the contractions of the parietes of the Organ effects a more or less complete reduction of it; some of its more nutritive components are dissolved by the Gastric Juice and prepared for immediate *absorption*, while others require the action of the biliary and pancreatic secretions; at last the components of the food are ready for reception into the Circulatory System: nearly all the nutritive portions are received into the Bloodvessels and Lacteals of the Alimentary Canal, the residue passes into and along the Intestinal Tube, the particles of nutritive matter being farther extracted from it in the passage, the indigestible matter is at last ejected from the body. Thus far the action upon the food is almost purely chemical, and is what is known as Digestion; the products are Chyle and Excrement.

The Chyle is now prepared for the process of Absorption, and is absorbed into the Bloodvessels and Lacteals. And now commences the important process of Assimilation. The portion absorbed by the Bloodvessels undergoes important changes in its passage through them and through the Liver, as also does that taken up by the Lacteals—both portions have entered upon the process of being organized, vitalized, and the Chyle is nearly in the condition of true Blood, when, passing into the Sanguiferous vessels, it is sent to the Heart which transmits it to the Lungs, and here the Respiratory function eliminates the superfluous Carbonic Acid and introduces Oxygen, the objective polar force, which, under the Life-principle already imparted, is to apply the now organized nutritive matter to the repair of organs, nerves, muscles, and tissues of every kind. Thus is the food taken into the mouth at last fully converted into "Vital Food." Meanwhile, the Lymphatics have gathered up the excess of Blood that has been left over from the repair of the tissues in their way, and bear it to and through the portions of the organism that depend upon them for sustenance.

Then returning from the Lungs to the Heart, the "Vital Food" is sent forth by that hollow muscular Organ to traverse the Organism, imparting Vital nourishment wheresoever it goes.

Note: to estimate the important influence and action of the circuitous circulatory course of the Chyle of the Lacteals, on its way from the Stomach to the Heart, we need but to compare its condition at the commencement and close of the journey: we find that, when first absorbed by the Lacteals, it shows no indications of Vitality or Organization, but in passing through the Mesenteric Glands the Albumen of the Chyle becomes vitalized into granules; this granular base becomes the granules and nuclei of Cells, the nucleus of a Cell being simply an aggregation of these granules. It is well known that no Cell can be formed without the granular base; the aggregation of granules into a nucleus of course increases the Vitality of a Cell. Now, as it has been demonstrated that nutritive matter must include or become Fibrin before it can become part of a Vital Tissue, it is not unreasonable to infer that this granular base is Fibrin. But of this we shall have occasion to speak presently. Nature appears sometimes unable to repair structure, and it is because of a low condition of vitality in the system which stops the formation of the granular base, without which the Blood is impoverished and incapable of developing Tissue.

There is scarcely a necessity for speaking specifically of the Organs of Reproduction, as our reader can readily see, first, that they belong to this general class, and, secondly, that they, like the others, are only in a limited degree dependent upon or influenced by the higher Organs, while they are entirely dependent upon each of the three lower Systems.

2. THE ORGANS PECULIAR TO ANIMAL LIFE.—In entering upon the consideration of our second general division, we recognize the fact at the very threshold that this System of Systems has a common centre of Vitality, the Brain, though we shall see that, unlike the preceding, it embraces one System which is, to some extent, in some of its functions, in-

dependent of that centre; in this division we shall find it best to commence with the Brain, and trace to and from it the Organic operations that find in it their final and initial termini; the Systems of this general division are comprised in the generic term: Nervous System. Employing the term Nervous System in this generic sense, we find it radiates into six Systems, each, as we have intimated, having its local habitation, or seat, in the Brain; these seats and Systems are:

1. The CEREBRUM, or Frontal Brain—the seat of the Psychical Faculties, and, as we shall see hereafter in specially considering our third division, in some respects of the Subjective Organs of Self-Consciousness, Conscience and Intuition, though, as we shall likewise see, the Subjective Faculties are not to be regarded as actually having an assignable habitation—like the Subjective Sun of the Universe, which manifests itself objectively only in and through the Astral Suns, the Subjective Organs of the Soul manifest themselves objectively in and through the higher Objective Organs, and in this view may be said to have their seat with them in the Cerebrum.

2. The SENSORY GANGLIA—the seat of the Organs of Sensibility and Special Sense, of Consciousness and Instinct.

3. The CEREBELLUM, or Posterior Brain—the seat of the Animal Passions and Emotions, and of Muscular Coördination.

4. The MEDULLA OBLONGATA—the seat of Organic Nerves of Respiration, Circulation (except that of the Capillaries) and Deglutition.

5. The SPINAL CORD—the seat of the Organs of Locomotion and of Manual Movements.

6. The SYMPATHETIC GANGLIA—the seat of the Organs that control the processes of Secretion, Assimilation, Capillary Circulation, Nutrition and Excretion.

The intimate relations subsisting between all these Organic systems, the very absolute character of their mutual dependence upon each other, is so readily discovered that the student of physiology is impressed with it in the first lessons he learns of the applications of Vitality in the Human Organism—indeed, it is scarcely possible to view a single Vital act as performed by one Organ or System. To separate the functions of the Nervous System, to study the specific functions even of the Organs of Locomotion or of Sensibility, one must go to the lower types of animated Nature, wherein the higher Organs are not found—as we have already said, as soon as a higher Organ is developed, it begins to influence all those beneath it, and in the successive types we observe that the higher the Organ the more pronounced is its influence upon those below.

A glance over the six departments of the Nervous System, with their respective functions, as given above, shows (1) that the Nervous System is the centre and source of Vital Energy for the Human Organism; and (2) that the Organs of the first general division, which we designated as "essential to Organic Life in General," and which Physiologists denominate "Organs of Vegetative Life," are in the animal and in Man brought under the control of higher Organs of the Nervous System—indeed, this supervisory authority over the lower functions constitutes an important part of the duties devolving upon the Nervous Organs. But this glance does not indicate another fact that it is indispensable to know and keep in mind if we would successfully apply medicines or other curative means to the Human Organism in disease: *i. e.*, that the sixth of the branches of the Nervous System does not have its seat in the Brain, and is actually an independent System in many important respects—it is absolutely dependent upon the Life-principle alone, and only in a remote or slight degree upon the distinctively Intellectual faculties.

The first five branches have their centres in the Brain and constitute the CEREBRO-SPINAL SYSTEM, the sixth has its centre in the *Semi-lunar Ganglion*, *at the back of the Stomach*, and is the Ganglionic or SYMPATHETIC SYSTEM. Its seat sufficiently indicates the character of the latter System—it is the aggregation of the Vegetative functions. The Cerebro-Spinal is the *Active-Vital* or *Animal-Life* System, while the Sympathetic is the *Still* or *Vegetable-Life* System. Notwithstanding the lower rank, however, of the latter, its value and importance to the Human Organism must not be underrated: upon its harmonious and regular functional working depends the maintenance of the integrity of the material form, and, as we have seen, upon the integrity of the form depends the perfect unfoldment of Life; hence, this system may be regarded as the homely foundation of the more or less elaborate superstructure—in other words, if the Sympathetic System, or one of its Nerves, refuses, in any measure, to perform its functions, just in that measure the Cerebro-Spinal System will be unable to effect its high purposes. The most illiterate and unthinking realize, if they do not understand, that a failure in the digestive apparatus to accomplish their work impairs the mental faculties in exact proportion to the extent of that failure; and this simple fact of every man's every-day experience or observation affords absolute proof of the value and importance to the Human economy of the humble Sympathetic System—in fact, functional derangements are all traceable to the Nervous System in some of its branches, and the Sympathetic certainly bears its full proportion of responsibility.

When Light came forth in response to the Will of the Almighty, its first act in bringing order and beauty out of chaos, Life out of Death, was the exercise of its polarizing power, in producing forms out of the universal *hyle* or *ether* that hitherto was "without form and void," and in the whole material-world the dual forces of polarizing and depolarizing, integrating and disintegrating, by their antagonism preserve and perpetuate motion, and motion is life. These dual forces are the only original forces in Nature—all other forces, call them what we may, are but modifications of these—attraction has its source in the polarizing, and repulsion in the depolarizing, principle of Light, and the centripetal and centrifugal "forces" are but attraction and repulsion. There can be no physical life without continuous change in material forms, and forms can only change by the operation of these two forces—the old polarity must make way for the new, the old form for the new; Life is a principle which cannot cease or wane—it wears out a body and yields it to decay, or it exhausts particles and demands their removal and the substitution of new ones as the condition of its continuance therein. In the outside world, the Sun is the direct actor—in the vitalized Animal and Human forms, the Nervous System is the actor, and in both there is a hidden, unseen but potent, Life-principle that guides the work of the two hands of the actor—in the outside world this Life-principle is an emanation from the Celestial Sun, in the Animal it is the same but abides within and in Man it becomes individualized in the Soul, and forms the Subjective faculties thereof. Thus the Nervous System is the objective Sun of the Animal and of the Human Organism. The Vital Force, imparted to and residing in each Cell, is concentrated in the Nervous System, the Ganglia become the reservoirs for the Organism and dispense the Vital Energies to the fluids and tissues, enabling each Cell and each aggregation of Cells to perform its part in the Physical and Psychical Economy. As the Sun in the exercise of his office requires conductors upon which his beams may travel to their respective destinations, so the Ganglia in the exercise of their functions require conductors for their beams; in the Solar System, the ether meets the demand and in the Human Organism the Nerves are the carriers. The Nerve-centres, or Ganglia, may thus be compared to a Vital battery and the Nerves to conductors.

Is the Nerve Force then, as formerly imagined, identical with Electricity? There are so many apparent identities in the characteristics of the two that we cannot either wonder at the mistake, or censure those who fell into it—but there are insuperable difficulties in connecting them: e. g., the immense difference in their velocity: the electric flash travels at the tremendous rate of 280,000 miles per second, Nerve Force at the rate of only from 32 to 40 yards per second—the former travels then 16,000,000 times as fast as the latter; again, a normal temperature of 98° is essential for healthy Nerve action, while electricity is retarded by the slightest access of heat, which expands the conducting wire and impairs its polarity.

Before attempting to define the nature of Nerve Force, however, it may be best to note its composition and construction: We have already declared the fact that the Life-principle manifests itself primarily in a simple Cell, and that the Human Organism is but an Aggregation of Cells. It is noteworthy, that, various as are the different tissues, fluids, etc. of the Human Organism, they are all composed by the Aggregation of Cells and the Cells themselves are all built up on the same plan; we find that in the development of a Cell, a cell-wall, more or less spherical, is formed, which contains and floats in the peculiar granular base of the Vitalized Chyle; the granules within, when there is sufficient Vitality present, combine into a nucleus, which increases as well as results from the Vitality already contained in the granules; as soon as a cell is thus developed it evinces its Vitality by that "perpetual motion" of which we have spoken.

But, how then is it that cells so alike in their construction, and whose base, as we have before shown, is the Vital Fibrin, act so differently, discharge so many radically different, even antagonistic, functions when aggregated into secretions, blood, flesh, nerves, ganglia, bones, tendons, muscles, etc? There is but one way to understand the diversity of action in similarly constructed Cells—it is to realize the presence of the Life-principle with a controlling influence and authority. It is this principle that assigns to each Cell its place and functions in the complex Organism.

The Nervous System is composed of these Vital Cells, combined into two tissues essentially different in structure and functions: in appearance one is white, the other gray—the white constitutes the Nerves, the gray the Ganglia. The Ganglion consists of nucleated Cells and granular matter imbedded in protoplasma and a fatty substance containing phosphorus, called phosphatic fat (the amount of phosphorus in the Nervous System is least in infancy and old age and greatest at the prime of life). The Nerves are tubular, consisting of a sheath containing protoplasma and phosphatic fat, and passing through the centre of this pulpy compound is a slender, delicate fibre called the *Axis Cylinder* of Rosenthal, which is the essential part of the Nerve; it is in this tension is excited in Nerve action. This is the conductor, and the pulpy compound through which it passes is the non-conducting insulator. A number of these Nerves, as they leave and enter the Ganglia, are united in a common sheath called Neurolemma.

But we must not omit to notice one very striking feature in the Nervous System: *i. e.* the remarkable vascularity of the Ganglia—they comprise Cells, granules and *bloodvessels*; the copious supply of blood has two evident purposes: to supply the necessary conditions of Nerve action, and to maintain its nutrition. In the Nervous System, as in all parts of the Organism, a sufficient supply of nutritive material to keep it in repair and in healthful vigor is of the utmost importance; as it is the chief centre of Vital Force, it is most subject to the wear and waste of Vital strain, and requires the most unremitting supply of Vital Food. The Excretions bear strong evidence of the great rapidity of the decay and repair of the Nervous tissues, in the presence therein of the products of the decay, while the cortical substance of the Brain shows Nervous tissue in all stages of preparation for replacing the decay; and these evidences are always proportioned to the functional activity of the System.

The Nerves are similar in structure, but very different in functional action: the *Sensory Nerves* carry impressions from without to the Ganglia, and *Motor Nerves* carry from the Ganglia to the various muscles and organs of the body—the former take their name from the fact that they receive *sensations*, and the latter theirs from the fact that they convey those sensations to the muscles and organs and command *motion* or action therein or thereby. Then there is another class of Nerves that connect the Ganglia, and are therefore called *Commissural* or Connecting Nerves; these not only connect the Ganglia, but also connect the Spinal Cord and Brain—thus establishing the unity of the Nervous System. The grand symmetry of the System may be realized when we see that thus an impression or sensation received from without the body finds a Nerve tension to the base of the Brain, where, in the *Sensory Ganglia* is the seat of Special Sense and Consciousness; thence another Nerve tension carries it to the *Cerebellum* to excite man's Animal Passions or Emotions, or to the *Cerebrum* to excite his Intellectual powers; thence, again a Nerve tension bears it to the *Spinal Cord* to produce visible motion or action. But there are motions sometimes in which neither the Animal propensities nor the Intellectual faculties seem to be consulted; *e. g.*, when the foot of a sleeping man is pricked or tickled, he draws it away, spontaneously, as it were, without awaking. On the other hand, a sound reaches the tympanum of a man's ear, a Nerve bears it to the Auditory Ganglion, and he becomes conscious of the sound; another Nerve bears it to the Cerebellum or Cerebrum, which communicates it to the Spinal Cord, and the Head turns, so that the cause of the sound can be made visible to the Optic Nerve; this receives the impression and conveys it to the Optic Ganglion, which sends its report to the Cerebrum, the man realizes that the sound proceeds from a falling building or a swiftly approaching Locomotive Engine, and that he is in peril; the Cerebrum having decided upon a means of escape, another Nerve conducts the command to the Spinal Cord, and from it another to the Muscles, whereupon the body is moved out of danger. The intimate relations of the Ganglia and their Systems of Nerves is such that all these transmissions are almost instantaneous. Then, again, the intimate relations, and the acknowledged superiority of the higher over the lower

Organs, may be illustrated thus: a man is made to realize, by the sense of sight, hearing or touch, that another man is about to inflict some bodily injury upon him; the Cerebellum suggests retaliatory action, but the Cerebrum counsels him to be content with merely protecting himself—it may be merely human intellect that gives this counsel on the ground of its being the safest or easiest course, or on some other purely selfish ground, or it may be the higher Subjective Faculty, "Conscience," that seeks to restrain his Animal Passions, on the higher ground of moral right. The reader needs not that we should remind him that the higher faculties of the human intellect may be so blunted by non-exercise or by continued disregard of their teachings, that the Animal Passions in time become the master of the man, converting him into a brute—of course, the "Conscience" may be so frequently disobeyed, or so entirely neglected, that its "still, small voice" will be silent, and give no warning. On the other hand, Conscience may be so cultivated and thereby developed in a man as to make his Animal Passions powerless for evil—even his thoughts, as well as his words and actions may be brought under the absolute dominion of Conscience.

The Cerebro-Spinal Nervous System is thus seen to be always, except in a limited class of spontaneous actions, under the control of the Brutalized, Humanized or Celestialized Will, but the Sympathetic Nervous System is, as a rule, independent of the higher Organs, and, in view of its functions, as before stated, it is well for the Organism that it is so—for, could the mind directly influence the important operations of structural repair and renovation, we should see a far larger number of instances of morbid growths and impaired Vitality resulting from idiosyncrasies of the Brain. The Sympathetic System is influenced by the Animal Passions or Psychical Faculties only indirectly through the influences they produce upon the body—the Sympathetic Nerves are indeed very quick to respond to the condition of the body: for instance, if the body be injured by even an external cause, loss of appetite soon announces a derangement of the Nutritive functions, resulting in a decreased demand for food, while the Liver, Kidneys or Skin is very apt to indicate a correspondent disturbance in the Excretory functions; a bruise on the flesh is sometimes followed by the growth of a Cancer, which is of course the direct effect of defective Nutrition caused by an *inscreation* of the Sympathetic System (all morbid growths are consequences of derangements of the Nervous System interfering with Nutrition.)

A familiar illustration suggests itself, in the discomfort experienced in the Stomach, and consequent faintness, resulting from the crushing of a finger or toe, or any part dependent upon capillary circulation; now, this is the Sympathetic System responding to an external injury—but note how it acts when it recovers from the first shock: it sets the proper Organs at once at work without consulting the Cerebrum or Cerebellum—of course, the Sensory Department has apprised its superiors, but they do not directly interfere; their only share in the cure is to keep the general tone of the body in a favorable condition, or restore it if it has become deranged, so as to prevent illness and physical prostration—or, at most, the Cerebrum suggests such assistance from without as may be acceptable to Nature, it may be the calling in of a Surgeon or Physician; but the charge of the actual repairs devolves on the Sympathetic System, under whose direction the Nutritive Organs and the Capillary Blood-carriers proceed to cure the hurt to the extent that it admits of cure, or if it be incurable they withhold the material for replacing the portion that is doomed, and it decays. When the assistance of a Surgeon or Physician will accelerate the cure or the removal of the wounded part, Nature accepts the assistance, but Nature will permit no undue interference—or at least will not coöperate with a meddler. Mortification, or gangrene, results from the inability of the Sympathetic System to carry on the Nutritive processes, either from its own impairment, or the condition of the part affected.

We pause here to remark: the Capillaries are operated by two sets of Nerves, called Vasa-motor, one set each from the Spinal and Sympathetic Systems; they form a minutely-anastomosing network; their office is to carry the Vital Fluid to the portions of the Organism not reached by the arteries; they receive the blood from the arteries and return it to the radicles of the veins. All the changes which take place between the blood and the surrounding parts, whether ministering to the operations of Nutrition, Secretion or Respiration, occur during its transmission through the Capillaries, and the larger trunks merely bring to them a constant supply of fresh blood, the supply being regulated by the demand created by the actions to which it is subservient, and to remove the fluid which has circulated through them. Still, it must not be supposed that Nutrition is only carried on by the Capillary Blood-vessels. Their importance to the essentially Vital tissues is seen in the fact that they traverse and re-traverse them constantly; in the Nervous System, e. g., they go in and out so frequently that they may be called part of the System. Their important service in Nutrition accounts for their being placed specially under the control of the Sympathetic department of the Nervous System.

What is Nerve Force, and how does it operate? We know that it is the Vital Motor, the Organizer, and the manager of the animated Organism; its presence is what converts *Still* into *Active* Life, and its progressive development constitutes the types of advancement from the inferior Animals upwards to Man, whose "crowning glory and honor" lie in the zenith of this System, the Cerebrum, with its grand Objective Psychical Functions and its grander Subjective Faculties. We know that it embraces a number of Vital Centres, each with its afferent and efferent Conductors of its Vital Principle—Conductors with an inward, and conductors with an outward, tension. We know, moreover, that the Nerve Force, excited by external or internal causes of a physical nature, in turn excites mental and physical motions and action, while, conversely, the mind, in certain conditions of activity, effects changes in the material fabric.

But all this knowledge does not satisfy our desire to learn what is the nature or character of the Force. We have seen that, while it resembles, it is not, Electricity; besides the insuperable obstacles to indentifying the two already given, the following occur to our mind: (1) A Nerve will conduct Electricity, but not nearly so well as copper wire, while the latter will not conduct Nerve Force under any circumstances; this has been clearly demonstrated by cutting out a piece of Nerve and inserting a corresponding piece of copper wire. (2) A ligature around a Nerve-trunk entirely suspends its power of conducting Nerve Force, while it does not in the least impair its conducting of Electricity. And (3) Nerve Force passes directly along the Nerve along which it is directed by the Ganglion, but Electricity cannot be confined to a single Nerve—it is apt to desert the Nerve for the first tissue that invites it.

It will be recollected that we demonstrated, in Chapter III., the identity and diversity of Electricity and Magnetism, showing that they were identical in their source and in essence, but diverse in their conditions of exercise (see pages 98, 99, 109, 118-122). And now we will add: The Nerve Force is correlated to Electricity and Magnetism, being more nearly allied to the latter—it is identical with them in its origin and similar to the latter in its exercise. The ancients knew this: Hermes and Pythagoras taught it; Synesius found it among the souvenirs of the School of Alexandria and sang it in his hymns—hear this: "One single source, one single root of Light flashes and spreads out in two branches of Splendor; one breath circles around the earth and vivifies under innumerable forms all parts of *animated* Nature." The discovery of "Animal Magnetism" has been wrongly ascribed to Mesmer, as we see; Mesmer simply rediscovered what had been known and forgotten in this branch, as Newton, Franklin and others did in other branches, of the Science of Light. Mesmer saw in elementary matter a dual force which in motion produced volatility, in repose fixity. It is the same force that dilates matter into vapor, congeals water into ice —a force that is forever and everywhere dissolving and congulating, repelling asunder and attracting together, disintegrating and integrating, depolarizing and polarizing; it is eternally destroying and creating, and never rests. Nerve Force is the dual principles of Light concentrated within the Animal and Human Organisms—in the latter ennobled by having intimately *combined with it* the Celestial Light of Life.

As we have said more than once, there is in all Nature, of every kind and form, a hidden but potent Life-principle—this principle is a direct emanation from the Celestial Sun—it controls and directs all motion, and its authority is recognized by the objective forces in the outer world, and in the inner world of Animated Organisms, and Man excels all other created beings simply because this Life-principle is individualized in his Soul, which thus becomes a *Personal* Manifestation of Celestial Light as that glorious Light is the marvelous Manifestation of Jehovah. It is this Life-principle that by sustaining equilibrium between the antagonistic destroying and creating forces, enforcing the Divine law of Harmony, maintains life, and just so soon as it withdraws its supervision, equilibrium is destroyed and Death succeeds.

To state our definition of Nerve-Force in the most concise terms, we would say:

NERVE-FORCE IS THE DUAL OBJECTIVE FORCES OF LIGHT HARMONIZED BY THE SUBJECTIVE LIFE-PRINCIPLE, ANIMALIZED IN THE ANIMAL, PERSONIFIED OR INDIVIDUALIZED IN MAN!

It must be borne in mind that the expressions Nerve Force, Vital Force, Vitality and Vital Dynamics are almost synonymous, all designating one *Force*, the only difference being that the first is applied specially to those developments of the Life-principle in which the Vital Functions are brought under the control of a Nervous System, while the other three may be applied equally to any kind of Life-unfoldment—Nerve Force comprehending simply a more complete and intensified Organization of Organic Life.

3. THE ORGANS THAT DISTINGUISH MAN FROM ALL OTHER CREATURES.—We come now to consider the "crowning" "glory and honor" of Man, the attributes that transform the Animal into Man, that make "Man a Living Soul" capable of unfoldment into the very image and likeness of the glorious Jehovah. The Subjective Sun works in exercising a supervisory control over the Objective Forces of Light in every department of Nature in our own and all other worlds of the Universe—it constitutes the Life-principle, the Vital Intelligence, in every created thing from a planet to the humblest, most insignificant worm, plant or organizing cell; it is incomprehensibly present in the simple Cell and in the highest type of form composed of Cells aggregated; it is the secret, hidden, but ever potent principle that controls

and directs the evolution of forms, which are all, from the simplest to the most complex, developed by it for its own manifestation; the Subjective Life-principle can only manifest itself Objectively in an Objective form, and the sole purpose of the creation of material forms is to manifest this Life-principle. The One Incomprehensible, Ineffable, Self-Existent Life, Jehovah, was as Infinite, All-Wise, Illimitable, Almighty in the Dark Abyss of Chaos as in the created, developed, unfolded Universe—but He willed to manifest His Infinitude, Omniscience, Omnipresence and Omnipotence, and the first expression of that Will was by His Word in the command "Let there be Light," and "Light was" forthwith and henceforth the sole manifestation of the Self-Existent Life, and the sole Life-principle in Heaven and in all the worlds of the Universe. It is that unique and universal Life-principle that Objectively manifests itself in the Astral Suns, and not only endows them with their Objective Forces, but controls and guides and directs them in the exercise of those Forces.

Now, as we have said, and iterated, the original and sole purpose of Jehovah when He first said "Let there be Light," was the Personal manifesting of Himself in "Man, the Living Soul," and in Christ this purpose was perfectly realized. We have shown how, step by step, from the simple Cell to the perfect Human Organism, this grand purpose of the Creator was evolved in Organic forms—how *Still* Life rose higher and higher until its highest type evinced the lower characteristics of *Active* Life—how Active Life unfolded from the merely pulsating Protozoa, one step at a time, until, in the highest types of Animal, Objective Faculties of the highest order manifested their presence—how, when the very highest type of material form was developed in the Human Organism, the germs of a higher Life than could be fully unfolded in a material body appeared in Subjective Faculties that demand an Immortal Life to attain their completest unfoldment. We have shown that the LIFE-PRINCIPLE *was and is one and identical in essence*, though diverse in the character and degrees of its unfoldment. In the forms of *Still Life*, it operates from without, and in the lowest forms of *Active Life* it does not yet find a centre within the form; but at length it developes Organic centres within material bodies, and in higher evolutions it concentrates the Organic functions into a Nervous System which it makes a mighty reservoir and source of Vital Energy. At last, in Man it individualizes itself into Faculties, becoming *part of his Organism*.

Thus, then, is Man's characteristic "crowning" "glory and honor": *The Subjective Life-principle is part of his Soul, not merely abiding therein and acting thence, but an integral part of it*. However, this is not only a "crowning" "glory and honor"—it involves a vast, *terrible responsibility*. In the inferior types, wherein the Life-principle is not part of the Organism, it acts but is not acted upon—there is no power of cultivating it in them, and hence they have no responsibility. But in Man, the Subjective Faculties, which are the Life-principle individualized, must be cultivated or they will be over-ridden and defied by the subordinate Objective Faculties—and Man is directly accountable for the cultivation and unfoldment of these Faculties. When the Subjective Faculties are cultivated, they unfold and grow in influence and power until they control and direct all the Objective Faculties to the attainment of higher unfoldment, and the entire Man is ennobled.

But let us note the peculiarities of these Subjective Faculties, wherein they differ from the Objective Faculties even of the highest Organs:

1. They cannot be assigned a specific *seat* or *habitation* in the Organism; being the Personal representative of the Celestial Sun, the Individualization of the Subjective Life-principle, they necessarily pervade or permeate the Organism throughout—they are Omnipresent in the Human System, just as Celestial Light is in the Universal System; as Celestial Light manifests itself Objectively only in and by the Astral Suns, so the Celestial Faculties of the Soul manifest themselves Objectively only in and by the Objective Organs. Thus, when the Organ of Anger prompts Man to a deed of violence, Self-Consciousness compels him to realize the influence of such a deed within and upon himself, Conscience to estimate the moral character of the deed, Intuition, Imagination and Prescience to see its ultimate penalty—if these triumph and the deed is unperformed, we only see the triumph of the Subjective Faculties as manifested in the operations of the Objective Organs.

2. They are peculiar to Man. But of this we have spoken fully enough, except that it may not be amiss to allude to the foregoing illustration as applicable as an illustration here: If the Organ of Anger in a Dog

prompts him to a deed of violence, he may be restrained by the sense of fear of immediate consequences; his instinct or low order of Intellect may tell him that the Dog or other object of his anger is too strong for him, and this may restrain him— but there is no one of the higher Moral Faculties to suggest nobler motives than physical fear or cowardice.

3. Duly cultivated, they open Man's Subjective Eye to see "the hidden things of the Spirit of God," which are "foolishness to the carnal-minded;" he is no longer " blind," but can see and know not only the true qualities of earthly things, but the mysteries of Heavenly things; no longer a "child of darkness" incapable of seeing anything beyond this fleeting, unsatisfying world of effects, he is "born again," a "new creature," with his " eyes opened" not only to "see the kingdom of God," but to understand "the breadth, and length, and depth, and height," and the ineffable glory of the "love of God," and to have a foretaste of the " unsearchable things that God hath prepared for them that love him." The highest earthly genius, the most comprehensive intellect, the most faithful investigation, cannot find out God or the things of the Causal World—the ablest, most painstaking philosopher, even the profoundest theologian, knows naught of true Celestial Light except he be enlightened by that Light in "the inner man"—and this illumination can only be secured by cultivating the Subjective Faculties of the Soul.

But 4. The grandest peculiarity of these Subjective Organs is the power they possess of morally and spiritually regenerating Man; were he the vilest wretch in the world, full of wickedness, possessed of a legion of Devils, these mighty Faculties can so utterly and absolutely transform him that he may truly be said to be "born again." A Man cannot be illuminated by the cultivation of his Celestial Faculties and fail to show the fact in his life; a "child of Light" must be a "Light of the world." As we have before shown, it is by cultivating and unfolding those Faculties Man assumes or acquires the image and likeness of God; he becomes, while still a resident of this "world of darkness," a citizen of Heaven, the "realm of Light." He has his "conversation in Heaven," "lays up his treasures in Heaven," and to him death is but a change of condition, a release from imprisonment in his material body, an escape from physical suffering and temporal sorrows, a glorious translation to "a land that is fairer than day," where "all tears are wiped from his eyes," where "there shall be no more death, neither sorrow, nor crying, neither shall there be any more pain," where "there is no need of the Sun, neither of the Moon to shine in it, for the Glory of God doth lighten it"— Jehovah is the "Everlasting Light" of that Celestial World. The Man whose "lamp is trimmed and burning," that is, whose Subjective Faculties are fully unfolded, when he passes through what is, to the dark-souled, the "dark valley of the shadow of death," will find it illuminated for him, and upon entering Heaven will not be a stranger there, but "forever at Home" amidst its glories and joys unutterable and that "never fade away."

The Subjective Organs, even when they are not cultivated, increase the capacity of the Objective Organs for a high unfoldment: hence, we see intellectual giants whose moral character is bad—*e. g.*, Francis Bacon; and many who pervert their Objective "talents" to the worst ends—*e. g.*, those who, like Voltaire, propagate infidel and ungodly notions. Hence, too, we find innumerable instances of men in whom the moral qualities are simply neglected, dormant, who yet attain great eminence as worldly scientists, and philosophers.

The Bible contains many Kabbalistic descriptive pictures contrasting the course of the Righteous, those whose natures are Celestialized by the cultivation of their Subjective Faculties, with that of the wicked. Solomon tells us: "The path of the Righteous as the glorious Light shineth more and more unto the Perfect Day [*i. e.*, that of Heaven]. The way of the Wicked is darkness; they know not at what they stumble." "The Light of the Righteous fills them with joy; but the candle of the Wicked shall be put out" [*i. e.*, they shall be left in utter darkness]. There are many other passages in the Old Testament, but the finest picture of the contrast between the Celestialized and lost Soul is drawn by our Saviour Himself in the Parable of Lazarus, the rich poor man, and Dives, the poor rich man—we can read the character of each in this world in his condition in the Eternal hereafter; the gulf that intervened was symbolic of the vast difference between a Carnal and a Godlike Soul. Then, what words could more strongly declare the importance of Soul-culture than the words of Jesus: "What is a man profited, if he shall gain the whole world, and lose his own Soul? or what shall a man give in exchange for his Soul?"

The one serious defect of what we call "education" in modern times, consists in the persistent effort to cultivate the Objective Faculties of the Mind, to the neglect, and too often at the expense, of the Subjective.

Our enlightened Republic is dotted all over with High-Schools, Seminaries, Academies and Colleges (to say nothing of the Public Schools almost innumerable), with thousands of thousands of tutors, professors, etc., all alike devoted to the cultivation of the Objective Mental Faculties of the young men and maidens of the land; Science, Oratory, Logic, Belles-Lettres, Music, and every conceivable branch of study calculated to develope the Objective Mind (to "improve the mind" is the popular phrase), are taught, and even the Animal Passions and Emotions are not neglected—nay, we have schools and gymnasia for the development of physical qualities. But not a School, however humble and insignificant in size, devoted to the unfoldment of the Subjective Faculties of the Immortal Soul, is there in all the United States. True, there are so-called *Theological* Seminaries sprinkled plentifully over East, West, North and South, but these, too, have more concern with the making of *educated* "clergymen" than with the true illumination of the people by developing their pupils into "lights of the world"—what time the professors can spare for distinctively *religious* instruction must be largely devoted to denominational and polemical specialties; the "educated clergyman" must above all things be able to defend and maintain the dogmas of the denomination that hires him; and in the churches the Objective Faculties are too much exercised in hairsplitting questions of form and doctrine, and even in inventing and seeking to establish doctrines that are in direct antagonism to the teachings alike of Nature and the Bible, when if men would but realize their own natural blindness and seek enlightenment from "the Father of Light," even the mysteries of Nature and Revelation would become plain.

We have no quarrel with any of these "educational" enterprises—the founders and promoters, and the instructors and pupils, all or nearly all unquestionably mean well, and they are really doing a good work; the cultivation of the Objective Faculties, the proper training of the Animal Passions and the developing of the physical form, are all proper, and those devoting money and time to these purposes are eminently worthy of esteem for so doing. But why are the highest, noblest, most elevating and ennobling Faculties of the Immortal Soul so universally neglected?

Were one tithe of the care and attention given to the due development of the Mind Objectively, bestowed upon its Subjective unfoldment, our sons and daughters would attain a plane of Moral and Mental excellence as far above the present popular standard as the popular standard of *Mental* culture in this country is above that of Africa.

Were the highest attributes of our citizens generally

cultivated and unfolded, would we be so often pained and shocked by dishonesty and depravity and turpitude in high places? The various projects for "Reform" can at most be partial and temporary in good results, because they are all superficial, and are about as likely to succeed permanently as would be an attempt to purify a stream while leaving filth in the fountain whence it issues. True Reform, public and private, in the body politic and the body individual, must commence with the raising of the standard of moral right, and this can only be effected by developing the Moral Faculties of the Soul!

When the Light of Truth, Justice and Moral Purity is thus made to shine in the Souls of the citizens of our favored Republic, we shall realize a true Reform that will pervade our domestic circles, our churches, our business marts, our political assemblages and elections, our municipal, state and national offices, and a millennium of Heavenly Harmony will bless us as a Nation, transforming the Nation itself into a "LIGHT OF THE WORLD."

"*Happy is that People whose God is JEHOVAH!*"

CHAPTER VII.

HOW TO ASSIST NATURE IN REMOVING DISEASE FROM THE HUMAN ORGANISM.

HARMONY is the unique law of Jehovah: In Heaven there is perfect, absolute Harmony; its uniform observance banishes sorrow and sighing, pain and suffering, disease and sickness, death and decay, and establishes joy and happiness, health and Eternal Life, in that Celestial World.

The Celestial Sun is glorious in white effulgence, because Harmony is the law of its glory.

In the Universal System, Harmony keeps the Solar Systems in their allotted positions, and maintains their requisite motions, in space.

In each Solar System, Harmony keeps the Sun, Moon, Stars and Peopled Worlds in their allotted positions, and maintains their requisite motions, within the periphery of the portion of space assigned them.

In the Peopled Worlds do we first find departures from Harmony, and commensurate with the extent of departure we find sorrow and sighing, pain and suffering, disease, death and decay.

Our world, the Earth, is called the World of Darkness because Man's disobedience interrupted the complete enforcement of the law of Harmony. But Man's fall from Light to darkness has not only brought the darkness of disharmony upon the world of his probationary abode, it also entails spiritual blindness and darkness upon his posterity. Spiritual Darkness in the world is the withdrawal of the visible presence of the Celestial Sun, and in Man it is the blinding of his Subjective Eye, the withdrawal of his Subjective Vision, the blunting of his Subjective Faculties.

In the world the true Light still Shines, though "the darkness comprehends it not," and in Man the Subjective Faculties still remain, though his blindness does not realize their presence and importance. In the world the condition of Spiritual darkness is attended with physical wear and waste, death and decay—the Objective Sun is permitted, by the exercise of his decomposing, depolarizing force, to dissolve or disintegrate forms; but the Celestial Light, as the hidden but potent Life-principle, is ever present to enforce the law of Compensation, a modification of the law of Harmony, by directing the same Sun in also exercising his composing, polarizing force, to recreate, reintegrate forms, or to replace old forms with new. In Man the condition of Spiritual blindness is likewise attended with physical wear and waste, death and decay, but the Celestial Light individualized in the Subjective Faculties of his Soul, is ever present enforcing the same law upon the Objective Forces of the Nervous System in the operations of disintegrating and integrating.

Perfect Harmony in Heaven, as we have seen, banishes death and decay—the Life of Heaven requires no change of forms, for "flesh and blood cannot inherit the kingdom of Heaven" and there is no material form there to demand perpetual decay and perpetual renewal; "bodies terrestrial" are "corruptible," and must be continually renewed, but "bodies Celestial" are "incorruptible" and never grow old. Therefore, the very nature of our mortal bodies is such that the law of Harmony must needs be modified into the law of Compensation, or Equilibration. In other words, absolute Harmony would perpetuate forms and prevent alike the disintegration of old particles to make way for new, and the creation and integration of new particles in place of old; but change, decay and renewal are essential to the development of material bodies to fit them for the unfoldment of the Life-principle, and hence the law of Harmony is adapted to our material world by being enforced as a law of Compensation or Equilibration. Absolute Harmony is adapted to a perfect Life like that of Heaven, not to a developing, unfolding Life like the probationary life of Man on Earth.

Now, he who has read with any degree of care and thought, the two preceding chapters, must understand that the body, or material form, of Man is merely the casket for a far more important something called the SOUL, *which is* MAN! the body, though the highest material form evolved in creation, and a grand wonderful piece of Divine mechanism, with a more wonderful complex system of motive, vital machinery within, is yet only mortal, destined, after at most a few years of vitalized existence, to dissolve into its many and different ingredients, while the Soul is immortal and must live forever and forever. Hence, the Soul should demand the first and most unremitting care to fit it for the immeasurable Eternity during which it must live after the frail body has passed away.

Having a realizing sense of the incalculable value of the Soul and the inestimable importance of promoting its best interests in time and Eternity, we have dwelt much upon the necessity and imperative duty of cultivating and unfolding its higher moral principles—indeed, our chief interest in cherishing and promoting bodily health and vigor arises from the knowledge of the fact that a healthful, vigorous body is conducive to healthy, earnest Soul-culture—a slight, delicate frame may indeed, and often does, encase a noble Celestialized, Godlike Soul-life, and a strong, vigorous form may, and too often does, contain a stunted, ill-cultured, nay a brutalized or even devilish, Soul; but a sick, diseased, pain-racked body is certainly not conducive to Soul-culture, except in so far as it reminds a Man of his mortality and calls upon him to prepare for Eternity.

While, on the one hand, a healthy physical condition is favorable to intellectual, mental and moral development, on the other hand, as is well known, intellectual, mental and moral health is equally favorable to bodily well-being. The Soul is, as we have seen, the Harmonizing centre, the Sun, of the Human Organism, and if it be out of tune there can be no melody in the body; peace and contentment of Mind are recognized universally as *essential* to health, and what is called "the Imagination" exercises an undeniable influence not only directly upon the body but even to some extent augments or diminishes the action of remedial means upon the body in disease. To acknowledge the influence of Mind upon the material form, is but to recognize the physiological fact that the Nervous System is the centre of Vitality, the reservoir and disseminator of Vital Energy, for the Organized System. But we claim much more, as our reader must know; we claim that a Soul attuned to Divine Harmony must so shape the manifestations of Life in action that even the most remote, the most menial, so to speak, parts will respond to its ennobling impulses, the whole character of the Organic Faculties and Functions, of the material members, and of every part of the Organism will be elevated, so that God's Will will become our will, and we shall honestly pray: "Thy Will be done." Then, in very truth, the Organism will be in a condition of health, and only external causes can derange this condition; even when deranged thus there will be a more emphatic bias within towards a restoration of health. And, at last, the time comes when, our work all done, the "good fight of faith" concluded, the "victory" fairly won over internal and external devils, we feel that "to depart is far better," as we are now ready to "lay down our Cross" and to "wear the Crown of Righteousness"—"the Crown of Rejoicing"—"the Crown of Life"—"the Crown of Glory that fadeth not away." Can any sane man question that such a condition of Celestialized Mind must conduce to bodily health?

Life is a continuous, unceasing antagonism, a perpetual Physical warfare. The two forces that constitute Vital Dynamics are necessarily antagonistic, or Life would be an inert quietude instead of incessant motion. Physical Life demands change, change, perpetual change! putting off the old, and on the new, casting aside and taking up. And to meet this demand, Nature must not only work two-handed, the two hands must oppose each other—one destroy, the other create.

The normal decay and regeneration, disintegration and integration, ever going on in the human form, as in all Natural forms, so long as the operations are regular and the Vital Force works in obedience to the law of Harmony, or rather the law of Compensation or Equilibration, are healthful, and promote bodily vigor and Life-unfoldment, but just so soon as the dual forces that constitute the Vital Force cease to work in unison a diseased condition of the System is at once evident, sometimes as the cause, and always as the consequence, of their want of coöperation. It is very easy to understand that a failure of the Stomach to perform its functions, or of the Lungs, Heart, Liver or Kidneys in the discharge of the duties devolving upon it, produces a greater or less general and more or less severe derangement of the entire Organism; but the consequences of like failures in the more directly vitalizing Glands or Organs are not so readily understood by those not familiar with physiology, though they are often more pronounced and more far-reaching than the others; often discomfort or disorder in the Stomach is directly caused by tardiness of action in the Absorbents or Secreting Glands or Membranes. The function of removing the products of disintegration and the non-nutritious ingredients of the food we eat is no less essential to health than the directly nutritive functions.

But, as we have seen, the Nervous System holds the reins of the Organism, more or less directly controlling all the inferior Organs; therefore we look to the Nervous System as responsible for a large proportion of the functional disorders of all parts of the Organism, and to it we usually direct our remedies.

Now, as our reader must ere this have discovered, the tendency in the Nervous System, as indeed in all Nature, is always to equilibration—not that the opposite elements of Nerve Force, or of Light, tend always to work equally, for then there could be no growth from the fœtus to manhood's prime, from the grain of corn to the "full corn in the ear"—but that, in submission to the Life-principle, each of the dual forces always tends to the performance of the proportion of work required of it. When any external or internal cause induces one force to perform an excess of work, the opposite is usually accelerated to attempt a compensative excess; and so, conversely, when one is retarded, the other appears to respond accordingly—thus Nature seeks to restore the equilibration of her dynamual Force. When either force varies so much from its allotted task that Nature cannot soon enough produce the compensation, the physician is called in to assist Nature. The physician who understands Nature and knows his own province never seeks to supplant Nature or to work independently of or in antagonism to her. He seeks to learn her ways and desires to follow her methods, to study and emulate her example in working within her domain.

The author of this little work fully recognizes this sphere of the physician, and, in recognition of the superior authoritative skill of Nature, has sought first to show the character and qualities of Nature's sole Actor, Light, in its dynamical Objective, and supervisory Subjective, aspects. He believes, not theoretically, but as the result of thirty years' earnest study, that Light is the Universal Motor; the Source of Vital Dynamics (therefore of Nerve Force); under and by authority of God, the Author, Sustainer and Promoter of Life. Believing, nay *knowing*, this, he cannot doubt that Light, when properly understood, will prove the one universal pathological agent—in fact, Light is the Source of the curative properties of medicines, and why should it not prove proportionately potent when its virtues are directly applied to the diseased system? But, to apply any remedy successfully, we must not merely realize its aggregate and specific qualities; it is equally essential that we have an accurate knowledge of the Human Organism to which we desire to apply that remedy. Hence, after defining Light in its various manifestations, and noticing its peculiarities as a whole and as separated virtues, we have gone into as full an investigation and exposition of the Human Organism as we deemed necessary to make intelligible the application of Light and its rays thereto.

Our reader has, we trust, learned to respect, as we do, the Ancient Sages, at whom modern Scientists, in their overweening self-esteem, their ignorant vainglory, are wont to scoff. No one who honestly studies the Kabbala, and its outgrowing literature, with a sincere desire to learn, can otherwise than venerate the marvelous men whose penetration, sanctified by humble devotion and illuminated by Celestial Light, discovered the truths of Nature and Nature's laws and principles, and actually fathomed many mysteries not only of the terrestrial world, but of Heaven and of the Almighty. Combined with this veneration, will be a warm, heartfelt gratitude for the vast stores of true learning treasured up in the old Philosophy. If Light is ever perfectly understood, it must be by an honest application of modern Scientific appliances and research to the teachings of the Ancient Philosophers.

In the department of Science comprehended under the generic designations of *Pathology* and *Therapeutics*, the Ancients had many eminent discoverers and teachers. In truth, the Ancients knew, in this as in other branches of Philosophy, much more than they are accredited with—much that has been lost and can only be rediscovered after a vast amount of study and investigation, while a large percentage of the *facts* of the Pathology and Therapeutics of our day have come to us from those old sources, and not a few of the discoveries heralded from time to time as made by this or that great man are revivals of old truths.

Paracelsus is recognized as a wonderfully learned man in true Philosophy and especially in Medical Science. He held that: "Man is made out of the four elements, and is nourished and sustained by Magnetic Power, which is the Universal Motor of Nature." We thus see that the therapeutics of Paracelsus reposes on the original Life-source, Light. So highly did the Ancients estimate Light as a curative agent that they called it "Fluid Gold," and "Potable Gold,"—to understand these terms, we must recollect the fact, before stated, that they could, by some method not now known, focalize and "fix" light in wine and oil, and thus administer it *as medicine*.

Paracelsus treated disease in two ways: Sympathetically and Antipathetically. There can be no question that he brought the Science of Medicine to a high state of perfection, and it is unfortunate that but a fragmentary trace of his system can now be found. Hahnemann, the father of Homeopathy, fully established the Antipathetic System of treatment, and the Homeopathic Practice is based upon that System. This mode of treatment may be explained and illustrated briefly, thus:

Every disease or derangement of the Organism, however general in its influential action, has some local centre, some one organ or tissue that it specifically attacks; it also has a clearly defined mode of attack, and indicates its character, *locale* and mode of attack by certain symptoms. Experiments upon a body in health show that a certain medicine exhibits precisely the same symptoms, and thus we infer that it attacks the same part in the same way. Then when this disease is indicated by the symptoms, we directly attack the disease itself by administering the medicine that produces the same effects in a healthy body. Now, it is evident that this medicine must go direct to the part affected, and we should infer it would augment the disorder—we find that if the dose be too large it actually augments the symptomatic indications for a while; then they abate, and in time, more or less according to the nature and extent of the disorder, the symptoms disappear and we know that their cause has vanished or at least been vanquished for the present. Hence, the proverb "Similia similibus curantur." So much for demonstration—but how may we account for the success of this treatment? Very simply, thus: Nature works by antagonism in all her operations; when one of her forces overdoes its work, disease or at least a local disorder is the immediate consequence; now, if we attack this force and overcome it, the opposite force has a clear field and may reässert its rights—thus equilibrium is restored, and *Equilibrium is Health.*

The Sympathetic System, instead of attacking the stronger force, sends recruits to the weaker one and enables it to recover its powers, or, if the disorder be the result of excessive tension of Nerves or Ganglia, a negative remedy may be employed to reduce the tension. Thus, too, equilibrium is restored, and *Equilibrium is Health.*

Of course, in each case, the Physician must be very careful in determining which plan of attacking the disorder is to be preferred. It may be that the loss of equilibrium is chargeable to the undue acceleration of one force, while the other is performing its normal duty—in that case, the former must be attacked and subdued, on the Antipathetic plan, by increasing the tension until it exhausts itself; or, on the Sympathetic, a negative medicine must be directed to the too-tense Nerve or Ganglion. It may be, on the other hand, that the loss of equilibrium is chargeable to the undue depression or weakening of one force, while the other is performing its normal duty—then, the depressed or weakened force must be assisted, strengthened. In either case, we observe that the Physician's aim is simply to assist in the restoration of the equilibrium.

Having determined upon the mode of attack, the next question for the Physician to decide is as to the violence of the attack. Here he finds that, though each case is liable to idiosyncrasies calling for peculiarities of treatment, there are certain general rules to guide him: the activity of the attack must depend upon the activity of the disorder. A sudden, severe, acute disorder requires more powerful remedies to produce prompt results: *e. g.*, a violent Fever, acute Rheumatism, etc. calls for a low dilution. A mild or sub-acute derangement demands a more patient, prolonged course of treatment, with a milder form of medicine, a higher dilution. A chronic disease can be reached only by very mild treatment and long-continued, patient care; the medicine must be of the thirtieth dilution at the least, and in many cases even this will fail to reach the disorder, when higher dilutions must be employed.

It is specially worthy of remark that often where a strong form of medicine utterly fails, a very much milder, higher dilution will immediately act. There has been no little controversy from time to time among Homeopathic Physicians, between the advocates of high and of low dilutions, and, as is often the case in such disputes, both have been right and both wrong. As stated above, the dilutions should be regulated by the severity of the disease. In an acute attack, Rheumatism, Neuralgia, active Fever, or whatever it be, a low dilution acts promptly, while if a higher one be employed it will be slow in its action, requiring the cumulative effect of several doses. On the other hand, in chronic diseases, the violence of the first attack, and even of the sub-acute stage has passed, and the disorder remains only as a slow poison in the system—a low dilution will, as it were, overshoot the mark, and fail to effect the desired result, and a twelfth or sometimes even a thirtieth will likewise fail, where a higher dilution will immediately affect the symptoms, proving that it has hit the foe.

This is certainly not incomprehensible: the chronic is the mildest form of a clearly defined disease, though the most difficult to expel from the system, and mild remedies, continued for a comparatively long period, come nearest to balancing the inactivity and the inveteracy of the disorder. On the contrary, an acute disease is quick and decided in its action—time may be very essential to subdue it before it gets unsubduable, and we use low dilutions. In the one case, the enemy is entrenched in works impregnable to direct assault; we therefore lay regular siege, cut his communications, prevent recruits or supplies from reaching him, and eventually compel surrender where direct assault would but ensure our repulse and perhaps ultimate defeat. In the other case, the enemy is in the field; his communications open, supplies and recruits continually arriving, time is all-important, as every hour of delay increases his power for mischief; we bring up all the forces at our command and fight him at short range or charge him with sabre and bayonet. We should not employ the famous Corliss Engine to run a single printing-press (even that on which this book is printed), though a press is mightier than the pen, which we are told is "mightier than the sword;" nor should we have attempted to supplant the Corliss Mammoth in Machinery Hall with an engine just powerful enough to run a press. In short, the means must be adapted to the end.

We have said the Homeopathic System is based on the Antipathetic plan of Paracelsus, and doubtless a word or two of explanation will not be out of place here. It must be understood that, as this work is specially designed to advocate and explain the employment of Light and its rays in therapeutics, we are not, in what we say here, advocating Homeopathy— in fact, we hope to see both the great systems give place to a true Natural System, with Light as its fundamental means;

Towards the close of the second century of the Christian Era, Claudius Galenus arose to great eminence as an Anatomist and Pathologist; he became the acknowledged leader of a "school," which, with a high character of excellence and a deservedly high reputation for its teachings, evinced an arrogant, overbearing dogmatism that would brook no opposition, and, when Paracelsus took issue with some of its founder's teachings, the leaders exerted their great influence and that of their adherents to crush the daring opposer; this so incensed Paracelsus that he, as an act of most unwise defiance, publicly burned Galen's works. As the Galen school was the "regular" and popular school of medicine of that day, their influonce was sufficient now to bring upon their adversary a bitter persecution, in consequence of which the world has lost the benefit of the truly wonderful knowledge of Nature and of Medicine that Paracelsus possessed—mere fragments of his teachings are now to be discovered. He was certainly not the inferior, in ability or acquirements, of Galen's disciples, or of any other Scientist of the time in Medicine, and in Nature he was without a rival.

Paracelsus maintained that the Book of Nature, written by the finger of God, was the only reliable source of Pathological and Medical knowledge. He taught two systems, as we have said: the Antipathetic and the Sympathetic. The latter, the chief remedy under which was Light, "fixed," as we have stated, in oil and wine, was his favorite system except in aggravated cases of excessive tension of the Nerves or Ganglia, when he attacked the offending part, on the theory of conquering it by Antipathy.

Hahnemann, in some respects like Paracelsus, especially in manly independence, exhibited, like his, in opposing the popular practice of his day, adopted the Antipathetic, and made it virtually his own System by amplifying the meagre information left by his teacher, into so complete and logical a System that many of the greatest minds of various parts of the world have since accepted it, and the great Homeopathic School is the result. All the blessings that Homeopathy has conferred upon the world, and they are too vast and numerous to be readily computed, are so many voices reciting the praises of Hahnemann.

Still, we believe that Paracelsus was right in preferring his Sympathetic System, as it appears the more rational; and we have not a doubt of its becoming the Universal System, so soon as the real nature and properties of Nature's own and only remedy, Light, come to be understood—the two are to each other in Pathology, much the same as in religion are the law of Moses and the law of Christ—the one was coercion, the other is persuasion; the one was evil for evil, "an eye for an eye, a tooth for a tooth," the other is "good for evil," "Love your enemies, bless them that curse you, do good to them that hate you, and pray for them which despitefully use you, and persecute you." Just as we believe the law of Christ is better than that of Moses, so we believe that the System of Sympathy, with Light for its base, is better than that of Antipathy.

In the following chapter, we shall show the application of Light, and especially of its Red and Blue rays, to the Human Organism, wherein it will be seen that in the therapeutic employment of Light the Sympathetic plan prevails, though in some cases the other may be found more efficacious.

CHAPTER VIII.

LIGHT AND ITS RAYS NATURE'S OWN REMEDIES FOR DISEASE—HOW TO APPLY LIGHT TO THE HUMAN ORGANISM.

GOD IS LIGHT! James, the Apostle, calls Him "the Father of Light." David, the Psalmist, exclaims: "Jehovah is my Light;" and, again he tells God: "Thou coverest thyself with Light as with a garment." But John, "the disciple whom Jesus loved," is more explicit—he says: "This then is the message which we have heard of him [Christ] and declare unto you, that GOD IS LIGHT!"

Surely, no Kabbalist could claim higher excellence and honor for Light than this! "Thou coverest thyself with Light as with a garment"—what is this but a declaration of the Kabbalistic doctrine that God manifests Himself in Light? And John affirms the same truth, only with special emphasis, in his declaration: "God is Light!" But we have, in the first chapter, stated the teaching of the Kabbala on this subject, and have shown that the Bible and true Science are in full accord in attesting the presence of Jehovah in Light as His manifester, His representative. We have shown that when God said "Let there be Light, and Light was," He simply sent forth a mighty creative agent, endowed with Divine Wisdom and Power to carry on forever the work He assigned it; that the work of creation was not limited to "six days," or "six periods of time," but was designed to be, as it is, a perpetual work, never ceasing until time itself shall cease; that, as "in the beginning" Light was the Almighty's chosen and only representative in creation, so it has been ever since, and must be until creation shall have been completed and time engulphed in eternity. We have no indication, in Nature or in the Bible, of God's choosing any other worker, or acting in or by any other instrumentality, than Light; hence, we have claimed, on the high authority of the Kabbala, and on the higher authority of Nature and the Bible, that Light is the Universal Motor, the original and only actual source of all Natural Forces —of Vital Dynamics in every phase, aspect or mode of exercise. We have clearly distinguished between this Celestial Power and its Objective manifestations, the Astral Suns, and have indicated the important differences between the Celestial or Subjective Sun, the fountain of Celestial or Subjective Light, and the Astral or Objective Suns, the reservoirs and dispensers of Objective or visible light. We have traced to the mighty Celestial Sun, through the Sun of our Solar System, all the so-called Physical Forces of the Earth, such as Attraction, Repulsion, etc., etc., and have shown that Electricity, Magnetism and Nerve Force alike are manifestations of Light. We have shown that, behind the dual Objective principles of Light, the Subjective Life-principle is ever present, controlling and directing every operation, and that upon the presence and influence of the latter depend the successful workings of the former.

In this chapter we propose to make practical applications of the knowledge we have epitomized in the preceding chapters, by showing how Light may be employed to banish disease from the Human Organism; but, by way of introduction to our specific subject, though our readers cannot actually require that we should do so, we deem it not amiss, and it will be interesting to most of our readers, to allude briefly again to the ancients, especially as our study of the old Philosophy gave us directly much of the information we have, and led us to the experiments from which we have acquired the rest:

The ancients, we have seen, knew well the properties of Light in all its manifestations, Subjective and Objective; they knew much more than we have yet discovered from the inimitable symbols which are the only record they left of their knowledge. Illuminated interpreters of later days have read many of the symbols more or less fully, but no doubt there are still important truths to be learned from them. We were favored some years since with the key, and have used it successfully so far as we have been permitted, but we have yet much to learn; nor are we at liberty to tell, for the present, all we have learned. The time may come, and we trust it may be not far distant, when we can tell more.

Every symbol of the Kabbala is a symbol of Light and its laws, in some of its manifestations. The ten Sephiroth we have reviewed at some length in the first chapter, and do not consider it advisable to notice them farther here. That Solomon, "the wise man," was a Kabbalist of a high order is unquestionable, and that he was familiar with the *Sephiroth* and their significance his " Books" of the Bible clearly attest; to see this, recall the facts that the first emanations from *En Soph* were Wisdom and Intelligence; the Celestial Light was described as " Wisdom" (*Sophia*); that the *Sephiroth*, as arranged in the Plate, were called the "Tree of Life"; and other facts noticed in our first chapter. Then read in the third chapter of "Proverbs"; "Happy is the man that findeth Wisdom, and the man that getteth understanding [Intelligence]. . . . Length of days is in her right hand; and in her left hand riches and honour [her right hand is Wisdom, her left Intelligence—see Plate]. . . . She is a tree of life to them that lay hold upon her, and happy is every one that retaineth her. Jehovah by Wisdom hath founded the earth; by understanding hath He established the heavens." [The Hebrew word translated "understanding" clearly means "Intelligence"—indeed, the English words are very nearly synonymous.] Then in the fourth chapter, read: "Get Wisdom, get Intelligence. . . . Wisdom is the principal thing [the word "thing" is not in the Hebrew]; therefore, get Wisdom: and with all thy getting, get Intelligence," etc. And so on throughout this "Book," and in the next we find the same—*e.g.*, "Wisdom giveth life to them that have it," and many more passages of equally strong Kabbalistic tone. The reader of Solomon's "Books" will find he very repeatedly uses the term "tree of life"—we have seen that he calls Wisdom a "tree of life," but so does he call "The fruit of the righteous," a proper "desire," " a wholesome tongue," etc. It will materially strengthen the Kabbalistic character of the cited and kindred passages to recollect that in the Septuagint, the Hebrew word *Chochmah* ["Wisdom"] is invariably rendered σοφία = *Sophia*.

But, as we have shown, the Bible is full of Kabbalistic terms, as, of course, we should expect when we bear in mind that the Kabbala was at the first an illuminated ("inspired") interpreter of Nature, and after the Bible was written the Kabbala likewise interpreted it. The passages notably that ordinary commentators are unable to expound, and get rid of by pronouncing them "figurative" (when this convenient make-shift will obviously not reach their confusion, they go so far as to pronounce them "apocryphal," "doubtful" or "an interpolation"), are strongly Kabbalistic, and he alone who comprehends the Kabbala can discover the exact signification. There are many passages in both the Old and New Testaments that baffle the commentators and pulpit divines, which can only be fully understood and explained by those who are illuminated by the Light of Truth in "the inner man."

"The Revelation of St. John the Divine" is especially full of these passages, "hard to be understood" to the unenlightened, and an ordinary commentary on this Book is more amusing and entertaining than instructive because of the evident difficulties the commentators experience in explaining what their Objectively trained Minds cannot understand, but he who knows the Kabbala encounters no such difficulties because the eyes of his Understanding or Intelligence are enlightened to perceive "all mysteries." We have alluded to one or two of these, one of the most striking being the record of John's vision of *Sophia* or *Isis*, "clothed with the Sun, and the Moon under her feet, and upon her head a crown of twelve stars"— our Frontispiece is the Kabbalistic symbol of this "woman" of John's vision, and affords a capital illustration of the idea of the Celestial Light "clothed with the [Objective] Sun" "as with a garment"—the Life-principle itself veiled, but revealing itself in an Objective form. The "Brazen Serpent," John's "Dragon," is excluded from the Sacred Circle.

Our title-page shows another of the most beautiful and impressive symbols of the Kabbala, the "flaming Pentagram" of the Ancients, "His Star" that announced to the Eastern Wise Men the dawn of the "Sun of Righteousness," the "Daystar" of Peter, the "Morning Star" and "Bright [Brilliant = Flaming] and Morning Star" of John. It is shown within the Objective Sun, the Life-principle within the Objective Orb. The letter A represents its Duality in Unity, the line across uniting the divergent lines, and the angle at the top being the point of unity where they emanate from the "All-Seeing Eyes" of the Supreme.

Other Symbols of the Kabbala are equally impressive and equally "orthodox" and "evangelical"— *i. e.*, equally in accord with "the Scriptures." For instance, we may mention, without illustrating: The "Pillars of Jokan and Boaz," one based upon water, the other upon land, the one white, the other dark, clearly tell of the dual properties of Light, and of the two principles of Moral Life, the "Good" and the "Evil." Samson, the strong, weak man, whose strength among men was no more marvellous than the sensual proclivities that made him a weak fool among women, furnishes the Kabbalists with materials for instructive symbolization: they consider that his strength lay in seven special locks of his hair, which represent the seven rays of the source of Strength, Light, and their being shorn from his head by the woman Delilah is the triumph of "Evil" in the suppression of Light; while his pulling down the pillars of Dagon's temple, involving as it did himself and all concerned in the temporary triumph of evil, indicates the electric restoration of harmony. Doubtless the Bible-reader is constantly struck with the force of the number "seven" in Scripture and its frequent occurrence as symbolical of might or excellence, but who of all the popular commentators has ever suggested the fact that the symbol is Kabbalistic? The "seven stars" repeatedly mentioned by John in his "Revelations," are the seven rays of Light.

According to the ancients, the colors of Light were symbolic of life and death: White is the color of the quintessence of Light; toward its negative pole, White is condensed in Blue, and fixed in Black; towards its positive pole, White is condensed in Yellow, and fixed in Red. Blue invites to repose, or is slumber, Black is absolute rest, the sleep of death; Yellow is activity, Red is absolute motion, the motion of life; and White is the equilibration of motion, healthful activity.

In Life-unfoldment, the progress is from Black to Red—Red is the zenith of manhood's prime; in the decline of Life the course is from Red to Black; in both unfoldment and decline, White is traversed, the healthful, elastic period of first maturity and of the medium stage of old age.

The White, of course, is the aggregation of Light, and the Black its absence; the three colors of the Life-scale, Red, Yellow and Blue, with the four not noted herein, constitute the Syllipsis, or Luminous Synthesis. Positive, *plus* Light in its extreme polarity is Life at its prime; Negative, *minus* Light in its extreme depolarity is Death.

The ancients declared that "Light is saturated with Life." They regarded the Red color of the Vital Fluid, the Blood, as a polarization of the most positive ray—polarized, fixed therein when the Oxygen of the air drives out and replaces the Carbonic acid introduced with the food and generated in the Excrementory Organs and Glands.

In our earlier studies of the old Philosophy we found so much that was not "dreamt of" by modern Scientists, that we were induced to commence a series of test-experiments; led to believe that there were invaluable virtues in Light that might be, nay should be, applied to the relief of sickness and suffering, we determined to find out, to discover, those virtues, and to learn how to cure disease with Nature's own specifics, the integral elements of the Light of Life.

Our experiments soon demonstrated the fallacy of

some of the popular theories of Light, and convinced us that Scientists have much to learn even in reference to the ordinary phenomena of Light and Life. For instance, we had been led to infer that the Actinic or Chemical ray was the sole or at least chief actor in producing molecular changes; we found this to be almost *contrary* to the facts of Light action; the Actinic element simply dissolves old forms, and prepares the molecules, or atoms of molecules, for the action of the Calorific ray, or rather for its next neighbor, the Red ray, which is the creator of new forms by imparting new affinitive attraction to the molecules or atoms prepared for it. These two principles form the two atomic forces, attraction and repulsion, the former being the Red, and the latter the Blue, in action, but the other rays are not inactive; they all have their respective shares in Nature's handiwork, though we cannot as yet assign to each its special functions; doubtless, the exact details will yet be discovered. As we have shown in the second chapter, Light works as an entity, though it works two-handed with five subordinate hands to assist its two principles. One ray, or two rays, or six rays, to the exclusion of the rest, cannot carry on the most simple operations in Nature. He who said "Let there be Light" deputed to this agent the work of creation, development, evolution—the business of carrying on the entire operations of Universal Life; within this one representative of His Wisdom, Will and Power, were all the forces—principal and subordinate—requisite for the creation of worlds, and for enriching them with every type of form for Life-unfoldment, and not a single principa.

or subordinate force is non-essential. Hence, while He permitted His agent to separate its forces and to assign to each its duty, not one could be ignored or pushed aside. When Nature or Light has a single operation to effect, a single object to attain, she employs one ray, but to evolve new forms out of old, Light must work as one, or rather it must use its forces in equilibrium—e. g., the single operation of disintegrating a body the Actinic Blue alone performs; the single operation of integrating a body the Calorific Red alone performs—but the dual operation of disintegration and integration must be effected by the two, while if the new be a form that requires more than mere integration, such as a plant which wants foliage, blossom and fruit, the other rays will be called for. It evinces an inexcusable stupidity or want of reflection for a scientist to attempt to effect the growth and maturing of a plant under the light of a single ray, be it Red, Yellow, Green or Blue; the grain of wheat, under Blue Glass alone, cannot grow, except a portion of the other rays steal in, or force themselves in, and then its growth will be proportionate to the quantity of these that gets to the roots and the growing stalk. We shall show, in the next chapter, that General Pleasonton's experiments were radically different from those of Professor Draper, Mr. Gladstone, and others who have utterly failed because they have not recognized the difference between augmenting the proportion of one ray and the exclusive admittance of but one. We shall show, too, that General Pleasonton's success was due to the single fact that the increased amount of chemical action upon the earth and air of his grapery enabled them to contribute more liberally to the nourishment of his vines; but the vines require more than food, and the other rays supplied the assimilating, polarizing power to supply the food, the coloring for the wood, leaves, blossoms and fruit, etc., etc. We believe, however, that with their increased number and size his grapes must prove deficient proportionately in quality and flavor—overfeeding can scarcely be desirable in plants more than in animals, hence care must be exercised not to carry the Blue Glass plan too far in vegetable development. But of this in the next chapter; our subject in this chapter is the application of Light and special rays to the Human Organism when it is diseased.

Our earliest experiments and observations convinced us that not only is Light the exclusive operator in the Mineral and Vegetable Kingdoms, but that in Animals and in Man as well, LIGHT IS LIFE. We realized that there is but one *original* force in the Universe, and that force is Light; that every created thing in the Universe is a manifestation of Light; that every material form is developed simply and solely to manifest Light. That Organic forms are developed to manifest LIGHT as LIFE—that Life is Light manifested within and by means of various forms; that *Still* or Vegetable Life is but the earlier Vital manifestation of Light, in which the visible Sun is the direct actor and the invisible Celestial Sun is the director of the actions of the visible Sun—the Celestial Sun being the Life-principle; that *Active* or Animal Life is an intensified development of the same Life—the Vital Power establishing within the Animal body a centre, called the Soul, and acting from within instead of from without the body; that *Human Life* is a higher manifestation of the same Life-principle, the Soul being now individualized by the Subjective Life-principle identifying itself with the Soul, and, in the character of Subjective Faculties, becoming an integral part of Man's Soul.

Thus, as the result of many years of patient study of ancient and modern Philosophy, with constant critical study of Human Life as seen about us continually, we are prepared to affirm: That the Human Organism, though "fearfully and wonderfully made," is simply and only an Objective manifestation of the Soul within: that the Organism comprises a frame or body with a complex system of motive apparatus called Organs; that these Organs are mutually related to and dependent upon each other, the highest upon all beneath, even upon the lowest, but nevertheless the higher Organs, as they ascend step by step in development, have a certain clearly defined authority over those below, and thus the Organs having their seat in the Brain are the rulers of the Organism, subject only to the Subjective Faculties, "Self-Consciousness, Conscience, Imagination and Prescience;" and that the Soul is the personification of Light.

We have demonstrated, in the sixth chapter, that Nerve Force is the dual properties of Light, acting within the Human System as they act in the world without, and Nerve Force is Vital Force. As soon as we had become convinced that Light is Life, in the earth, in the Plant, in the Animal and in Man, and observed how Light worked in visible operations, we felt assured that in Man the same Force must work in precisely the same way. We have distinctly advised our readers that the ancients fully understood not only the Science of Light (which we have shown comprehends all science, Physiology and Pathology, no less than Astronomy, Natural Philosophy, etc.), but were peculiarly expert in the employment of Light in restoring equilibrium and health to the Human Organism; their teachings induced us to make our first experiments in Light, and now that we had confirmed, to our complete satisfaction, their views of Light as the sole Universal Source of Dynamics, Physical and Vital, we felt no doubt of their correctness in regarding Light as Nature's own and only specific for disease of all kinds—indeed, it seemed most reasonable that the source of Life must be best calculated to prolong Life by maintaining equilibrium in, or restoring it when impaired by disease to, the Organic System; and to strengthen this inference we have the fact that the virtues of medicines are largely received from Light. But we are not left to inferences, however reasonable; we have the testimony of the ancients, and the convincing success of careful experiments, to prove that Light, and separate rays thereof, are really invaluable curatives, especially in diseases arising from defective or excessive action of either factor of Nerve Force. When we take into account the fact that not less than four-fifths of all the ailments, serious or otherwise, must be traced to impaired or accelerated action of the Nervous System, we cannot but see the incalculable value of a remedy that acts directly upon the Nerves and their Ganglia. We entertain not merely an opinion, but a hopeful confidence, that the results already achieved are but the incipient tokens, the harbingers, of a glorious revolution in Therapeutics and Pathology—that Light will ere long completely revolutionize the methods of treating diseased Human beings and families throughout the world; that it will drive all the death-laden nostrums and medicines of violence rather than beneficence from the *materia medica* of our day, and overwhelm the innumerable and infamous army of empirics and quacks that are an unconscionable blot on Human Nature and an inestimable curse to the world. Pretenders in any walk of life are worthy of contempt, but those who dare intrude unfitted into the philanthropic profession that cares for the sick and suffering should be scouted and flouted by every person of respectability—nay, Light itself could vouchsafe to the Human race no greater blessing than by the exercise of its *Fire* element to consume in a universal empyrosis the whole horde of ignorant or worse beings of prey who make suffering humanity their amusement and victims to their greed. We hope, however, to see Light triumph even over the prejudices of *regular* born and trained physicians, and believe, in very truth, that the day is not far distant when Light will secure its just position as the chief and sovereign "cure-all" for all "the ills that flesh is heir to."

It is well known generally that all functional diseases of the Human Organism result more or less directly from the derangement of one or the other of the two great Nervous Systems that control the

Human Economy. It would be out of place here to attempt to notice, or even to mention, the thousands of diseases that rise in or immediately involve one of these centres of Vitality.

We have already in the sixth chapter portrayed the Human Organism at as great length as the character and design of our work demands or would justify, and have shown that the sole condition and characteristic of health is Harmony, or rather a well-regulated Compensation and Equilibration, between the Organs, Nerves, Muscles, Fluids and all the functional centres and Vital apparatus—nay between everything within the body or identified with it. That disease is the direct consequence of every or any infraction of the law of Equilibrium, and must be proportionate to the extent of the infraction. As every part is essential, not even the most trival can be ignored nor the most important can be permitted to exceed its required office without more or less serious damage to the complex and delicate Human Machine. The finger pricked with a pin or crushed does not confine the momentary pain or the more serious consequences to itself—the little toe alone may be visibly injured and yet the injury may prove fatal.

Paul in his letters to the Romans and to the Corinthians repeatedly alludes to the mutual dependence of the members of the body—n. b., "The body is one and hath many members, and all the members of that one body, being many, are one body;" "The body is not one member, but many;" "much more those members of the body, which seem to be more feeble, are necessary;" "there should be no schism in the body;

but the members should have the same care one for another, and whether one member suffer, all the members suffer with it," etc. This is all true, and would be no less true were we to substitute "Cell" for "member."

The body is an aggregation of millions of Cells, each Cell endued with Life, and capable of living independently; but so soon as two or more of these living Cells combine, they become one *Life*, whether they be two or millions—they no longer live, or can live, independently; each Cell that lives *in* a body as part of it lives *for* the rest, and so no Cell can suffer except its associate Cells suffer with it. An aggregation of Cells must have a Life-centre—an Organ; an aggregation of Organs into a system must have a Life-centre—a System-Organ; an aggregation of Organic Systems must have a Life-centre—a Soul, with its Nervous System comprising Vital centres and conductors of Vital Energy; this Soul unfolds until, in Man, the Life-principle Organizes itself with it, and it becomes an Individualized or Personified Soul, with authority and responsibility peculiar to itself. [We have treated of this at some length before, and only iterate here so far as it seems necessary to the elucidation of our present subject.] But note: In all these successive unfoldments, the Cell-life continues the base; each Cell is an entity, but in submitting to aggregation with other like entities loses its independence, its individuality, and becomes part of the aggregate entity, so that if it suffers the others suffer in sympathy, and if another suffers it too sympathizes in the suffering.

As the Nervous System is the reservoir and centre

of the Vital Energy of all the Cell-lives, so it is the reservoir and centre of the suffering, the disease, of the Cell-aggregration, the Organism. We have shown that the Subjective part of the Human Soul is the Subjective Life-principle Personified, and, therefore, the regulator of the Life of the Organism, the harmonizer of the Forces that move the Machine; we have shown, too, that when the Subjective Faculties control absolutely the Life-forces, there must be absolute harmony, or rather absolute Compensation and Equilibration, within Man; where these are thus absolute, disease cannot arise from within, and when introduced from without, absolute Compensation and Equilibration tend immediately to banish it; if the power within were always superior to the evil introduced the Man could not die. But, as to every Man the time must come when "to depart is far better," when, his work all done, his mission accomplished, he desires to lay aside his earthly material form and pass into the Eternal Celestial World, God has kindly and wisely "appointed unto all men to die" physically. A few, a very few, die simply from "old age" without disease, but even the most Godlike seldom escape sickness and suffering—hence, we need not only to teach men to cultivate the Subjective Faculties of the Soul, as the most important remedy, but to discover remedies to apply from without to assist the Life-principle within in ejecting disease, and, hence, too, the need of skilled, careful Physicians to advise and direct in the application of these remedies.

The functional diseases of the Human Organism, then, have their centre and often their source, in the Nervous

System. If it be in the Cerebro-Spinal System, it is usually at once recognized as a "Nervous affection," even by those who know little about the import of the term; they recognize it because there is an evidently augmented or decreased action of the Nerves—an acceleration or a depression of Vital Energy. The simplest form of the former consists in the condition we call "Nervous"—as when we see a person unduly excited, it may be to tremulousness, we say: "He (or she) is nervous." So, too, one who is subject to excitement is called "Nervous." The simplest form of the latter consists in that condition of lassitude, indisposition to move, even to think perhaps, that so often succeeds an unusual strain upon the system—it is not laziness, but merely a *relaxation* of the system.

This word "relaxation" explains the whole matter. Nerve action is *tension*—in health, the tension is normal, or natural, in disease there is an *intensifying* or a *relaxing* of the *tension*. We have seen, in the second chapter, that tension is polarity—hence, disease is an abnormal disturbance of polarity, either in excess of polarization or excess of depolarization. Healthy physical life is a perpetual and regular polarizing and depolarizing, disease is the loss of this *regularity*, death a depolarization of the Nerve-tension, decay the ultimate depolarization of Life-forms. It is important to bear this in mind, because every remedy must be administered upon this basis. On the Antipathetic plan, if the Nerve-tension be too great we exhaust it by augmenting it; apply a remedy that increases the tension, knowing that tension carried beyond its limit exhausts itself. On the Sympathetic

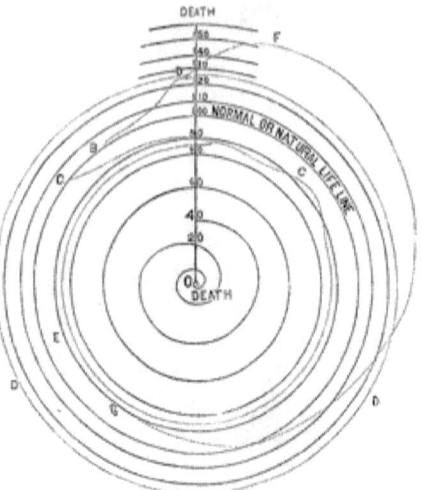

Plate IV.—Nerve-Tension in Health and Disease.

plan, we relax the tension by applying a negative remedy that partially depolarizes it by drawing to itself a part of the tension, repeating the application until the tension is reduced to the normal standard. Or, if it be a case of abnormal relaxation, the Sympathetic plan is the safest and we apply a positive remedy to increase the polar-tension.

On page 105, we gave a circle, with a dotted line showing variations in Atmospheric Electricity, and facing this we give a "Biometric Life-Circle" to illustrate variations in Nerve-tension. It will be observed that 100 indicates the "Normal or Natural Life Line" of Nerve-tension; from that to 0 indicates relaxation of tension, and from 100 upwards shows stages of acceleration. When Nerve-tension has fallen to about 40, Nature, even with the aid of the most skillful Physician and the best available remedies, can seldom restore tension, the system rapidly declines until at 0 Physical Death supervenes—so utter is the prostration sometimes that the mortification or final decay commences before death.

In low forms of Typhus and Typhoid, and other Malarial and sluggish Fevers, in Consumption and kindred diseases, in Cholera and kindred diseases, and in many other diseases where there is little or no inflammation, the Nervous System relaxes, and, as a rule, the Physician directs his remedies to the assistance of Nature in bringing the tension up to the normal 100.

On the other hand, in Neuralgia, Rheumatism, and inflammatory diseases generally, in active Fevers, and in very many diseases where there is a pronounced tendency to excitement, the Nervous System becomes tense, and the Physician seeks to assist Nature by the Antipathetic plan of direct assault on the tension, or by the Sympathetic plan of allaying the excitement, soothing the excited Nerves, drawing off the tension.

The extreme state of tension is found in Tetanus, or Lockjaw, when the line runs up to 150 or upwards; the corresponding extreme of relaxation is found in the Congestive Chill, in which the prostration reaches 20 or below—in either case Death can scarcely be averted; in the one because the polarity is so high, the Nerves so "fixed," in the other because the tension is so nearly destroyed, the System so near collapse, that equilibrium cannot be restored.

Derangements of the Sympathetic System are of the same nature, arising from excessive tension or relaxation, but do not manifest themselves externally in the same way; this System, it will be recollected, controls the "Vegetative Organs," wherefore, diseases having their centre in it affect the Nutritive functions directly and through them the entire Organism; the early symptoms are discomfort in the stomach and parts adjacent, in the bowels, the kidneys, etc., with pain of the character of dull ache; later, the symptoms become more aggravated, internal fevers, and sometimes external, inflammation of stomach or other organs connected with the Nutritive processes, and general debility, and eventually a gradual, at times rapid, decline, follow. As we have before stated, Cancers, Scrofulous affections, Ulcers, Skin-diseases generally, and all morbid growths are due to disease in some part of the Assimilating, Eliminating or Excreting Organs, and as the Sympathetic Nervous System is the manager of these, they are all evidences of augmented or relaxed tension in this branch of the Nervous System.

Now, we must remind the reader that Nerve Force like all Natural Forces, comprises two principles, a positive and a negative, a giver and withdrawer of polarity—as in the outer world, so in Man, there must be a Compensatory and Equilibratory relation between these two opposites, or Nature cannot carry on her work successfully. In Man, if the Soul-superintendent be not kept in a state of healthful activity, this relation will be suspended and disease is the result : if the Soul perform well its part, this relation can be disturbed only by external causes, such as excessive physical or mental effort, irregular habits of life (i. e., eating at irregular intervals, too much or too little, not having regular hours of sleep, etc.), dissipation, eating unwholesome food, going too much into society, an isolated, sedentary life—in short, excess of any kind in any direction; the external causes may be beyond our control, such as exposure to contagious or infectious disease, excessive heat or cold, excess of positive or negative Electricity in the Atmosphere, or any one of many causes. When the Soul is attentive to its controlling authority, and disease is introduced from without, there is evident an immediate effort to expel it by restoring the equilibrium, if the disease be slight or within the power of the Soul, equilibrium is restored with ease—unless the Nerve Force is too much relaxed or intensified to permit it, the Soul, unaided, can effect the reëquilibration, otherwise external assistance is rendered. The tendency to Compensation and Equilibration is seen in the Fever that follows a Chill, or the proportionate prostration that succeeds a Fever—in this, Nature is restoring Equilibrium by making one excess compensate for the other.

We have in the preceding paragraph alluded to the fact that among the external causes that suspend equilibrium within Man is excessive labor of Body or Mind. The American people are naturally extremely devoted to business—of course, there are very many who "rust out," but the American Simonpure is far more likely to "wear out." The American is distinguished, the world over, for qualities aptly expressed in vulgar parlance by the word "push"—he is an excitable "go-ahead" sort of a creature that is far too apt to become so engrossed in his chosen pursuit that Body, Mind and Soul, even the Subjective Faculties, are placed in requisition, made contributory, if not actually subservient, to the one idea, until he becomes an intense moving machine, almost automatic in the one direction. Now, extravagant concentration upon one pursuit is *waste* of Nerve Force. To say nothing of the depreciation of the Mind and the lowering of the standard of Soul-Life that inevitably result from this one-idea excess, the damage to the Nervous System is incalculable, permanently impairing the individual Organism throughout, and transmitting, by a natural "law of entail," appalling evils to his offspring and even to his posterity to "the third or fourth generation," in the shape of hereditary taints and predisposition to disease that Nature, even with the assistance of the Physician and the Divine, can seldom remedy or alleviate. During excessive application there is an excessive strain upon the Nerves and Nerve-centres that fearfully accelerates natural, healthful disintegration, and either the integration soon falls behind, or the strain of keeping it up exhausts the Organs thus driven to undue labor, and in some way or other Nature will enforce her law of Compensation—in the Man himself so far as his self-abbreviated life-span will permit, and in those who receive the taint of his weakened Vitality. The Cerebro-Spinal System is peculiarly delicate, and therefore susceptible to the effects of over-work, but the Sympathetic also inevitably becomes involved, the Man becomes an early wreck, and his unfortunate offspring have no "constitutions" to withstand external influences or to overcome internal predisposition to disease.

So important do we consider these facts, in the light of the fearful havoc already visible in this "go-ahead" Republic of ours, that we have in preparation a book expressly devoted to this subject, dedicated with earnest heart and profound sympathy to the best welfare of the land we love with patriotic ardor and the fellow-citizens we regard with true fraternal feelings. There is no human foresight that dare venture to penetrate the future and foretell the *Physical, Mental and Moral Whirlwind* that we shall reap as a people if we do not cease in the mad sowing of the *wind* of excessive Nerve-strain.

Every exercise of Nerve Force produces a proportionate disintegration of life-tissues, and so long as it is not excessive, is beneficial to the Organism in that it favors regeneration and revivification in the necessary integration of new tissues. A normal decay and renewal is always healthful—an occasional excess of mental or physical effort, if not carried too far, is doubtless beneficial rather than hurtful, in awakening the functions to zeal and energy, but even the most ordinary intellect must accept our caution against persistent, perpetual excess.

As soon as a Man feels himself becoming, on the one hand, "Nervous" (i. e., unduly excitable, irritable, "touchy"), or, on the other, subject to the "Blues" (i. e., low-spirited and apprehensive of evil), careless, indifferent to any subject that should interest him, let him pause and examine himself—he is in peril and must determine its source and end, and see how the threatened evil is to be averted. Before seeking relief in Medicine or Light, the Man of common sense will ascertain the cause of his "Nervousness" or "low spirits," and, in so far as the cause is under his control, will remove it—no remedy can counteract an evil by attacking the *effect* while the *cause* continues to produce it. Trimming the top of a Tree will not make it healthy and productive, while the worm is at its Root—depurating the Stream will not make the water healthful while the poison is in the Spring—or, to use a simile that may be more apropos, when we learn that the Sunlight hurts our eyes, we do not stare at the Sun while applying remedies.

There are two methods of applying Light as a remedy for disease—an indirect and a direct: by combining its virtues with Medicines, and by the application in "Sun-bath."

Our reader will recall the fact that the ancients, by a secret process unknown to the Science of our day, but which we trust will yet be rediscovered, converted ordinary wine and oil into "Fluid Gold," or "Potable Gold," by concentrating or focalizing Light and "fixing" it in them—this we cannot do, but many years ago, when our experiments with Light had convinced us that the "accepted" Scientists were in error in supposing it was the ray or rays reflected by an object that caused it to have the appearance of color—when we came to be assured that the color of an object was part of the object, given, not lent, to it by the Sunbeam; that a ray or rays passing into an object polarized its ether-conductor therein, thus making itself with its virtues an integral part of the object; that objects thus treated by Light were endowed with the essential property or properties of the ray or rays that took up their abode, or "fixed" their chosen conductors, therein; that objects in themselves soluble in the fluids of the body and capable of imparting their properties to those fluids or to the more or less solid tissues, endowed with the virtues of certain rays, thus became efficacious as Medicines; that, in short, the virtues of Medicines were due to the Sunlight or its action.

When we became thus convinced and assured, we conceived the plan of preparing certain Medicines under special rays of Sunlight, not to color them, for they already had received their color from Nature, but to augment the specific virtues of the ray used within each Medicine, to increase its action in the desired direction. We have tested this plan most satisfactorily, and have established the correctness of our hypothesis, and now we prepare certain positive Medicines exclusively under Red, and certain negative Medicines exclusively under Blue, Light. We find such Medicines to act with special effectiveness in harmony with the rays applied externally, and attribute our most gratifying success in the direct employment of colored Glass to the assistance of Medicines so prepared. It would be manifestly out of place here to specify the Medicines thus treated, or to give the details of our method.

The direct mode of applying color-rays is, of course, by compelling the Sunlight to pass through Glass the pores of which are filled exclusively with ether that will conduct only the color-ray desired, and will "throw down" the rest. We have already explained how Glass is made to pass the Blue or the Red ray, and have stated that Glass cannot be made absolutely exclusive—that the Blue will permit fragmentary portions of the Indigo and the Violet, and an infinitesimal amount of the Green, rays to slip through with the Blue; and that the Red is equally friendly to its Orange and Yellow neighbors, while each absolutely excludes its opposite. As we have shown, in applying a color-ray to vegetable propagation, it will not do to exclude all but a single ray, and the same is in a measure, but not equally, true in the application of a color-ray to the Human Organism. Our colored plates show that we do at times, in special cases, exclude all but one color, but, as it will be seen hereafter, we usually only augment the proportion of one color while admitting the rest, by employing a number of Blue or Red panes, more or less according to the exact effect we desire to produce, in conjunction with plain Glass. In either case, it will also be seen in due time, we are exceedingly careful not to carry the treatment to an extreme—we apply the ray in *baths of greater or less power, and of greater or less duration,* according to the condition of the patient and the exact result we propose to attain. In the use of Medicine, no skillful and successful Physician need be told that the results achieved depend not more upon the qualities of the Medicines than upon the methods of administration and quantity administered—and the same is equally true of Light as a therapeutic means.

As to the color to be employed, we can state the whole truth in a single sentence: To ACCELERATE the Nervous System, in all cases of relaxation, the RED ray must be used, and to RELAX the Nervous System, in all cases of excessively accelerated tension, the BLUE ray must be used.

We have clearly demonstrated the fact that these two rays produce the two opposite forces, or principles of Light—the Red the positive, polarizing, integrating force or principle, the Blue the negative, depolarizing, disintegrating force or principle. We have also demonstrated that relaxation of the Nervous System means the relaxation of its tension, or the depolarization, disintegration of the centres or conductors of Vital Force, and that excessively accelerated tension means the excessive polarization, integration of the centres or conductors of Vital Force. Hence, to counteract the former we employ the POSITIVE RAY, and to relieve the latter we employ the NEGATIVE RAY.

But, as in the outside world, to act efficiently Nature must have everything in a favorable, concomitant condition, so in applying Nature's forces to Man we must be careful to have the surroundings conduce to, not hinder, the end sought. The room, the atmosphere, the companions and attendants, nay the very clothing must be harmonious; there must be nothing antagonistic in drapings, furniture, atmosphere, associations, or in the patient's clothes, for just in proportion to the antagonism there must be difficulty in effecting the purposed cure. The matter of clothing is of the highest importance, for, as any one may see, a Black garment would "throw down" the color, whether Red or Blue—i. e., it would not permit the ray to reach the patient; a Blue garment would repel the Red ray and a Red garment would repel the Blue ray. The clothes, inner and outer alike, should be either white or of the color applied. Where the disorder is specially localized, promptly beneficial effect is often best secured by applying the ray directly to the part affected—any article of clothing intervening must weaken the action of the ray or delay it.

When we first commenced our experiments with Light-rays upon the Organism in disease, we had a sash made to occupy the lower half of a window. Our first trials were of Red, Blue and Violet Glass, but we soon found that the Blue and Violet were so identical in action that one would serve to represent the Actinic or Chemical principle, and, as Blue appeared to act with more promptness and uniformity, we discontinued the use of Violet. The Red and Blue Rays, then, constitute the entire *materia medica* of the Light System of Therapeutics, or all that our experience and investigation as yet seem to indicate as desirable.

As before stated, iterated and reiterated, the Red ray contains the positive, active, polarizing principle of Light, to which all Nature owes it power of combination; it is the positive element of Physical Force, the Attraction that enables Atoms to draw and cling to Atoms, forming Molecules, Molecules to draw and cling to Molecules, forming Masses of inorganic matter; it is the positive element, the Objective life element, of all Vital Force, that, in the shaping hand of the Subjective Life-principle, imparts to the particles of alimentary fluid that peculiar property that is called Vitality and converts it into the granular base of the Vital fluid; that makes these particles combine into nuclei; that forms the nuclei into Cells; that causes the Cells by their Vital motion to combine into organized bodies; that continues, still and always controlled and guided by the Subjective Life-principle, and assisted by the Blue co-worker, causes the simplest Cellular Organisms to unfold from type to type into the perfection of material forms in the Human Organism, and that, now under the responsible Personified Soul, continues to keep the Cells united, and to integrate with them the new particles that keep them in condition of Vitality; hence, when the positive within the Human Organism loses any portion of its power or influence, we employ the same Red ray to recruit and strengthen it, or to coöperate with it, in the restoration of the equilibrium of health.

And the Blue ray contains the negative, passive, depolarizing principle of Light, to which all Nature owes its power of dissolving exhausted, worn-out, effete forms; it is the negative element of Physical Force, the Repulsion that prevents the eternalization of material forces and the stoppage of Motion and Life that its opposite, the Red Attraction alone would produce; it is the negative, the death and decay, element of Vital Force, that, controlled by the Subjective Life-principle, goes before her Red colaborer preparing the way for his renewing work; but for the Blue, the Red would soon die himself, and Vital Energy would cease; old forms must be dissolved to make way for new, old, dying particles of continuous forms sloughed off to make place for fresh, new living particles—death and decay are just as essential to progress and development, as are generation and creation, death and decay are the germ of generation and creation, and the Blue element of Light is the source of death and decay; but for her, Nerve Force would become powerless for Life-work, as the Nerves and Ganglia, under the Red alone, would become set, fixed in tension and incapable of transmitting or conducting Vital Energy—hence, when we see a tendency to such an extreme of polarity in the Nervous System, we know that the negative force within requires assistance to prevent the fixity of death, and we employ its original author, the Blue ray, to go to its assistance.

Knowing the properties of the two rays in visible Nature, we find by experience that they act within the

APPLICATION OF RED LIGHT, Full Bath.

APPLICATION OF RED LIGHT, Partial.

Human Organism as without. Hence, the Red ray awakens all the dormant Vitality in the Nervous System, and, if administered at the right time and in the right way, produces healthful activity within when disease has reduced the Vitality below the health standard; in all cases where external symptoms show that the Nervous System, or any one of its parts, is, as it were, neglecting or losing its vivifying, vitalizing work, we awaken and spur it to action by means of the Red ray. Of course, great care must be exercised not to let our agent become our master, not to let it overdo the work we desire—in other words, if applied in excess, either as to amount or time, the Red Light over-excites the Nervous System and may produce dangerous Fevers or other disorders that may prove as troublesome as the evil we are seeking to correct. We seldom employ Red Light to the exclusion of the other rays, and it should never be so employed except in extreme cases when prompt action is the first consideration, and then very guardedly—indeed, it is extremely dangerous to attempt the exclusive Red-bath without a skilful Physician to watch the results and prevent excess. In employing Red Light, as in the use of medicines, each case must dictate the amount and duration of the bath; but, where a Physician is not available, it may be well at first to try alternate panes of Red and plain glass; if this be found too exciting a proportion of one Red pane to three or four plain ones may be tried; in either case, the bath should not extend beyond a couple of hours. By thus commencing with moderate doses, an intelligent person may learn the amount and time of bath required.

The same cautions are equally applicable in the use of Blue Light. Its action is as pronounced in reducing, as that of Red is in producing, Nervous excitement. If administered in small doses, say through a proportion of one Blue to four plain panes, it acts as a gentle sedative, creating a disposition to sleep, but so soon as this effect is reached the bath should cease. In cases of extreme Nerve-tension, when prompt action is imperatively demanded, we employ a pure Blue bath, but this is rare, and as there is always danger in so large a dose, we are very careful to note the momentary effects lest the patient be reduced to a condition of extreme prostration—sometimes, as may be readily understood, the lapse from intense excitement to an extreme prostration is sudden. As a general rule, a dose in ordinary cases would be a bath of about two hours through a window containing alternate panes of Blue and plain glass. It is safer, in aggravated cases especially, to consult a Physician, in the use of Light as in the use of Medicines.

As stated earlier, we are in the habit of administering Medicines, specially prepared for the purpose, in connection with the Red or Blue bath.

Before citing a few of the cases in which we have most successfully employed Red and Blue Light, we deem it our duty to offer a few cautionary suggestions:

In all ages and all climes, there have always been notorious empirics and quacks, who, without knowing either the Human Organism or even the first principles of Pathology or Therapeutics, have set themselves forward as wonder-working "Doctors"—their nostrums are pronounced *by themselves* sovereign remedies

APPLICATION OF BLUE LIGHT, Full Bath.

APPLICATION OF BLUE LIGHT, Partial.

for certain maladies, sometimes they are positively declared to be "cure-alls," but usually perhaps they are simply worthless, often dangerous, seldom efficacious, compounds; but, whatever their actual nature, it is extremely rash to risk the consequences of their use, no matter how many "Certificates" avouch their marvelous properties. The tendency of Nature to equilibrium in some persons is so strong, that she restores them to health in spite of pernicious drugs, and when they recover the "Patent" or "Proprietary" nostrum receives the credit of Nature's work. But our present interest is not with these quacks.

It was to be expected that, when the virtues of Light as a curative agent began to be known, some persons would seek wrongfully, fraudulently to make money out of the discovery. And we find this has actually occurred. It is not our purpose, as it is not our province, to mention any of these Light "Quacks" by name; but it is our province to caution the public, in general terms, against attempts to defraud them. All we propose to say, however, in this work on the subject is that: 1. There is no special virtue in one Blue pane of glass over any other of the same shade; Cobalt Blue is the best, and glass colored in the process of manufacture is better than *painted* glass, because the pigment applied externally imparts more or less opacity to the glass. 2. There is no special advantage in any particular method of arranging the glass in any particular sort of frame; an ordinary sash placed *upright* in the window-frame is as good as any other frame in any other position. 3. The Blue Ray cannot be focalized—it refuses to be modified, or changed, or concentrated, by the most powerful lens. The Red may be focalized by a suitable lens, but not by any arrangement of a pane or panes of glass, while the Blue *cannot be focalized by any means yet discovered.* 4. The idea that, when the Blue ray passes through, and the others are "thrown down," because the rejected Calorific Ray heats the glass, there is any special opening of the pores to admit Electricity, is simply absurd. The Electricity of the atmosphere is no more disposed to pass through Blue than plain glass—glass is *per se* a non-conductor.

But we must proceed to cite a few of the cases in which we have applied the Red and Blue rays:

I. Mrs. B., aged 44, had been, for many years, a sufferer from SUBACUTE RHEUMATISM; aggravated by stormy or even threatening weather. Had tried numerous Physicians and a vast quantity of Medicine, without more than the most transient relief. We placed her in a bath of alternate *Blue* and plain panes. Within *one* week the pains ceased, and within a fortnight the last symptom vanished. The stiffness of joints for a time returned occasionally in unfavorable weather, but within three months all tendency to stiffness ceased, and now nearly five years have passed since the last most remote indication of Rheumatism.

II. Mrs. L., a widow, aged 32, had been a severe sufferer, for several years, from SCIATICA, with extreme tenderness in the lumbar region. We instructed her to sit daily for about two hours in a bath of all *Blue* panes, with her back bared to the Light. After the third sitting, the tenderness along her spine was almost entirely gone, while the distress and pain in her hips sensibly abated. This treatment continued but for ten days, when all symptoms had disappeared.

III. Mr. W., aged 52, was afflicted with a dull ache and stiffness in his right shoulder, partially extending to his finger-tips; at times, the ache and stiffness in his fingers were intense, especially in the joints; occasionally, he experienced wandering RHEUMATIC pains in his back, the sides of his chest, and across the hips—the trouble was, however, generally confined to his upper extremities. *Blue* glass, in one-half proportions, brought relief at the second sitting, and he continued to improve at each sitting; the pains and stiffness having disappeared, he neglected the baths (though he continued to take the Medicine), and there were indications of the return of the difficulty; but, resuming the sittings, within three months the trouble had entirely vanished, and has not returned since, though a sense of tension occasionally causes him to imagine it is returning and he finds relief in a Blue bath.

IV. Mrs. H., aged 35 years. This was a case of CONSUMPTION *in the third stage, with both lungs involved*, the left hepatized with mucous râle through the upper third, and crepitation in the apex of the right lung; sputa copious, amounting to half a pint in twenty-four hours; her expectoration was a yellowish, ropy and frothy mucus and pus, a portion of which sank in water; she had severe night-sweats, and chills or "creeps" regularly at 11 o'clock, A. M., followed by fever with flushed cheeks; at times there was great dyspnœa and prostration—the latter so utter that she could sit up only an hour or two at a time. To increase the difficulty of successful treatment, there was a strong hereditary predisposition: her father, mother, brother and several sisters had died with Consumption; but one sister survived who was strong and robust (though troubled somewhat with Rheumatism). I placed Mrs. H. under *Red* baths regulated by the effects produced. In two weeks, improvement began to manifest itself in all her symptoms; in another week, the mucous râle became a submucous, then successively a crepitant and a bronchial; soon respiration was resumed through the entire left lung, and the crepitation at the apex of the right lung disappeared; expectoration improved, and the cough became less frequent and less distressing; with the improvement in these symptoms, the chills and fevers and the dyspnœa disappeared, and her strength rapidly increased; in two months and a half the only remaining trouble was a slight hacking cough arising from an irritated throat. Mrs. H. was from Boston, and had come to Philadelphia, to her sister's home, expressly for treatment; in the spring after her recovery she returned to her own home; she was so entirely cured, that she continued to enjoy excellent health even throughout the ensuing winter, though the climate had never agreed with her before. Her husband was subsequently unfortunate in his business, and she had become so hearty that she undertook to help him by opening a boarding-house; however, though still apparently well, she was overtaxing her recently acquired strength and, late in the fall, caught a severe cold which developed into Pneumonia which was very rapid in its advances; she was brought again to this city, but too late for treatment—she was already a dying woman sustained solely by stimulants.

In an active and extensive practice covering more than thirty years, we have never known or heard of a case of Consumption at so advanced a stage successfully treated. Her recovery was absolute and entire, and her subsequent attack of Pneumonia and death in no way derogate from the proven fact that *in Red Light is found an exceptionally reliable remedy*, with some assistance from harmonious Medicines, *for Consumption in almost its fatal stage.*

V. Master F., aged 8 years, had a tedious convalescence from a severe attack of Diphtheria, which was suddenly interrupted by a very severe attack of PARAPLEGIA; the paralysis was almost complete; he could not walk, and could only stand when supported by a table or chair. We had him arrayed entirely in white and placed in strong *Red* baths, from one to two hours at a time; soon after being placed in the Red Light, he would fall asleep and a profuse perspiration burst forth, saturating his underclothing; in three weeks he was walking firmly, and in two months was perfectly well. More than two years have since elapsed, and he has continued in perfect health.

VI. Master H., aged about 18 months. This was a severe case of CHOLERA INFANTUM, and MARASMUS brought on by teething in extremely warm weather; he had been under treatment by an excellent Physician for some time, but was steadily declining. As the last faint hope we determined to try the *Blue* treatment; he had been exceedingly irritable, but the Blue Light immediately soothed him into a gentle sleep, and he came out of the bath calm and refreshed. Two months' treatment made of him a fine, healthy-looking child, with full, rosy cheeks and happy temper. We are confident that but for the Blue ray this child must have died—no ordinary treatment could have saved him.

But the Blue Light was to effect farther wonders in him: his anterior frontinal had shown no evidence of closing, and one year subsequent to the above, while he was with his parents at the Seashore, he became suddenly very ill, the difficulty being confined to the Brain; the cerebral derangement increasing, the Physician in attendance advised the parents to hasten to Philadelphia and take him to their family Physician, saying that he had done all he could, and unless relieved he could not live forty-eight hours; they sent a messenger to see us, and we ordered the child to Philadelphia without delay. Upon his arrival, we found he had actual CEREBRAL MENINGITIS, with strong indications of Effusion; we placed him again under Blue Light treatment, and the most favorable effects were immediate; in one week, he had so far recovered that his parents, with our consent, returned to the Seashore. This child is now a fine, rosy-cheeked boy.

VII. Mr. R., 45 years of age, an overtaxed and (previous to treatment) prematurely worn-out man of business; the house of which he was principal became involved in the financial troubles that grew out of the panic that burst upon and ran riot through the country in 1873, and his anxieties and efforts to save his credit and standing produced an exhausting strain upon his mind, indeed the actual physical strain of sleepless nights and ceaseless work was enough to break him down—mind and body were continuously on the rack, he could neither eat nor sleep normally, and at last complete physical exhaustion and Nervous prostration naturally came upon him, for Nature would endure no more. The first warning was severe pains in the back of his head, soon followed by shortness of breath, flutterings of heart, compressible pulse, loss of appetite, constipation and phosphatic urine. He was properly advised, at the first token of the approximating peril, to leave business for a time and seek relief in travel; this advice he naturally was loth to follow, on account of the condition of his business, which he felt would soon be overwhelmed by the general financial ruin without his head to guide. Failing to persuade him to this, unquestionably the wisest, course, we determined to try the *Red* Light treatment, especially as his prostration was unattended by any indication of morbid irritability, and in all our experience as a Physician, we have never witnessed more remarkable beneficial results than were at once produced by the Red ray in this case. The very first bath had the most encouraging effect—it acted as a tonic both upon mind and body, dispelled his gloomy apprehensions and gave vigor to his physical functions. Commencing with small doses, we gradually increased them until assured that we had reached the most effective dose in proportion of Red to plain panes and in length of bath. [In Light as in Medicine there can be no invariable standard for doses, determined alone by the symptoms; in each case, the Physician must take into account the tone of body, the normal tension of the individual Nervous System and the entire temperament of the patient in health—a proper dose for one often proves insufficient for a second and an overdose for a third, even where the symptoms are identical.] Mr. R. rapidly improved, notwithstanding his continued attention to business. From the first, he slept more refreshingly, ate with better relish, his bowels became regular, and the secretions of his kidneys recovered the healthy appearance. Three weeks' treatment sufficed, and there have been no signs of relapse.

VIII. Mr. T., aged 35; in consequence of long-continued excessive physical and mental exertion, his Nervous System was entirely disordered; unlike Mr. R., the derangement manifested itself in " Nervousness" and trying irritability; he could not sleep at night, was disturbed by frightful dreams; his appetite was variable, sometimes ravenous, at others the very sight of food was an annoyance; his bowels varied, too, at times constipated, at others lax; he had frequent pains in his head, the least excitement unnerved him, and he was inclined to extreme despondency. His irritability forbade *Red* Light, and we determined to administer *Blue* Light with Red Light Medicine. The beneficial results were immediate; his entire system improved rapidly; five baths actually restored a healthy tone to his Nervous System, and he has since experienced no symptoms, even of " Nervousness," though his life is one of constant physical and mental activity.

IX. Mrs. G., aged 40 years, was worn out by over-gestation and too-long nursing. Her Nervous System was so shattered that she was compelled to lie abed a considerable part of the day; the most pronounced symptoms were intense spinal irritation, almost constant "Nervousness," and frequent palpitations of the heart; she had no appetite, and evinced very little interest in those domestic duties that had always been her delight hitherto. In her case, the prostration and listlessness called for *Red Light*, but her extreme susceptibility to the least excitement, with the tendency to palpitation, would be aggravated thereby—therefore, we employed Blue baths with Red Light Medicine. Two months' treatment restored her to perfect health which has continued to the present time; she says that she "was never better in her life." We should remark here that Mrs. G.'s normal temperament is calm, with marked sensitiveness to external influences—just the sort of system that often baffles medical skill, and that demands the utmost caution, and we feel confident that her recovery would have been tedious under any purely medicinal treatment.

X. Mrs. S., 45 years of age, had naturally a frail constitution, was from youth weak and delicate, with a tendency to Nervous prostration; easily despondent, and ready to "give up" when ill. Her natural weakness had resulted in, and been augmented by, Uterine difficulties which had continued for ten years, and had at last broken down her entire system when she called on us for professional advice. Her condition was such that the slightest exertion completely overcame her and sent her to bed for days at a time; the influence of "the change of life" had brought on the crisis, in an illness that kept her bedfast, which was directly attributed to a brief visit to the Centennial Exhibition; but this last was but a feather in the balance—the attack was impending and the excitement of the visit only hastened it. We applied the *Blue and Red Light* treatment, alternating, not at equal intervals, but according to variations in her symptoms. Her recovery was rapid and permanent—a whole day at the Centennial some time afterwards did not overfatigue her. She has enjoyed better health uniformly since the treatment than ever before.

But, why should we multiply illustrative cases? we have cited only ten, and these are all, in their distinctive features, only typical cases of classes treated. To multiply citations would but swell our little work without strengthening its effect or advancing its purpose to show that the Light-rays are unrivalled as remedial agents in the cure of diseases of almost all classes, especially those more directly incident to accelerated or relaxed Nerve action.

In closing this chapter, we must reiterate our declaration that we firmly believe and earnestly hope that SUNLIGHT and its rays are destined to become the UNIVERSAL MEDICINE. Light is God's grandest gift to Man, and the half is not yet known of its incalculable worth. "Truth is mighty and must prevail!" Light is mighty—it is truth—and must prevail over prejudice and self-interest, to the glory of its Source, God, and the inestimable benefit of His creatures of the Human race!

CHAPTER IX.

LIGHT IN THE VEGETABLE KINGDOM.

A MAN may by observation or by experiments, or by both, discover great truths in Nature, and yet not be a Scientist; a man may be a Scientist of high repute, with all the theories of popular Science at his tongue's end or pen-tip, and be unable to discover great truths or even to distinguish a truth, a fact, among theories. Because a great truth, or fact, in Nature is discovered by one who shows, in his attempts to impart his discovery to others, that he is not a Scientist, is it an evidence of mental acuteness, of superior Scientific knowledge, to reject the truth? Suppose eminent Scientists have for years been experimenting in the same direction only to fail—suppose they have actually woven whole webs of theories in conflict with the truth, and demonstrated those theories by innumerable experiments that have resulted only in showing that the theorists did not discover the truth simply because their experiments were guided by preconceived notions—suppose, even, that the newly discovered truth is calculated to explode the theoretic Science of a century and a half's growth! What then? Must we reject the truth in the interest of theoretic Science? or, must we reject the truth simply because neither Tyndall, nor Huxley, nor Schellen, nor some other Scientific "authority" discovered it? But, suppose our non-Scientific discoverer has demonstrated his truth by experiments that have produced results that will not, cannot be gainsaid! and suppose that truth is calculated to prove a blessing to mankind, an inestimable advantage to us, and our land, and to the world! Must we, dare we, reject or discredit the truth, decry the discoverer, rob ourselves and our land and the world of the benefits of the discovery—and that on no better ground than the non-discovery of the truth by a Scientist, or the blunders of the discoverer in his effort to explain his discovery?

Nay, rather, let us accept the truth and be grateful to its discoverer! We shall be no less worthy to rank with Scientists because we accept a truth at the hands of a non-Scientific discoverer! And so far as the theoretic Science that is wounded by this truth is concerned, it will be the better for the wound—like the tree or the vine that the husbandman prunes for its good, Science cannot suffer by having some of its theories pruned away by the sharp knife of truth, even if an unscientific hand applies the knife!

We believe that General Pleasonton is entitled to the grateful esteem of all men, Scientific and unscientific alike. He has rediscovered a great, important truth, and this truth when it comes to be understood in all its possible applications will prove the greatest blessing, to the entire world, of the nineteenth century. That the General is utterly and absolutely mistaken in his theories in attempting to account for the virtues of Blue Light is indubitable, *but the virtues are real no less!* That he does not know *why* or *how* Blue Light does certain things, does not derogate the high honor due him for demonstrating that it really does them. That he attributes to the sky the virtues of the BLUE RAY OF SUNLIGHT may readily be pardoned in consideration of the true service he has rendered to "the TRUE SCIENCE OF LIGHT" in directing attention to those virtues and inducing others to investigate the great subject—even his mistakes can be productive only of good results in inviting investigation. No one disputes Sir Isaac Newton's title to grateful admiration because some of his theories have been disproved by later researches, nor because his greatest discoveries have been found to have been forgotten truths known centuries before.

We have already shown that Light is the source of Vegetable, as of all, Life, and have not only demonstrated that the Blue ray has an important mission, which it faithfully fulfils, in the economy of Nature, but have explained how it performs its work. But, having come now specifically to consider "Light in the Vegetable Kingdom," we shall be pardoned for such repetitions as are unavoidable to make this branch of our subject clear and this chapter comprehensive.

It must be distinctly recollected that the chief difference between Vegetable, or *Still*, and Animal, or *Active*, Life, is that: In the one, the Vital Force acts entirely from without, without responsive or coöperative action from within; in the other, the Vital Force establishes a centre of vitality within, and by reason of this centre, the Animal responds or coöperates in the processes of Nutrition, etc. In the plant, the Sun is the actor, the plant merely the recipient of the action; in the Animal, the Nervous System, deriving its power from the only original source of Vital Dynamics, the Celestial Sun, is the actor, with a more and more complete (in the successive types) system of motive machinery acted upon and coöperating with the Nervous-centre. Bearing this difference in mind, we understand why the members of the Vegetable Kingdom, as a rule, live only in the Sunshine—it is their life in a special sense; it is essential to every operation in them, for it performs every operation; the Sun feeds the plants, eliminates mischievous elements from its food, assimilates the nutritive elements, applies the nutritive products, and removes the excrementitious matter (so to speak).

Now, note: in these operations, the Sun is the actor—not one Ray or two, but the seven rays, nay the nine, all have their proportion of work to perform in the unfoldment of life in a plant, and in the development of the root, stalk, branches, leaves and blossoms, which manifest that life. The Blue ray and its Actinic associates no doubt have a large proportion of the work devolved upon them—we reasonably infer this from the fact that they form 100 out of 170 parts of every Sunbeam, as it reaches the earth; but whatever its proportion of the work, it must perform that and no more. The Blue, with all its Actinic aiders, cannot take the place of the Red as the polar, integrating ray; nor of the Yellow as the supplier of the *chlorophyl* that colors the foliage; nor even of the colorless Calorific as the imparter of the genial warmth that is as essential to plant-life as food itself—*e. g.*, the chemical properties of Sunlight are just as active in winter as in summer, only the Calorific are overborne by the cold, and plants live not in winter but in summer; and, as General Pleasonton himself declares, vegetation is far more luxuriant in the tropics than in temperate regions, although the chemical properties are not more prompt or constant there. We believe that the Orange and even the Green rays are not idle spectators in Nature's laboratory, though their special functions have not been identified as yet; the Indigo and Violet are more charged with actinism than the Blue, and possibly this is why Blue is preferred in vegetable propagation.

We have declared our conviction that when the Human Organism is in a state of harmony or equilibrium, the Sunlight, pure, simple, undivided, is better than any single ray as a preserver and promoter of that harmony or equilibrium which is health, and that, only when that equilibrium is disturbed, must we employ the ray best calculated to restore it. And we believe the same is true in regard to Animals and Vegetables. Then, asks a critic, how do you account for the success of General Pleasonton? With little difficulty: He did not exclude the other rays, but augmented the Blue one-eighth; this increased the supply of food, and at the same time increased the appetite, or demand, for the food—the first by separating a larger amount of nutritive matter from the soil and atmosphere, and the second by accelerating the disintegration of exhausted particles from the vines; farther, it facilitated the transformation of elements from stage to stage until the ripened fruit was ready to be plucked; but it was the Red ray, passing in with the undivided Sunlight through the plain panes, that fed the vines with the food prepared by the Blue, and the Yellow that produced the coloring for the leaves, and the other rays fulfilled their respective functions. We doubt much whether the augmentation of the Blue in the Light admitted to a Greenhouse (or Bluehouse perhaps we should say), for fruit-culture will not eventually prove as much of an injury to the fruit as overfeeding is to Animals and Men—but of this we know nothing from personal observation, as our duties in caring for the sick leave us little time to practice or even to observe fruit or vegetable culture. This we do know, however, that over-large fruit is never as palatable as the medium, nor indeed have we a special liking for "forced" products of any sort.

It must be noted that Professor Draper, Mr. Gladstone, and other eminent Scientists have clearly demonstrated the impossibility of cultivating grain or vegetables under a single color of Light, and General Pleasonton did not attempt this; he simply, we repeat, by putting one Blue pane to every seven plain ones, increased the Blue element of the Light within his grapery one-eighth.

Before proceeding to speak connectedly of plant-development, we must notice one other Pleasontonian idea, viz.: "The magnetic, electric and thermic powers of the Sun's ray reside in the violet ray, which is a compound of the blue and red rays." After a careful second reading of the General's argument, we are at a loss to understand how he discovers anything *thermic* in the Violet, or gets the Violet from the combination of the Blue and Red. That these two colors blended in certain proportions do produce a Violet color—but the Violet ray has not a trace of calorific character, and no process that we know of can get heat out of it; filtered through a Violet glass it is purely actinic and much cooler than solid Sunlight, very much cooler than the Red, or even the Yellow; but, farther, the Red is the least refrangible of all the color-rays, and the Blue is the fifth of the scale—now, in common sense, how can a combination of these two produce the most refrangible, the seventh of the scale? That negative electricity "resides" in the Violet ray, or rather in the four actinic rays, we have shown, though perhaps "resides" is not *the word* to express the correct idea; still, accepting the "residence," how can the dual force Magnetism "reside" in *one* ray? how can positive electricity "reside" with negative in the same ray? In a bar of iron or steel, when *magnetized*, the two electricities take the opposite ends, called the poles, with a neutral *equator* midway; is the Violet ray, then, thus magnetized? We fear the General claims more for the Violet than it ever claims for itself. This is scarcely more remarkable, however, than his theory that Electricity is the agent of Light in promoting vegetable growth and that heat is the product of Electricity, when we consider that in January the mean tension of Atmospheric Electricity is 605°, while in July it is but 49°, as shown in M. Quetelet's table cited on page 107; nor is this as remarkable as the discovery that the "Blue color of the sky" has *functions*. The Blue ray of the Sunbeam does *deoxygenate*, but even it must have the aid of the Red to *sustain* any sort of life; and, moreover, oxygen is not the property of the Blue, it *belongs to the Red*, as we have demonstrated. We admit that "without these chemical powers [the properties of the actinic rays] there could be no vegetation." But neither could there be without the polar Red, or the colorless Calorific—the latter may be substituted by artificial heat, as in a Hot-house, but we know of no substitute for the Red. The General's plan of operations is nearer correct than his explanations: as we have explained, he admits all the rays to do their portions of the work. By-the-way, we admit that there is heat generated in the earth, as there is in the Human Organism and in the Animal—the source is the same in all, Light: its dual forces in active exercise generate heat, when in the Animal, in Man or in the earth; and the opposite Electricities do "evolve" (or *evosue*) heat in coming together, but here too the two Light-forces are in action. It is the faculty of generating heat within the body, consequent upon the presence of a life-centre within, that gives to Animals and Man a more certain tenure of life than plants; the latter having no internal warmth are nipped by the first frost—some forms of Animal-life in which the heating apparatus are not developed cannot stand the least cold, and upon the approach of winter suspend life until the return of Sunwarmth, much as what we call *perennial* plants do.

We have seen that, as soon as God's representative, Light, had precipitated Earth from the waters under the firmament, and had thus caused the "dry land" to "appear" from their midst, the Earth was made to "bring forth grass, the herb yielding seed, and the fruit-tree yielding fruit after his kind, whose seed is in itself, upon the Earth." We have demonstrated that it was the action of the *two hands* of Light upon and within the Earth that enabled it to bring forth, or *give forth* vegetation. This demonstration included evidence that the dymannal Life-principle was more essential to the development of vegetation than the seed; for it created the seed-germs from the inorganic elements of the soil when as yet there was no grass, herb or fruit-tree to yield seed "after his kind;" that if all vegetation were blotted out, this Life-principle could again produce the myriads of species from the same original elements by the same original processes, while without this dymannal Life-principle no one species could perpetuate or renew or repeat itself— without either *hand* of Light, or without the *guiding principle*, no seed could be made to germinate and develope into the blade, the stalk, the leaf, the blossom, etc. At the first evolution of a plant-form, this mighty Life-principle, with its two objective hands, had to form the seed-germs, and then cause them to unfold to manifest its power as God's worker, and then it made provision for the continuance and perpetuation of all the species by imparting to each the Organs of Reproduction; but we saw that plants, not having functions of locomotion, are left dependent upon means without themselves for the necessary copulation; then, when the new life is implanted in the germ-cell, the development into a perfect germ goes on, independent of outside interference; but when the germ is to be made to unfold, some intellect must see that the soil, temperature, and general auxiliary surroundings are favorable, especially if it be a plant that we deem worthy of *cultivation* (*i. e.*, evolution into higher perfection), in which case Man takes a hand in the soil-preparation, seed-planting, and other processes of cultivation, otherwise the great Life-principle still directs; but even if Man works the soil, plants the seed, harrows and tends the unfolding plant-life, the germ cannot be made to germinate without the direct assistance of the two objective hands of Light—the one to break up, dissolve the seed-particles, the other to refix, repolarize the particles into the new forms, each "after his kind;" in this germinating process the two Light-forces are within the germ, placed there as the germ-life essence, but, as soon as the young plant peeps forth out of the ground, the Sunbeam becomes the actor with its two principles, under the Life-principle, the one preparing the nutritive materials, drawing them from the soil, the water, the air, etc., the other "fixing" these materials, feeding the plant; then, in the continuous processes of development, the same two hands must continue the one to provide food for the other to posite, assimilating, eliminating, removing the excretory matter, and thus carrying the plant to its completed development; then, if it be a plant that Man or Animal uses, he destroys, not the particles, but the form, and the same two forces continue to act in Man or Animal, and after these forces within Man or Animal are done with the respective ingredient-particles and cast them forth, the same forces still act in restoring the particles to the soil, water, air, etc., to be again applied in Life-unfoldment; or, if it be a plant not applicable to Human or Animal use, the same two forces proceed to disintegrate its particles, it decays, and to convert them to new developments. Thus, always under the Life-principle, the two hands ever act, whether directly in the Sunbeam, in the germ, or in the Vital Force of Animate Nature, and the entire economy of Nature ever goes forward in motion, motion, change, change, decay and regeneration—but all the time, there is but one Life-principle variously unfolded, but one dymanual objective force working from various centres.

Thus, we find *seven* (or *nine*) rays, *two* principles, *one* Light. Nature has regulated the proportions of the several rays, the powers of the separate principles, and decreed that the two shall work in *harmony* or *equilibrium* as *one* Light-power. If, under any influence, either force exceed its share of the aggregate work of Light, we observe at once that life is imperiled—in plant, Animal or Man, and, if Nature require our assistance, we render it by sending a special messenger to strengthen the weaker force or to check the stronger—it is but the part of wisdom, when we know the source of each force, and have that source at command, to apply that source: if it be the negative force we wish to reinforce, we employ the Blue, Indigo or Violet, if the positive force demands help we employ the Red.

This is the whole secret of the true utilization of Light-rays, whether in Vegetable, Animal or Human Life: we must employ the Red or the Blue, or whichever ray we find best adapted, to assist, not supplant, Nature, to restore, not subvert, Equilibrium. We firmly believe that Man, Animal or Plant, when in health, requires the pure, unadulterated, undiluted Sunlight; when disease indicates the loss of equilibrium within, and then alone, we should apply the ray or rays that will assist in restoring health, and as soon as we have attained the desired end, health, the treatment should cease, and it should be sustained with pure Light, pure Air, pure Water. We should as soon modify or alter the air we breathe by increasing the amount of Oxygen or Nitrogen, as modify or alter the Light, when the Organism is in a condition of health—we do modify or alter the air when impure, and so we would modify or alter Light when impure, not otherwise. Nature provides stimulants in sufficient variety and sufficient amount for healthy Men, Animals and Vegetation, and only when her supply fails shall we attempt to make up the deficiency.

In the ensuing chapter, with which we close our present work, we propose to review the ground we have traversed and sum up the lessons we believe we have imparted.

CHAPTER X.

LIGHT THE SOLE SOURCE OF LIFE—LIGHT THE DEVELOPER OF MATERIAL FORMS—FORMS DEVELOPED SOLELY TO MANIFEST LIFE—LIGHT NATURE'S MEANS OF PRESERVING LIFE— HENCE, LIGHT NATURE'S MEANS OF BANISHING DISEASE BY RESTORING THE EQUILIBRIUM THAT CONSTITUTES HEALTH.

We have established the important Fact that Light is NATURE'S SPECIFIC FOR DISEASE—that is, Nature employs no other means or instrumentality in the cure of Disease. But let us take a brief survey of the ground we have traversed, and note the main facts that we have demonstrated :

Light is the original Source of Life. Motion is Life and Light is the Universal Motor. There is no force in Nature that is not directly derived from Light: 1. the Physical Forces, Attraction and Repulsion, with all their modifications, are the positive and negative principles of Light, acting in matter— they are the Objective Forces of Light as they operate in creating and dissolving inorganic material forms. 2. The Vital Forces that constitute what we call Life —are the same positive and negative principles of Light acting in organic forms, acting in Still or Vegetable Life only from without and in Animals and Man becoming Nerve Forces because in each Active or Animate Life-form there is established a Nervous System as a centre of Vital Energy. Like the Physical Forces, the ordinary Vital or Nerve Forces are Objective, and are derived from the great Light-source and Light-power, the Celestial Sun, through the Objective Sun of our Solar System; the Objective Sun is not the Source of Light, but the reservoir and disseminator of Light to the worlds of its System, and of the Nervous System in Animals and Man the same is true—it is the receiver and dispenser of Vital Energy for the Organism. 3. The Subjective Life-principle is an emanation from the Celestial Sun; as that original Luminary controls the Astral Suns in their motions in space, so this Life-principle is ever and everywhere present, guiding and directing the dissolution of old and the generation of new forms, according to established types.

When Jehovah first decreed the creation, He constituted Light His agent, representative, manifester in the creation of the Universal System: all was chaos—infinite Space was one vast, immeasurable, incomprehensible abyss of absolute, utter darkness; but when Light came forth in response to the Divine Will, forthwith all was changed: darkness gave place to effulgence; ugliness to beauty; voidness, vacuity to orderly fullness; formlessness to Suns and Planets; stillness, inertia to motion; boundless death to countless manifestations of Life. Light was the active producer of all this glorious change, and Light alone prevents the return of the universe to chaotic darkness and stillness and death. Time began, was separated from Eternity when God said "Let there be Light, and Light was," and Creation began with Time; Creation is coeval with Time—it began, and can only end, with Time; as Time rolls on from age to age, Creation goes forward from stage to stage: Light begot and maintains Time, and Light began and continues Creation. But Time is not eternal, it shall cease, shall be engulphed in Eternity, and Creation is not eternal, it shall cease, shall be engulphed in chaos. Time is for material existences to be measured and gauged by—there is "a Time to be born and a Time to die," physically, and Creation is a work of material development—where there is death there must be Creation or material forms and physical life would cease, Life would no longer be manifested in matter. There is no Time to die in the Celestial World—there is an Eternity of Life there, and there is no Creation there, because "flesh and blood cannot inherit the kingdom of heaven"—there are no material, "corruptible" bodies there to die and decay and be regenerated. Time and Creation belong only to the material world, because only in the material world are beginnings and endings and renewals. There is Life in the Celestial World, but no death, hence no Creation—there is Eternity there but no Time, all is Eternal Life in that World because the Harmonious Light of Health and Life shines unceasingly there—God is Light, the Light of Life, the Light of Heaven.

Creation was designed to manifest the Light of Life in Objective Form. When God decreed Creation, and His Word proclaimed it, it was not to produce a new Life-principle—He was the Light of Life, self-existent from Eternity, and there could be no new Life, for

"He filleth Eternity." When the Omnipotent Light of Life, by His Supreme Will, decreed Creation, His sole purpose was to manifest the Light of Life in Objective Form—material Creation is simply and purely the Objective manifestation of the Light of Life. The Suns, Moons, Stars are manifestations of Light—the Planets, or Peopled Worlds, with all their countless living forms or bodies, are manifestations of Light, the Light of Life!

Without recapitulating in detail, let the reader recollect that from the first manifestation of Light in Creation, the one ultimate purpose of Jehovah was the manifestation of the Light of Life in PERSONAL FORM: in short, that the successive forms from the lowest to the highest—MAN—were but steps in the progressive visible unfoldment of Life. The material forms were developed, not for themselves, but for the unfoldment of Life. Recollecting this, bearing it constantly in mind, we can the more readily understand how with Man the work of development ceased. Matter was incapable of higher development—no grander, more perfect material casket for the Light of Life could be evolved—material development had reached its zenith, and it only remained to "breathe into his nostrils the breath of Life," when "Man became a Living Soul," "in the image, after the likeness" of God Himself—that is, with Attributes or Faculties within him that could be unfolded into so high a degree of perfection as to make Man Godlike. Of course, as we have seen, the material form of Man could not be "in the image" or "after the likeness" of God, who "is a Spirit." No amount of development could make "corruptible flesh and blood" like God.

Hence, " Man is not a material body" that is only his casket—"Man became a Living Soul," and the "Soul is Man." And hence, for Man to lose his Soul is to lose himself.

The Light of Life is Eternal—Immortal! Life cannot cease—the body dies, when the Light of Life, the Life-principle, ceases to occupy the casket. This is true of the simplest plant, the humblest worm, no less than of the noblest Human Organism, and of the noblest Human Organism no less than of the humblest worm and the simplest plant. Realizing this, that *the body is only the perishable, nay perishing, casket for the temporary habitation of* MAN, THE SOUL, we have dwelt at considerable length, and repeatedly upon the importance of Man's cultivation of the Subjective Faculties of his Soul—this was the one and only purpose for which he was made, this *the one duty God enjoins upon Man*. The care of the body is a duty, but only to fit it for the higher development of "the inner Man." "God is Light"—"the Light of Life!" "Know ye not that your body is the temple of the Living God? . . . . . . If any man defile the temple of God, him shall God destroy; for the temple of God is holy, which temple ye are! . . . . . . Therefore, glorify God in your body, and in your spirit, which are God's!" Man is called a *responsible being* because the Almighty Jehovah has implanted in him the germ of Godliness, Faculties which if diligently and devoutly unfolded, until they shape and control the Objective life, will elevate him and make him worthy to be regarded by God Himself as "in His image and after His likeness"—and He has assigned to Man himself the duty of cultivating and unfolding these high and holy Faculties. When Paul calls the Human body the temple of God, he means no more and no less than that these Faculties of Man's Soul are Godlike, are Divine. Just in proportion as these Faculties are unfolded and rule the Organism, Man becomes Godlike—the "child of Light" is the "child of God," for "God is Light." God is "the same yesterday and to-day and forever"—Redemption is but the crowning act of Creation, the act that opens the way for Man to fulfil the grand, original purpose of God in Creation, the development of Godlike Men to manifest Him; Christ was the perfect realization of "the Light of Life," "God manifested in the flesh," the "Word made flesh," "Emanuel," "the Son of God." Christ was not only sent to be our example in Life-culture but our Helper. But of this we have spoken very fully in earlier chapters.

The duty of taking care of our bodies is second only to the highest duty of Soul-culture—in some senses it is part of that higher duty. We must "glorify God" not only in "our spirits," but in "our bodies"—the first by cultivating our Godlike Spiritual Faculties, the second by keeping our bodies free from every taint of sin and of disease. But we cannot entirely escape sin, nor can we keep free of disease —then, let us strive to fulfil our duty as nearly as we may by living soberly, wisely and in conformity with the laws of God's two Revelations of His Will, in the Book of Nature and in the Book of Books, the Bible

—both are from God: in the one, His agent and representative, Light, has manifested His Will, directly, in the other, the same agent and representative has illuminated Men to declare His Will. May the same agent and representative of Jehovah illuminate us to read aright His Will in both Revelations, and to comprehend the lessons imparted therein!

As there is one God, so there is one Life-principle—"God is Light," "the Light of Life," and Light is the Life-principle. God manifests himself in Light, and Light manifests itself in Life, and Life manifests itself in material forms. Hence, the Life manifested in Vegetation, in Animals and in Man, is alike in its source and origin, which is Light. The Light of Life as witnessed in Heaven is perfect in Harmony, but as manifested in material forms, the law of Harmony is modified into the law of Compensation and Equilibration, because material forms must necessarily be continually decaying and renewing; perfect Harmony would not permit decay, and where there is no decay, there can be no renewal. The law of Compensation and Equilibration consists simply in maintaining an equilibrium between the dual forces of Light, and this is done by the Life-principle, which is Subjective, *i. e.*, invisible to the physical eye, and is only recognized Objectively in the operations of the Objective Forces, Physical or Vital. In the exterior world, these forces are forever at work, under the supervision of the Life-principle, dissolving and creating. In Man, they are constantly at work, under the Individualized Life-principle, the Soul, disintegrating effete particles and integrating new particles, so as to keep the tissues, the

Organs, the entire System in a healthful condition for the unfoldment of Soul-Life within. In the external world, so long as the two forces work in equilibrium, the one dissolving only exhausted forms and the other creating new forms to take their places, Nature moves forward in orderly beauty; in Man, so long as the two forces work in equilibrium, the one disintegrating the particles exhausted by the operations of Vital Energy, the other replacing them with new particles, there is a condition of perfect health throughout the Organism. In the external world, the law of Equilibration does not require that the integrating right hand shall do no more than just repair the decay produced by the left, —for then there would be no progress; it requires only that each force shall obey the Life-principle to do just what is required of it. So, in Man, we find that the right hand of Light does more than the left during the period of growth from the fœtus to the prime of manhood, and then the two work equally for a time, and then, during the period of decline from the prime to old age, the left does more than the right —yet there may be evident health during each of these three periods, provided the two forces precisely obey the Soul-superintendent. In other words, the two forces are the hands to tear down and build up, and the Soul is the head to direct, and, so long as each regards its proper station and duty, health is the delightful result.

As we have seen, with the Soul in absolute control, and the forces in Equilibrium, disease cannot arise within the Organism, and when introduced from without there is at once apparent a strong tendency to cast out the evil influence by restoring the disturbed Equilibrium. Hence, Soul-culture is of incalculable advantage from a purely physical point of view, as an invaluable means of promoting health. But, even the most-highly developed Soul does not insure physical health, and Nature cannot always preserve or restore equilibrium within the Organism; often Nature demands assistance, and it is our duty to render her all the aid we can, for, as we know, the care of the body is a duty second only to the cultivation of the Soul. Of course, to render acceptable and effective assistance, we must understand the Organism and Nature's ways of working therein; if we do not possess this essential knowledge, we may thwart and hinder Nature—we may increase the disturbance of equilibrium so that it cannot be restored at all—we may kill instead of assisting Nature to cure. It is to render timely assistance to Nature in the cure of disease men are educated to become Physicians, and if special, specific training is needful to enable a man to become a master-carpenter, a capable machinist, a successful merchant, or to succeed in any pursuit, much more is it absolutely essential, indispensable to enable a man to become a Physician—not only because his work is the care of bodies created by God for the manifestation of His glory, but because he can only see his work in its effects, and then when the effects are evident it may be too late to rectify a mistake. It requires no argument to demonstrate the importance of a thoroughly trained and educated Medical Ministry, and yet how many are far less careful in the selection of a Physician than in the selection of a mechanic.

When we learn that Nature works under the one law of Compensation and Equilibration, and that, when disease indicates the disturbance of this law, she at once seeks to banish the disease by restoring Equilibrium—we should render assistance on the same plan. When we learn that Light is the only means she employs in all her operations, and that Light is her only remedy for disease—we should strive to learn how we may best assist her by applying the same remedy. The ancients knew far more about the therapeutic properties of Light—as of the causal workings of Light in every particular—than we have yet discovered.

But we believe the great learning of the ancients will yet be equalled in these later times, and that the entire Science of Light will be made plain. The Light shines, and we reap its benefits, we know not fully how, as yet—the darkness comprehends it not! But the day is dawning, the Light of Truth is bursting through the clouds of prejudice and error and all evil. Not only the prevalent conceptions of Pathology and Therapeutics, but of all branches of Science, even, it may be, of Theology, shall ere long be swept away, and the Light of Truth, the Light of Life, the Light of Heaven, shall illumine the whole earth, to the glory of God and the temporal and Eternal wellbeing of Man!

"GOD IS LIGHT!"

INDEX.

"ACCEPTED" theories unsatisfactory, 62.
Atomic element of Light Dissolves solid forms, and prepares the Atoms and Molecules for the Polar Rod, 240.
Acute Diseases require more Powerful Remedies, 236.
Advent substituted in reading for Jehovah, 46.
Advice to the "Nervous" and those troubled with the "Blues," 264.
Albumens, 172.
Albuminous Compounds, 171.
Ancient Philosophy and Modern Science, 155.
Ancients Peculiarly Expert in Employing Light as Medicine, 252.
Angle of Inclination, 128.
Animal Magnetism, the Discovery of, Wrongly Ascribed to Mesmer, 244.
Antagonistic Forces, 141.
Antipathetic System, 224, 238.
Antiquity of the Kabbala, 17.
Apocalypse of John proves him a Kabbalist, 22.
Ascending Nature, 263.
Astral Soma, 24, 40, 43.
Atmosphere under a Clouded and a Serene Sky, (Table), 109, 108.
Atoms Miniatures of the Earth, 125.
Atoms Angular in Inorganic, Spheroidal in Organic matter, 124, 145.
Atoms, the Polarity of, 174.
Attraction and Repulsion known to Pythagoras, 50.
Attraction and Repulsion of Electricities, 131.
Authority of Organs, 190 to 191, 194, 201, 218, 253.
Authority of the Soul, 229.

BALL-LIGHTNINGS, 213.
Baths of greater or less Power, and greater or less Duration, 263.
Bezesda, the "Miracle of," 39.
Bible and the Kabbala, 23, 24, 248.
Bible Full of Kabbalistic Terms, 248.
Black the absence of Color, or the presence of two or more inharmonious Colors, 75.
Blue and Red Light Treatment combined, 280, 282.
Blue and Red Rays the entire Materia Medica of Light Treatment, 268, 269.
Blue Bath, the Proportions Most Desirable, 273.

Blue Bath, we Seldom Employ a Pure, 272.
Blue Glass a Non-Conductor of Electricity, 274.
Blue Glass better than Violet, 268.
Blue Glass Cures, 274 to 282.
Blue Glass, When we use, 270.
Blue, Indigo and Violet, the, the Negative Rays, 61.
Bluemonde Glass Better than Painted, 275.
Blue Ray cannot be Focalized, 279.
Blue Ray cannot Usurp the place of the Red, or Yellow, or Colorless Calorific, or even of the Green, etc., 286, 289.
Blue Ray cannot Sustain Life in any form, 289.
Blue Ray, the Character and Action of the, Clearly Explained, 270, 271.
Blue Relaxes the Nerve-centres by decreasing the Polarization of the Ice-tenant Ganglion of Nerves, 267.
Bluish silver of Clouds, 78, 86.
Body, the, an Aggregation of Millions of Cells, 235.
Body, the Material, Analyzed, 145.
Book of Nature and the Bible, 306.
Book of Nature the only True Source of Pathology and Therapeutics, 229.
"Bright and Morning Star" of John, 246.

CATOMETRIC Substances, or Heat-Producers, 169.
Cancers, Scrofulous Affections, Ulcers, Skin-diseases, Morbid Growths, 280.
Capillaries, 241.
Cohesion and Exhalation, 148.
Chaotic, 173.
Chaos Chaos, 274 to 282.
Causes and Effects from the Beginning, 132.
Cautions and Advice, 264.
Celestialized Mind must conduce to Bodily Health, 229.
Celestial Light Individualized, 238.
Celestial or Soul World, 46.
Celestial or Subjective Light, 43.
Celestial Sun, 28.
Celestial Sunlight the Original, Perpetual Source of Vital Dynamics, 135.
Cell, each, of an Aggregation no longer lives or can live Independently, 186, 236.
Cells, Granular Base and Nuclei, 199.

INDEX.

Cell, the Simple, the Type and Base of Organization, 146, 185.
Centre of Centres of Vitality, 187.
Centre of Vitality Essential, 186.
Cerebellum, 208.
Cerebral Meningitis, with Strong Indications of Effusion, Cured by Blue Light—Case Cited, 275.
Cerebro-Spinal System, 202, 205.
Cerebrum, 200.
"Change of Life," see Case X., 281.
Cholera and Gastroenteric Diseases promoted by Excessively Negative condition of the Air, 169, 258.
Cholera Infantum and Marasmus, Hopeless Case of, Cured by Blue Glass—Case Cited, 277.
Cholera never attacks Men working in Copper, 115.
Cholesterin, 199.
Chondrin, 178.
Christ our Example in Life-culture and our Helper, 300.
Christ promised immediately after the Fall, 64.
Christ the Living Embodiment of Light, 191, 300.
Christ the Perfect Fulfilment of Jehovah's Original Purpose, 216.
Christ "the Son of God," 161, 300.
Chronic Diseases require Mild Remedies, 246.
Circulatory Course of the Chyle, 198.
"Civil Service Reform," 274.
Classification of Nervous Centres, 200.
Classification of Organic Constituents of the Human Organism, 169, 171.
Classification of Organs, 188, 195, 192.
Clothing must be White, or of the same Color as that applied, 288.
Cloud-light, 72, 80.
Cobalt Blue the Best, 273.
Colored Spectacles and Eye-glasses, 95.
Color—Facts opposed to popular Theories, 74.
Colors of Objects, 72, 73.
Colors of Sun-light, 81.
Commentators, Difficulties of Ordinary, 30, 245.
Compass, Some Uses of the, 122.
Compass, the, Known in the Second Century, 125.
Compensation and Equilibration the Conditions of Health, 227, 257, 300.
Congestive Chill, 280.
Conscience, 201, 200, 209.
Consciousness, 151, 180.
Constituents of the Actual Living Tissues, 169.
Consumption and Kindred Diseases, 239.
Consumption in the Third Stage, with Both Lungs Involved, Cured by Red Baths—Case Cited, 275 to 277.
Contrast between the Motive in Man and Animal, 218.
Creation Coëval with Time, 296, 297.

Creation Developments, 127.
Creation in "Six Days," 134.
Creation, What, was Designed for, 297.
Cultivation Developments, 127.
Cures by Red and Blue Light—Cases Cited, 274 to 280.

Darkness, the World of, 43.
Dark Soul, the, 20, 157.
"Dark Valley of the Shadow of Death" Illumined, 220.
Darwinism Repudiated, 128.
Dawn and Twilight, 17, 80.
"Daystar," of Peter, 246.
Death and Decay necessary to Physical Life, 127.
Death an Entire Depolarization of Nervousness, 259.
Decay and Regeneration continually going on, 177.
Decay the Ultimate Depolarization of the Life-forms, 258.
Diamagnetic bodies Electric, 121.
Differences between Still and Active Life, 182, 264, 265.
Differences in Action between Ganglia and between Nerves, 207.
Difficulties of Scientists in defining Light, 55.
Direct Mode of Applying the Red and Blue Rays, 206.
Disease an Abnormal Disturbance of Polarity, Excessive Polarization or Excessive Depolarization, 258.
Diseases caused by Excess of either Electricity, 117.
Diseases with little or no Inflammation, 259.
Dissent from "Accepted" Theories, 62, 263.
Diurnal Variations in Electric tension (see Plate III., p. 105), 104.
Divine origin of the Sabbath, 28.
Draper, When Professor, has Demonstrated, 285.
"Dry land," 132.
Dual Force of Light, 263.
Dual Functions of some Organs, 192.
Duality of the Human Soul, 26, 27.
Duty, 159, 300.
Dynamical Life-principle more Essential than Food, 294.

Earth, How created, 45, 85, 132.
Earth, the, a Magnet, 121, 122.
Educated Physicians Indispensable, 268.
Education of our day Seriously Wrong, 223, 245.
Effects of American Excess in Business Application, 262.
Electric and Magnetic bodies, 124.
Electrization, the two, are the Two Forces of Light, 100.
Electricity and Magnetism defined, 99, 119, 121.
Electricity, How a flash of, travels, 112.

INDEX.   307

Electricity known to the Ancients in its Source and Phenomena, 97.
Electricity not the Agent of Light in promoting Vegetable Growth, 298.
Electricity of the Violet Ray, 299.
Electricity, Source of, 99, 100.
Electro-Magnetic Current to sit at the Poles, out at the Equator, illustrated, 123.
"Emission Theory" discarded by "authorities," 64.
Empirics and Quacks, 254.
Equator of a Magnet, 129.
Equilibration, the Law of, 227.
Equilibrium in Health, 196, 227.
Equilibrium of Organs, Nerves, Muscles, Fluids, etc., 251.
Eternity alone in the Celestial World, hence no time, 297.
Ether neither a fluid nor a solid, nor yet a gas, 64.
Ether, the Rule of the Ancients, 63, 64.
Ether the only perfectly transparent substance, 75.
Ether-wires, temporarily polarized for the transmission of Light, 59, 74.
"Everlasting Light," 162.
Evolution Being a Manifestation of Light, 251, 306.
Evolution, Material, 118.
Evolution of Animals, 135, 136.
Evolution of Life, 138, 139, 185, 216.
Evolution of Vegetation, 133.
Evolution of Wheats, etc., 133.
Evolution, Progress, Investigations, a Caution concerning, 108.
Exosmose-athious Substances, 109, 142.
Experiments Custom Teachings of the Ancients, 230.
Experiments with Red, Blue and Violet Glass, 209.
External Causes of Disease, 251.

Fact, a Scientific, to take the place of the "Emission" and "Wave" theories, 60-72.
Facts and Theories of Science, 55, 69.
Fallacy of some Popular Theories of Light, 248.
Fall of Man and its Consequences, 45, 161, 291.
Fibrin the most Important of the Albumen Group, 214.
Fire, God manifests Himself in, 42.
Fire-worshippers, so-called, 45.
Flaming Protoplasm, the, the "Star of Bethlehem," 31, 32.
Forked-Lightning, 113.
Fuel of the Sun's interior Incandescence, 91.
Functional Diseases result more or less directly from Derangement of the Nervous System, 200, 251, 257.

Galen's School and Paracelsus, 228.
Gelatin, Not an Atom of, in the Blood or Healthy Fluids, 178.

Gelatinous Compounds, 176.
Germination, the Process of, in Vegetable Life, 291.
Gladstone, What Mr., has Demonstrated, 209.
Glass, Light passing through, 82.
Glass made transparent chiefly to one Color, 76.
Glass, Red and Blue, 206.
Globe of the Sun chiefly Water, 94.
Globulin, 174.
Globe-Lightning, 115.
Glucose, 189.
Gluttin, 171.
God in Nature, 123.
"God is Light," 241.
God still manifesting Himself in Light, 29, 129, 150, 305.
God's Two Revelations, 306.
Gold, Fluid and Potable, 244.
Gravity at the visible boundary of the Sun, 90.
Greeks and Romans not "the Ancients," 97.

Hamavin the Representative of the Polar Force of Light, 173, 195.
Hanemann, 176.
Hahnemann and Homeopathy, 228.
Harmony abounds in Heaven, 32, 105, 196.
Harmony, "God's unique law," 27.
Harmony, Illustrations of, 27.
Harmony in Heaven, in the Celestial Light, in the Universal Systems, in the Solar Systems, 720.
Harmony in Nature, 28.
Harmony in the Moral World, 29.
Harmony in the Universal and Solar Systems, 27, 88.
Harmony of the Kabbala, 26.
Harmony, the Law of, relaxed by God for our good, 45, 59.
Healthful Season, 197.
Healthy Physical Life a popular Polarization and Depolarization, 208.
Heat in the Earth, in the Bodies of Animals, in the Human Organisms, and Everywhere, "Evolved" or Generated only by Light, 299.
Heat-Lightning, 115.
Heaven not to be discovered by the aid of the Telescope, 95, 137.
Hereditary Taints, 252.
Histogenetic Substances, or Tissue-Creators, 168.
Hogarteen, Dr. Chas. L., in Appletons' Cyclopedia, defines light, 61.
Homely Foundation, 262.
Homeopath, 134, 228.
How Color is imparted, 72, 74.
How Light travels, 79.
How sunlight affects the Atmosphere, 77, 80.
How the Earth was Enabled to "bring forth" Vegetation, 291.
How to Color Glass, 76.

INDEX.

How to Elevate the Standard of Moral Light, 223.
Human Organism only an Objective Manifestation of the Soul, 232.
Human Soul, the, 74.
Hydrogen the Negative Polarization of Ether, 132.
Hyle the Ancient Name for Ether, 129.

ILLUSTRATION, 36, 37, 137, 218.
Illustration of Action and Development of the Sympathetic Nervous System, 249.
Illustration of Nerve Action, 208.
Illustration of the Authority of the Higher Organs, 208.
Illustration of the Principle that Disease is sought of Remedies, 227.
Illustrative Circle of Nervousness Described, 250.
Imagination, Influence of, on Health and on action of Medicines, 228.
"Impulse and Tension," 69–72.
Indigo Ray, 53.
Ineffable Name, the, of God, 46.
Inflammatory Diseases, 250.
Inorganic Constituents of the Human Organism, 163 to 165.
Inspiration of the Bible and of the Kabbala, 58.
Instinct and Consciousness of Animals, 178, 179.
Intellect, 146.
Intelligence, 25, 151.
Interesting Ancient Ideas of the Colors, 247.
Intimate Relations of Ganglia and their Systems, 208.
Iron in the Human Organism, 167.
Isis, "Clothed with the Sun," etc. the "wonder in Heaven" of John's Vision, (See Frontispiece), 246.
Isis, Lifting the Veil of, 35.

JAH, or YAH, 47.
JAHVEH or YAHVEH (יהוה) the correct vocalization of the Ineffable or Four-Letter Name of God, 47.
JEHOVAH or YEHOVAH (יהוה) the Ineffable Name of God, 46.
JEHOVAH the Everlasting Light, 162.
JEHOVAH the One Self-Existent, Independent Life, 139, 153.
Jupiter, 57.

KABBALA and Kabbalistic teachings—the assistance that they have rendered and that they might render to "discoverers," 69.
Kabbala, debt of the world of all ages to the, 17.
Kabbala, Ignorance in reference to the, 57.
Kabbala, Source of the, 18, 27.
Kabbala, the, as authorized Interpreter and Expounder of Nature and the Bible, 23, 24, 245.
Kabbala, the, comprehends Religion and Philosophy, 79.
Kabbalistic Pictures in the Bible contrasting the Righteous with the Wicked, 220.
Kabbalistic Theosophy, Light the foundation of, 40.
Kabbalist, the, recognizes God's Will as Supreme, just as truly as the most "Orthodox" Theologian, 123.
Key to Kabbalistic Symbolism, 19, 25, 62.
Kingdoms of Nature, 141.
Knowing One's Self, 130.

LACTIC ACID, 162.
Lassitude, Relaxation, 208.
"Liber de Causis, or the Book of Causes," 25.
Life against Death, 290.
Life-Kingdoms of Nature, 140.
Life of Heaven and Earth Contrasted, 290, 291.
Life-principle, the, and the two Objective Hands of Light, 296, 291, to 295.
Light and Fire, 41.
Light and its Color rays, Kabbalistic knowledge of, 55.
Light and its Rays Invaluable Curatives, 163.
Light and its Rays unrivalled in Materia Medica, 95, 292.
Light a sublime aggregation of Marvelous Virtues, 94.
Light a unit, 67, 245.
Light began and continues Creation, 297.
Light begot and maintains Time, 297.
"Light, Children of," 96, 97, 157.
Light-conductors, 70.
Light does not feed but gives ("Rays") Color, 74.
Light God's agent in Creation and Providence, 54, 149.
Light "in the Beginning," Now and Hereafter, 242.
Light invisible, 42.
Light is Life, 251.
Light not Spirit, 38.
"Light is Saturated with Life," 208.
Light must Triumph over Prejudice, 254.
Light Nature's Specific, 290.
Light of Life, the, is Eternal=Immortal, 290.
Light Quacks, 271.
Light, Scientific "authorities" in trouble about the nature of, 60, 61.
Light Soul, the, 39.
Light, Subjective and Objective, the distinction, 38, 62.
Light the first and still the Manifester of God, 139.
Light the Fountain of Life, 58.

Light the Great Electro-Magnetic Po-
  larizer, 124.
Light, the laws of, comprehend the
  laws of Nature, 57, 58.
Light, the nature of, 59 to 62.
Light, the only, independent of the
  Sun, 28.
Light, the positive Power or Force in
  Nature, 62.
Light the universal Medium of the
  Ancients, 59.
Light, the, we see is the Apparition of
  Celestial Light, 63.
Light is because the Universal Mod-
  icine, 292.
Light, transmission of ("accepted"
  theories rejected), 64, 70.
Light, undivided, undiluted for those
  in Health, and its Red and Blue
  Rays for the Sick, 95.
Lightning (see Chapter III.), 106, 107,
  110, 111, 115.
Lightning, but one kind of, 112.
Lightning-Rods were used Four Cen-
  turies before Christ, 97.
Lightning understood by the An-
  cients, 97.
Lime in the Human Organism, 165.
Limit of our Sun's Vital or Creative
  Energy, 186.
Liver the chief Fat-factory, 175.
Lockjaw, 260.
Luminiferous ether, 64.

Magnetic and Electric bodies, 124.
Magnetic Meridian, 122.
Magnetism and Electricity one Mani-
  festation of Light in two Aspects,
  108, 119, 121.
Magnetism, How, is produced, 118,
  120, 121.
Magnetism is Electricity Equili-
  brated, 106.
Magnetizing, 120.
Magnets, Magnetic bodies, etc., 120,
  124.
Man " been blind," 44, 137.
Man Excels all other Created Beings,
  143, 130, 214.
Man's Body "the Temple of the Liv-
  ing God," 229.
Man not a Corruptible Body, but an
  Immortal Soul, 229.
Man's Lamp "Trimmed and Burn-
  ing," 229.
Man's Subjective Eye Opened, 219.
Man the "Light of Life" in Objective
  Manifestation, 229.
Man the only Responsible Creature,
  270.
Marasmus and Cholera Infantum,
  Hopeless Case of, Cured by Blue
  Baths—Case Cited, 277.
Margarine, 175.
Mars, 66.
Masonic Symbols Kabbalistic, 12.
Masterpiece of Creative Skill, 160.

Material Forces developed Simply and
  Solely in Manifest Light, 254.
Materialism of Ordinary Evolution
  Theory, 189.
Materia Medica of Light System, 308.
Means Adapted to the End, 216.
Medical Ministry, 305.
Medicines Prepared under the Red
  and Blue Rays, 266.
Medulla Oblongata, 200.
Mercury, 66.
Mesmer's Rediscovery, 254.
Mineral Kingdom, 244.
Mistakes of General Theosomics, 283
  to 294.
Mistakes of Scientists, 27, 93.
Moisture, Influence of, upon Electric
  condition of the Atmosphere, 109.
Morbid Growths, 269.
Most Trying Case, where there was
  no Constitutional foundation to
  build on, see Case X., 291.
Motion in Life, 193.
Mutual Dependence of Organs, 201.
Mystics—the extent of their Know-
  ledge of Light, Heat, Electricity,
  etc., 56, 129.

Name, the Power-letter, of God, the
  Key to the Kabbala, 25, 46.
Natural System to Supplant both Al-
  lopathy and Homoepathy, 278.
Nature must work Two-handed, 226.
Nature owes its every Item and fea-
  ture of Life to Light, the Unit, 86.
Nature's Own Specifics, 246.
Nature, Laws of, change not, 27, 191.
Nebula Nuclei of New Worlds, 193.
Negative condition of the Earth's sur-
  face neutralized, 108, 116.
Negative Electricity from Negative
  Rays, 107.
Neptune, 68.
Nerve Force Defined, 204, 211, 212, 213,
  238, 261.
Nervous Conductors of Vital Force or
  Energy, 204, 212.
Nervous Affections, 258.
Nervousness and General Prostration,
  with Irritability, Variable Appetite,
  Variable Bowels, Sleepless Nights—
  Very Trying Case, Cured by Blue
  and Red Light Treatment—Case
  cited, 289.
Nervous Prostration and General Re-
  laxing of System, Very Trying Case
  of, Cured by Red Lights—Case cited,
  275 to 280.
Nervous System, 240 to 265.
Nervous System Broken Down, and
  little or no Hope or Interest, Constitution naturally frail, and al-
  together a case to defy ordinary
  treatment—Cured by Red and Blue
  Baths alternating—Case cited, 281.
Nervous System Center of Vital Energy, and therefore of Disease, 257.

Nervous System Shattered, see Case IX., 280.
Neuralgia, Rheumatism and other Inflammatory Diseases, 253.
Newton and the Kabbala, 56, 57, 60.
Nine Organic Systems, 108, 260.
No Constitution—Weak and Indicate from youth, see Case X., 281.
No Invariable Standard for Doses, 278.
North Pole, the, Positive, 122.
Number of Suns and Worlds, 68.
Nutritive Processes, 186 to 189.

OBJECTIVE SUNS, 38, 43.
Obligations to Modern Scientists acknowledged, 103.
Ozonition, thirty years' study of, and what we have learned, 56.
Obnoxious Compounds, 178.
Obolu, 178.
One God and One Life-principle, 303.
One Light, Two Principles, Seven (or Nine) Rays, and Harmony or Compensation and Equilibration, 293.
One Original Force, Light, 208, 209.
Opposite Processes of the two Life-Kingdoms, 149.
Optics but a Fragment of the Science of Light, 234.
Organic Compounds in the Human Organism, 160 to 162.
Organic Distinctions in two Life-Kingdoms, 147.
Organization in Life, 183.
Organs Essential to Organic Life in General, 190 to 199.
Organs Peculiar to Animal Life, 199 to 218.
Organs that Distinguish Man from all other Creatures, 218 to 234.
Overfeeding not desirable for Vegetation any more than for Animals, 151.
Oxidation and Dexidation, 149.
Oxygen the Objective Polar Force, 198.
Oxygen the Positive Polarization of Ether, 172.
Oxygen the Property of the Red Ray alone, not in any sense of the Blue or Violet, 295.

PALPITATION of the Heart and Excessive Nervous Prostration—Bedfast, and tending to Decline, Cured by Blue and Red Light Treatment—Case Cited, 280.
Paracelsus's Knowledge almost Lost, 233, 269.
Paracelsus's two Systems, 234.
Paralysis, Complete, 127.
Paraplegia, an Extreme Case of Cured by Red Glass—Case Cited, 277.
Patent Medicines, 172.
Pathology, What the Ancients Knew of, 236.
Pentagram, the Flaming, the "Star of Bethlehem," etc., 21, 246.

Perpetual Motion, 122, 123.
Phlodem russia, 106.
Photosphere of the Sun, 98.
Physical Force, Vital Force and Nerve Forces, all of Light, 242.
Physical Life generated in Death, 127, 170.
Physical Life the result of Motion, and manifested in a Physical Form or Body, 127.
Physicians Should be Consulted when Accessible, 272.
Physicists Theorize too much and Study the Ancient Philosophy too little, 100.
"Pillar of Mercury," 31.
Plain Statement, 127.
Plato's Enigmas, 50.
Plea for Phrenology—he has Rediscovered a Great Truth, 283, 284.
Phenonotation Ideas, Some Absurd, 216.
Pleasanton's Success and Draper and Gladstone's Failures, 286, 287.
Polarity, 293.
Positive Electricity other teasely polarized, 100.
Positive Electricity from Positive Ray, 192.
Priest, the, 82.
Processes of Creation realized, 234.
Progress of Life-unfoldment, from Black to Red—Decline, from Red to Black (with Illustration), 247, 248.
Proportions of the Rays, and of the Positive and Negative Principles, in Protein-Compounds, 171.
Psychical Functions Cultivated at expense of the Subjective, 221.
Pure Light! Pure Air! Pure Water! 294.
Purpose of God, 133.
Pythagoras and his views, 45, 49.

QUACKS and Humbugs, 272.
Quetelet's Observations (Table, p. 107), 106, 108.

RAINBOW, the, 80.
Reciprocal Influences of Soul and Physical Health, 228.
Red Aesthenice the Nerve Force, Increases Tension, 267.
Red and Blue the only Independent Colors, 93.
Red and Blue the only Rays we consider Desirable in Disease, 259, 268.
Red Attraction, Blue and associate Repulsion, 246.
Red Bath, the Proportions most Desirable, 271.
Red Bath, we Seldom Employ the, without More or Less of the other Rays, 175.
Red Color of the Blood, 176.
Redemption the Crowning Act of Creation, 300.

INDEX.

Sun, the Astral or Objective—What they are, of what made, what the nature of their Luminosity, Whence they derive their Light, and how they disseminate it, 48, 49.
Sun, the extent of the domain of our, 83, 86.
Surroundings must Favor not Hinder the end sought, 300.
Survey of the Ground Traversed, and Facts noted, 290 to 304.
Syllipsis or Luminous Synthesis, 245.
Symbolism of the Colors, with Ancient Illustration, 247, 248.
Sympathetic Ganglia, 263.
Sympathetic Nervous System, 261, 262, 263, 269.
Sympathetic, the, Medical System more Rational than the Antipathetic, 237, 239, 270.
Synthesis of Material Creation, 102, 103, 104.
Synthesis of the Universe, 132, 140, 294.

TALISMANS, 81.
Tension is Polarity, 279.
Tension of ether into Light-conductors, 70, 87.
Tension, the Comparative, of the several Rays, and why the Red is the most and the Violet the least tense, 82, 83.
"Tension Theory" explained, 73 (see "Impulse and Tension").
Tenure of Life on the Planet Uranus, 27.
Tesseus, or Lockjaw, 280.
"Tetractys," the, of Pythagoras described, 46 to 49.
Theories only admissible where Knowledge is unattainable, 65.
Therapeutics, What the Ancients Knew of, 258.
Therusic property of the Violet Ray, Imaginary, 286.
Thunder—what it is, 110, 114.
Time a moment of Physical Life, 287.
Time and Creation belong only to the Material World, 287.
Time and Creation Coeval, 286.
Time shall Cease, 286.
Time the Measure of Creation, 134.
Tissues of the Ganglia and Nerves, 296.
Transparency—what it is, 75.
"Tree of Life," the, 96, 244.
True Doctrine of Evolution or Development, 132.
Two hands of Deity, 28.
Two Methods of Applying Light, 264.
Tyndall definition of Light ("the sensation of light"), 66.
Tyndall unable to declare the Origin of Magnetism, 122.
Types of Evolution, 132.
Typhus, Typhoid, and other Material and Sluggish Fevers, 258.

ULCERS, 280.
"Undulatory Theory," see "Wave Theory."
Unfoldment of Life, 139, 185, 186.
Unity of Light fatal to the "Wave Theory," 90.
Unity with Diversity of Nature, 182.
Uranus, 87.
Uterine Difficulties, see Case X., 281.

VACUUM in Nature, 65.
Vapors absorb two-thirds of the Calorific Ray, 108, 114.
Variations in Electricity (see Plate III., p. 160), 104 to 108.
Vascularity of the Ganglia, 296.
Venus, 86.
Vesuvius, the Vapor from the Crater of, 172.
"Vibrations" of ether, see "Wave Theory," and pp. 56, 67.
Violet Ray, not a Combination of Blue and Red, 298.
Violet Ray, see Blue, Indigo and Violet.
Vital Dynamics, 174.
Vital Flood, 298.
Volta and the Voltaic Battery—an interesting Query, 55.

WATER a powerful Absorber of Positive Electricity, 105.
Water Everywhere and in Everything, 43, 138, 163, 165.
Water Generated by the Sun, 43, 152.
"Wave Theory" of the "authorities" exploded and shown to be entirely unsatisfactory, 64 to 69.
Weakness of Man Physically, 139.
What we Believe, and Know, 292.
Wheat cannot grow under Blue Glass alone, 299.
White the harmonious combination of all the Colors, or of two or more "complementary Colors," 79.
Why the Red Ray is the most Heating and the Violet the most cooling of the color-rays, 83.
"Wisdom," in Hebrew Chochmah (חכמה), in Greek Sophia (Σοφία), 28, 30, 243.
"Wise Men" of the East, of the olden time, 49.
Woman's Soul, the, and Satan, 44.
"Woman, the, clothed with the Sun," etc., 32 (see Frontispiece).
World of Darkness, 229.
Wormswood, the Star, 31.

YELLOWISH cast of Clouds, 78, 86.
Yellow, the, the most Luminous Ray, 81.

ZENITH of Material Evolution, 102.
Zigzag-Lightning, 105.
Zöllner's view of the Astral or Objective Suns, 45.

www.ingramcontent.com/pod-product-compliance
Lightning Source LLC
Chambersburg PA
CBHW030742230426
43667CB00007B/814